A NEW, EXPANDED

GUIDE TO THE BIRDS OF ALASKA

A NEW, EXPANDED GUIDE TO THE BIRDS OF ALASKA

ROBERT H. ARMSTRONG
AND THE EDITORS OF ALASKA® MAGAZINE

ANCHORAGE, ALASKA

First Printing: 1980
Revised Edition: 1983

Library of Congress cataloging in publication data:
Armstrong, Robert H
A guide to the birds of Alaska.
Bibliography: p.
Includes indexes.
1. Birds — Alaska — Identification. I. Alaska. II. Title.
QL684.A4A75 598.29798
80-20882
ISBN 0-88240-254-4

COVER: BALD EAGLES (Robert A. Henning)

Photographs by Robert H. Armstrong except as noted.
Paintings by John C. Pitcher

Alaska Northwest Publishing Company
Box 4-EEE, Anchorage, Alaska 99509

Printed in U.S.A.

CONTENTS

TEREK SANDPIPER
(Rick Austin)

FOREWORD

Watching birds is fun! Being able to identify the birds you are watching increases this pleasure. And watching birds in Alaska has its special excitement, both for resident observers and visitors.

This photographic book on Alaska's birds is designed to assist everyone in their enjoyment of birds, helping in bird identification and telling something about their habits and where one may expect to find them.

Seeing birds that have adapted to the harsh environments of the boreal forest, tundra and sea ice of the North and that cannot be seen farther south is one exciting aspect of observing birds in Alaska. Even those bird species that visit more southern climes during migration and winter often look and behave quite differently when on their northern breeding grounds. Not only may their plumage be strikingly different than in winter, but they may occupy entirely different habitats (e.g., many sandpipers and other shorebirds nest in Alaska's mountains, far from seashores and marshes) and they may be singing and executing various courtship antics that are performed only on their northern breeding grounds.

In addition to the northern-adapted species, two other groups of geographically restricted birds add particular zest to birdwatching in Alaska. The first is a group of endemics which apparently differentiated, historically, in the Bering-Chukchi sea area ("Beringia") in isolated glacial refugia. These birds still have their centers of abundance in this relatively inaccessible region, and many have not extended their ranges much beyond the Aleutian Islands or southcoastal Alaska. Hence, it is necessary to visit Alaska (or Siberia) to see many of these geographically restricted species (e.g., Red-faced Cormorant; Emperor Goose; Red-legged Kittiwake; Aleutian Tern; Parakeet, Least and Whiskered auklets; and McKay's Bunting).

The second group is sometimes referred to as the "Asiatics," birds that have their origins in Asia and most of which can be seen in North America only in Alaska. Some are regular breeders (Bar-tailed Godwit, Bluethroat, Arctic Warbler, White Wagtail and Yellow Wagtail), but most are migrants or are casual or accidental visitants. The occurrence of these Asiatics is facilitated by the nearness of Siberia, with some species passing across parts of Alaska—especially the western Aleutian Islands and the islands of the Bering Sea—during migration. A few even straggle occasionally as far as mainland Alaska (e.g., Spot-billed Duck, Common Crane, Common Ringed Plover, Eurasian Dotterel, Wood Sandpiper, Terek Sandpiper, Great Knot, Sharp-tailed Sandpiper, Hoopoe, Eurasian Wryneck, Common House-Martin, Eye-browed Thrush, Dusky Thrush, Fieldfare, Brambling, Eurasian Bullfinch, etc.).

One of the most exciting aspects of watching birds in Alaska is that there is so much yet to be learned about them. We are still at the frontier of knowledge about so many aspects of Alaska's bird life that any observant bird watcher has a good chance of contributing new and valuable information about them—range extensions; dates of migration, eggs, young, fledglings; clutch and brood sizes; food habits; flight speeds and distances; habitat requirements during nesting, migration, winter; behavior relative to others of their own species, to different species and under various kinds of stress, including that caused by man; behavioral means of adapting to the rigors of northern life; and *ad infinitum.*

Watching birds is indeed fun, whether you watch birds casually or seriously. Whether your enjoyment comes from watching birds through a window of your home as they sing or feed; from adding new kinds of birds to your life list; from seeing birds with different plumages, habits and behavior patterns; from studying the natural history or ecology of a species; or from matching wits with game birds during the hunting season, you will be glad to have this Alaska bird guide, with its beautiful illustrations, close at hand.

Brina Kessel
Professor of Zoology and Curator,
Terrestrial Vertebrates Collection,
University of Alaska, Fairbanks
23 July 1979

ACKNOWLEDGMENTS

The help of many people made this book possible. Frank Glass, an attorney and self-taught ornithologist, reviewed the manuscript and offered useful suggestions and ideas. Jim King, U.S. Fish & Wildlife Service biologist, reviewed the sections on swans, geese and ducks and added items based on his extensive experience with this group in Alaska. Ed Bailey, U.S. Fish & Wildlife Service biologist, reviewed the seabird sections of the book and provided additional information.

The timely publication of this book was made possible by receiving a copy of the manuscript on the *Status and Distribution of Alaska Birds* several months prior to its publication from Dr. Brina Kessel, professor of Zoology and curator of Terrestrial Vertebrate Collection, University Museum, University of Alaska, Fairbanks. She also worked up a seasonal checklist of birds for the eastern interior of Alaska which helped a great deal in compiling the status and distribution charts for each species. Many others provided information on local abundance of birds which helped in compiling the charts: Bruce Paige, National Park Service biologist, for Glacier Bay National Monument; John C. Pitcher, for the Anchorage area; Richard MacIntosh, National Marine Fisheries Service biologist, for Kodiak Island; and Doug Murphy, ornithologist and former seasonal ranger at Mount McKinley National Park, for the Mount McKinley area.

Technical reviewers made significant contributions to the quality of this book. Dr. Dennis Paulson, zoologist, instructor and consultant in Seattle, Washington, added considerable information to the identification section for each species, commented on the format and content of the manuscript, and provided valuable assistance in selection of the photographs. Pete Isleib, commercial fisherman and self-taught ornithologist, filled out status and distribution charts for all species not covered by *Status and Distribution of Alaska Birds*. Dr. Don McKnight, research chief, Game Division, Alaska Department of Fish & Game, and working under funding from Federal Aid in Wildlife Restoration Program, reviewed the entire manuscript and offered useful suggestions.

We are grateful to Dan Gibson of the University Museum, University of Alaska, for his constructive criticism of the manuscript and for his review of the photographs.

Special thanks go to the many photographers who allowed us to tie up their photographs for many months through the selection and printing process.

To John C. Pitcher, whose excellent paintings enabled us to reach our goal of illustrating all of the bird species that occur in Alaska as of June 1979, we are especially grateful.

Many voice descriptions used in the book are from *The Audubon Society Field Guide to North American Birds, Western Region,* (1977), text by Miklos D. F. Udvardy, and reprinted here by permission of Alfred A. Knopf, Inc.

Assistance in updating the 1983 version of the book was received from several people. Dan Gibson reviewed the text changes and new photographs and provided references for status and distribution changes. Richard Gordon of Juneau assisted in updating the status and distribution charts for Southeastern Alaska. Bob Day of the University of Alaska, Fairbanks, provided new information on seabirds. Jim King, U.S. Fish and Wildlife Service, provided new information on swans, geese and ducks and made other helpful comments. Dan Timm, game biologist, Alaska Department of Fish & Game, Anchorage, provided new information on the status and distribution of Canada Geese subspecies in Alaska. Dr. Richard Chandler, photographic consultant for British Birds, assisted in the location of several photographs of the new Asiatic species. The help of all of these people is greatly appreciated.

INTRODUCTION

This new, expanded *GUIDE TO THE BIRDS OF ALASKA* covers the 405 species of birds known to have occurred in Alaska as of February 1, 1983. Information on identification, status, distribution and habitat is detailed on 355 of these species. The remaining 50 are accidental in Alaska. These species and where they have occurred are listed in the back of the book.

This book was designed to aid in the identification of birds of Alaska and to provide the reader with information that is unavailable in other guides. We have used photographs for many of the species and paintings for those species for which we lacked photos. As much as possible, we have attempted to present birds in a natural setting as they would normally be viewed at close range. The adult male is depicted unless otherwise noted. Not all of the photographs were taken in Alaska but the species shown are the same as those that do occur in the state. While we feel that the illustrations will help in field identification, we also realize the limitations of the photographic approach. Paintings of similar-looking birds, with size relationships and appropriate field marks emphasized, will and should remain the standard approach to field identification guides for birds. For this reason the reader may also want to use, in conjunction with this book, one of the other field guides on the market when attempting to identify birds in the field.

Individual species are organized by families. The reader is encouraged to become familiar with family characteristics as this can save a great deal of time when identifying birds in the field. The order in which the species appear and their common and scientific names generally follow the American Birding Association checklist (1982). The length of each bird is an approximate average from the literature and represents a measurement taken from the tip of the bill to the tip of the tail of museum specimens. For identification we encourage the reader to use the text with the illustrations. For most birds the photograph or painting will provide the basic descriptive features and we have added information only on field marks important to identification. Voice descriptions are included where we feel they aid identification. Written descriptions of a bird's voice, while helpful, often vary among those describing the voice and are difficult to interpret. We encourage readers to learn voices through actual field study and by listening to recordings. Once learned, most birds can be readily identified by voice alone. For some species, learning the voice is essential for positive identification.

The status and distribution of each bird in Alaska is presented according to the 6 biogeographic areas (see page 4) recognized by Kessel and Gibson (1978). Knowing when a particular bird occurs in an area and its status can be helpful in narrowing the

RUFF
(Rick Austin)

choices leading to final identification. This information on distribution is based on Kessel and Gibson (1978), Gabrielson and Lincoln (1959), several published checklists and the knowledge of individuals familiar with specific areas. For simplicity and to make the areas more comparable, we have combined some of the terms presented by Kessel and Gibson (1978) and others.

The habitat in which a bird usually occurs is included for most species. For some, especially rare and casual species, we present the locations within the region where they have been found rather than their habitat. Most designations are understandable and need no definition. Exceptions are inshore and offshore marine waters. Inshore refers to all marine waters within 3 nautical miles of the outer coast and islands of Alaska including all waters of the inside passages of southeastern Alaska. Offshore marine waters encompass all marine waters beyond 3 nautical miles of the outer coast and islands of Alaska.

In summary, many factors are useful in identifying birds. In conjunction with field marks, learning a bird's voice, habits and habitat can be very helpful. Also knowing where and when individual species normally occur and their status in selected areas of Alaska are important. We hope this will be a useful guide and that appreciation of Alaska's birds will be enhanced through the use of this book.

THE SIX BIOGEOGRAPHIC REGIONS OF ALASKA

Delineated by dotted lines
Status and Distribution charts accompanying the text outline the distribution of individual species within these regions.

Key to National Wildlife Refuges

numbers corrrespond with those on the map

1. Alaska Maritime NWR
   In addition to the Aleutian Islands Unit the refuge includes an enormous number of offshore islands, islets, rocks, reefs and spires.
2. Alaska Peninsula NWR
3. Arctic NWR
4. Becharof NWR
5. Innoko NWR
6. Izembek NWR
7. Kanuti NWR
8. Kenai NWR
9. Kodiak NWR
10. Koyukuk NWR
11. Nowitna NWR
12. Selawik NWR
13. Tetlin NWR
14. Togiak NWR
15. Yukon Delta NWR
16. Yukon Flats NWR
    This map reflects the addition of about 53 million acres to the existing 23 million acres of National Wildlife Refuges in Alaska by the Alaska National Interest Lands Conservation Act of 1980. Bird lists for some of the refuges and other information is available from the Regional Director, U.S. Fish and Wildlife Service, 1011 E. Tudor Road, Anchorage, Alaska 99503.

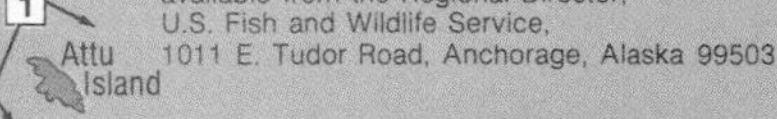

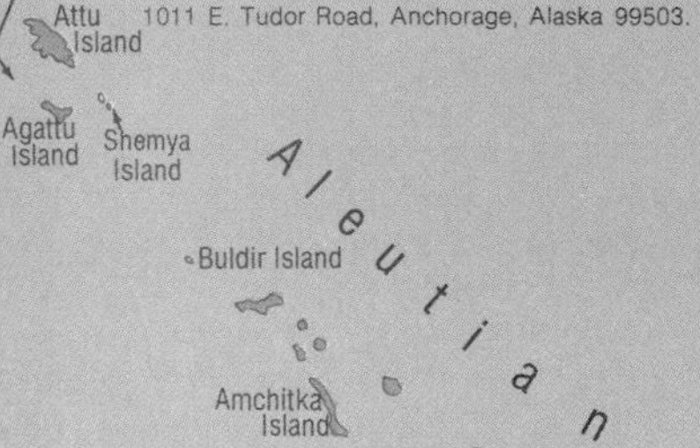

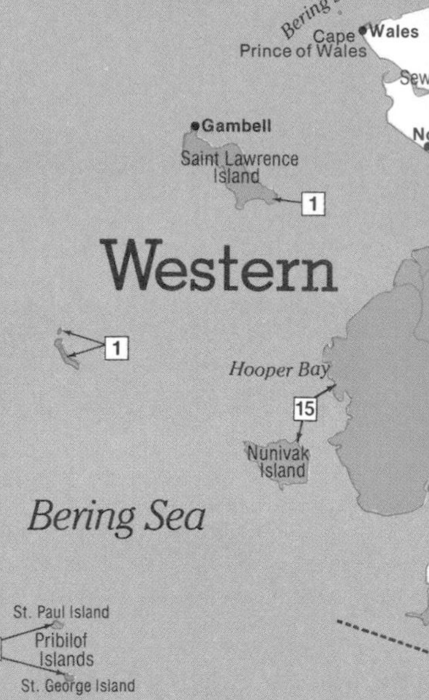

TOPOGRAPHY OF A BIRD

Although birds will vary radically in the specifics of their anatomy, they all share the same basic structures. Shown here are the basic features (far right) and wing feathers (right).

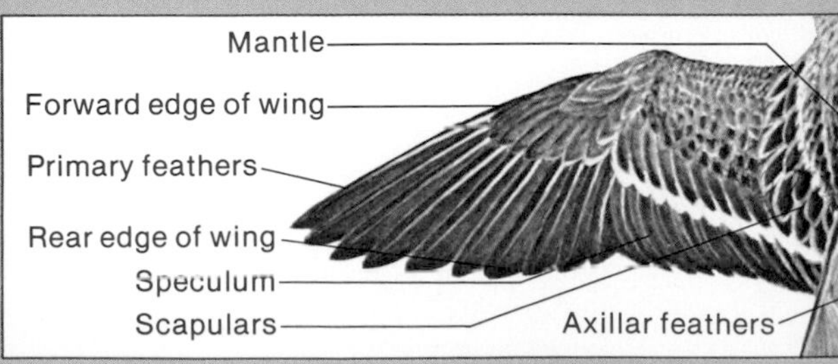

Illustrations by John C. Pitcher / CartoGraphics by Jon.Hersh

A GUIDE TO THE FAMILY HEADINGS AND STATUS AND DISTRIBUTION CHARTS

Each family of birds is introduced by the family scientific name and the number of species with casual or more frequent occurrence and the number of accidental species. For example:

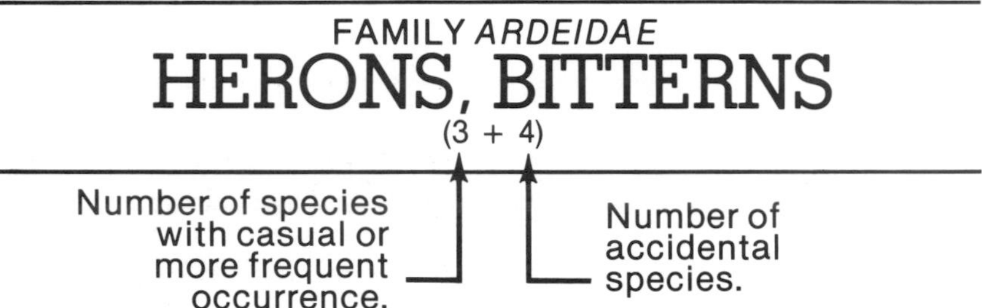

The total of the 2 numbers is the total number of species from that family occurring in the state.

The Status and Distribution Charts outline the occurrence in various biogeographic regions of Alaska (see map, pages 4 and 5) of individual species. Symbols for the charts and their meaning are:

C = **Common.** Birds normally considered abundant, common and most of those considered fairly common.
U = **Uncommon.** Birds normally considered uncommon and some of those considered fairly common.
R = **Rare.** Includes all birds considered rare or very rare.
\+ = **All birds considered casual or accidental.**
— = **Not known to occur.**
★ = **Known breeder or probable breeder in a region.**

Definitions for the terms, taken from *Birds of the North Gulf Coast — Prince William Sound Region, Alaska* by M. E. Pete Isleib and Brina Kessel (Biological Papers Of The University of Alaska, Number 14, November 1973) are:

Abundant — Species occurs repeatedly in proper habitats, with available habitat heavily utilized, and/or the region regularly hosts great numbers of the species.
Common — Species occurs in all or nearly all proper habitats, but some areas of presumed suitable habitat are occupied sparsely or not at all and/or the region regularly hosts large numbers of the species.
Fairly Common — Species occurs in only some of the proper habitat, and large areas of presumed suitable habitat are occupied sparsely or not at all and/or the region regularly hosts substantial numbers of the species.
Uncommon — Species occurs regularly, but utilizes very little of the suitable habitat, and/or the region regularly hosts relatively small numbers of the species; not observed regularly even in proper habitats.
Rare — Species occurs, or probably occurs, regularly within the region, but in very small numbers.
Casual — Species has been recorded no more than a few times, but irregular observations are likely over a period of years.
Accidental — Species has been recorded only a time or two; it is so far from its usual range that further observations are considered unlikely.

CHECKLIST OF ALASKAN BIRDS

This is a list of all birds found in Alaska, including Accidentals (A), as reported by Gibson (1982). Readers may wish to use this list to record the species they have seen.

_ Common Loon
_ Yellow-billed Loon
_ Arctic Loon
_ Red-throated Loon
_ Red-necked Grebe
_ Horned Grebe
_ Western Grebe
_ Pied-billed Grebe
_ Short-tailed Albatross
_ Black-footed Albatross
_ Laysan Albatross
_ Northern Fulmar
_ Pink-footed Shearwater
_ Flesh-footed Shearwater
_ Buller's Shearwater
_ Sooty Shearwater
_ Short-tailed Shearwater
_ Manx Shearwater
_ Mottled Petrel
_ Cook's Petrel (A)
_ Fork-tailed Storm-Petrel
_ Leach's Storm-Petrel
_ American White Pelican (A)
_ Double-crested Cormorant
_ Brandt's Cormorant
_ Pelagic Cormorant
_ Red-faced Cormorant
_ Great Blue Heron
_ Cattle Egret (A)
_ Great Egret (A)
_ Chinese Egret (A)
_ Snowy Egret (A)
_ Black-crowned Night-Heron
_ American Bittern
_ Tundra Swan
_ Trumpeter Swan
_ Whooper Swan
_ Canada Goose
_ Brant
_ Emperor Goose
_ Greater White-fronted Goose
_ Bean Goose
_ Snow Goose
_ Ross' Goose
_ Mallard
_ American Black Duck
_ Spot-billed Duck
_ Gadwall
_ Northern Pintail
_ Falcated Teal
_ Green-winged Teal
_ Baikal Teal
_ Garganey
_ Blue-winged Teal
_ Cinnamon Teal
_ Northern Shoveler
_ Eurasian Wigeon
_ American Wigeon
_ Wood Duck
_ Common Pochard
_ Canvasback
_ Redhead
_ Ring-necked Duck
_ Greater Scaup
_ Lesser Scaup
_ Tufted Duck
_ Common Goldeneye
_ Barrow's Goldeneye
_ Bufflehead
_ Oldsquaw
_ Harlequin Duck
_ Steller's Eider
_ Common Eider
_ King Eider
_ Spectacled Eider
_ White-winged Scoter

_ Surf Scoter
_ Black Scoter
_ Ruddy Duck
_ Hooded Merganser
_ Smew
_ Common Merganser
_ Red-breasted Merganser
_ Turkey Vulture (A)
_ Northern Goshawk
_ Sharp-shinned Hawk
_ Red-tailed Hawk
_ Swainson's Hawk
_ Rough-legged Hawk
_ Golden Eagle
_ White-tailed Eagle
_ Bald Eagle
_ Steller's Sea-Eagle
_ Northern Harrier
_ Osprey
_ Gyrfalcon
_ Peregrine Falcon
_ Merlin
_ American Kestrel
_ Eurasian Kestrel
_ Blue Grouse
_ Spruce Grouse
_ Ruffed Grouse
_ Willow Ptarmigan
_ Rock Ptarmigan
_ White-tailed Ptarmigan
_ Sharp-tailed Grouse
_ Common Crane (A)
_ Sandhill Crane
_ Sora
_ Eurasian Coot (A)
_ American Coot
_ American Black Oystercatcher
_ American Avocet (A)
_ Common Ringed Plover
_ Semipalmated Plover
_ Little Ringed Plover (A)
_ Killdeer
_ Mongolian Plover
_ Lesser Golden-Plover
_ Black-bellied Plover
_ Eurasian Dotterel
_ Black-tailed Godwit
_ Hudsonian Godwit
_ Bar-tailed Godwit
_ Marbled Godwit
_ Eskimo Curlew (A)
_ Whimbrel
_ Bristle-thighed Curlew
_ Far Eastern Curlew
_ Upland Sandpiper
_ Spotted Redshank
_ Marsh Sandpiper (A)
_ Common Greenshank
_ Greater Yellowlegs
_ Lesser Yellowlegs
_ Solitary Sandpiper
_ Green Sandpiper
_ Wood Sandpiper
_ Willet (A)
_ Terek Sandpiper
_ Common Sandpiper
_ Spotted Sandpiper
_ Gray-tailed Tattler
_ Wandering Tattler
_ Ruddy Turnstone
_ Black Turnstone
_ Wilson's Phalarope
_ Red-necked Phalarope
_ Red Phalarope
_ Common Snipe
_ Jack Snipe (A)
_ Short-billed Dowitcher
_ Long-billed Dowitcher
_ Surfbird
_ Great Knot
_ Red Knot
_ Sanderling
_ Semipalmated Sandpiper
_ Western Sandpiper
_ Rufous-necked Stint
_ Little Stint

- __ Temminck's Stint
- __ Long-toed Stint
- __ Least Sandpiper
- __ White-rumped Sandpiper
- __ Baird's Sandpiper
- __ Pectoral Sandpiper
- __ Sharp-tailed Sandpiper
- __ Rock Sandpiper
- __ Dunlin
- __ Curlew Sandpiper
- __ Spoonbill Sandpiper (A)
- __ Broad-billed Sandpiper
- __ Stilt Sandpiper
- __ Buff-breasted Sandpiper
- __ Ruff
- __ Pomarine Jaeger
- __ Parasitic Jaeger
- __ Long-tailed Jaeger
- __ South Polar Skua
- __ Glaucous Gull
- __ Glaucous-winged Gull
- __ Slaty-backed Gull
- __ Western Gull (A)
- __ Herring Gull
- __ Thayer's Gull
- __ California Gull
- __ Black-tailed Gull
- __ Ring-billed Gull
- __ Mew Gull
- __ Common Black-headed Gull
- __ Franklin's Gull
- __ Bonaparte's Gull
- __ Ivory Gull
- __ Black-legged Kittiwake
- __ Red-legged Kittiwake
- __ Ross' Gull
- __ Sabine's Gull
- __ Common Tern
- __ Arctic Tern
- __ Aleutian Tern
- __ Caspian Tern
- __ Black Tern
- __ White-winged Tern (A)
- __ Common Murre
- __ Thick-billed Murre
- __ Dovekie
- __ Black Guillemot
- __ Pigeon Guillemot
- __ Marbled Murrelet
- __ Kittlitz's Murrelet
- __ Ancient Murrelet
- __ Cassin's Auklet
- __ Parakeet Auklet
- __ Crested Auklet
- __ Least Auklet
- __ Whiskered Auklet
- __ Rhinoceros Auklet
- __ Horned Puffin
- __ Tufted Puffin
- __ Band-tailed Pigeon
- __ Rock Dove
- __ White-winged Dove (A)
- __ Mourning Dove
- __ Common Cuckoo
- __ Oriental Cuckoo
- __ Common Barn-Owl (A)
- __ Oriental Scops-Owl
- __ Western Screech-Owl
- __ Great Horned Owl
- __ Snowy Owl
- __ Northern Hawk-Owl
- __ Northern Pygmy-Owl
- __ Barred Owl
- __ Great Gray Owl
- __ Long-eared Owl (A)
- __ Short-eared Owl
- __ Boreal Owl
- __ Northern Saw-whet Owl
- __ Jungle Nightjar (A)
- __ Whip-poor-will (A)
- __ Common Nighthawk
- __ Black Swift
- __ Chimney Swift (A)
- __ Vaux's Swift
- __ White-throated Needletail
- __ Fork-tailed Swift

- __ Common Swift (A)
- __ Ruby-throated Hummingbird (A)
- __ Anna's Hummingbird
- __ Rufous Hummingbird
- __ Belted Kingfisher
- __ Hoopoe (A)
- __ Eurasian Wryneck (A)
- __ Northern Flicker
- __ Yellow-bellied Sapsucker
- __ Red-breasted Sapsucker
- __ Hairy Woodpecker
- __ Downy Woodpecker
- __ Black-backed Woodpecker
- __ Three-toed Woodpecker
- __ Eastern Kingbird
- __ Western Kingbird
- __ Say's Phoebe
- __ Yellow-bellied Flycatcher (A)
- __ Alder Flycatcher
- __ Least Flycatcher (A)
- __ Hammond's Flycatcher
- __ Dusky Flycatcher (A)
- __ Western Flycatcher
- __ Western Wood-Pewee
- __ Olive-sided Flycatcher
- __ Eurasian Skylark
- __ Horned Lark
- __ Violet-green Swallow
- __ Tree Swallow
- __ Bank Swallow
- __ Northern Rough-winged Swallow
- __ Common House-Martin (A)
- __ Barn Swallow
- __ Cliff Swallow
- __ Purple Martin
- __ Gray Jay
- __ Steller's Jay
- __ Black-billed Magpie
- __ Common Raven
- __ Northwestern Crow
- __ Clark's Nutcracker
- __ Black-capped Chickadee
- __ Mountain Chickadee
- __ Siberian Tit
- __ Boreal Chickadee
- __ Chestnut-backed Chickadee
- __ Red-breasted Nuthatch
- __ Brown Creeper
- __ American Dipper
- __ Winter Wren
- __ Northern Mockingbird (A)
- __ Brown Thrasher (A)
- __ American Robin
- __ Eye-browed Thrush
- __ Dusky Thrush
- __ Fieldfare (A)
- __ Varied Thrush
- __ Hermit Thrush
- __ Swainson's Thrush
- __ Gray-cheeked Thrush
- __ Mountain Bluebird
- __ Northern Wheatear
- __ Bluethroat
- __ Red-flanked Bluetail (A)
- __ Siberian Rubythroat
- __ Townsend's Solitaire
- __ Wood Warbler (A)
- __ Dusky Warbler
- __ Arctic Warbler
- __ Middendorff's Grasshopper-Warbler
- __ Golden-crowned Kinglet
- __ Ruby-crowned Kinglet
- __ Red-breasted Flycatcher
- __ Siberian Flycatcher (A)
- __ Gray-spotted Flycatcher
- __ Siberian Accentor
- __ White Wagtail
- __ Black-backed Wagtail
- __ Gray Wagtail
- __ Yellow Wagtail
- __ Water Pipit
- __ Brown Tree-Pipit (A)
- __ Olive Tree-Pipit
- __ Pechora Pipit
- __ Red-throated Pipit
- __ Bohemian Waxwing

_ Cedar Waxwing
_ Brown Shrike
_ Northern Shrike
_ European Starling
_ Red-eyed Vireo
_ Philadelphia Vireo
_ Warbling Vireo
_ Black-and-white Warbler (A)
_ Tennessee Warbler
_ Orange-crowned Warbler
_ Yellow Warbler
_ Magnolia Warbler
_ Cape May Warbler
_ Yellow-rumped Warbler
_ Townsend's Warbler
_ Black-throated Green Warbler (A)
_ Bay-breasted Warbler (A)
_ Blackpoll Warbler
_ Ovenbird (A)
_ Northern Waterthrush
_ Kentucky Warbler (A)
_ MacGillivray's Warbler
_ Common Yellowthroat
_ Wilson's Warbler
_ Canada Warbler (A)
_ American Redstart
_ Bobolink (A)
_ Western Meadowlark
_ Yellow-headed Blackbird
_ Red-winged Blackbird
_ Rusty Blackbird
_ Brewer's Blackbird
_ Common Grackle
_ Brown-headed Cowbird
_ Northern Oriole (A)
_ Western Tanager
_ Scarlet Tanager (A)
_ Savannah Sparrow
_ Dark-eyed Junco
_ American Tree Sparrow
_ Chipping Sparrow
_ Harris' Sparrow
_ White-crowned Sparrow
_ Golden-crowned Sparrow
_ White-throated Sparrow
_ Fox Sparrow
_ Lincoln's Sparrow
_ Swamp Sparrow (A)
_ Song Sparrow
_ Lapland Longspur
_ Smith's Longspur
_ Snow Bunting
_ McKay's Bunting
_ Little Bunting (A)
_ Rustic Bunting
_ Gray Bunting
_ Pallas' Reed-Bunting
_ Common Reed-Bunting
_ Brambling
_ Hawfinch
_ Evening Grosbeak
_ Eurasian Bullfinch
_ Common Rosefinch
_ Purple Finch
_ Pine Grosbeak
_ Rosy Finch
_ Oriental Greenfinch
_ Hoary Redpoll
_ Common Redpoll
_ Pine Siskin
_ Red Crossbill
_ White-winged Crossbill

THE FAMILIES

FAMILY *GAVIIDAE*

LOONS

(4)

Loons are large swimming birds with webbed feet and sharply pointed bills. In flight their head is held lower than their body giving them a hunchbacked appearance.

COMMON LOON
Summer
(Don Cornelius)

COMMON LOON
Winter
(Dennis Paulson)

COMMON LOON

(Gavia immer)

LENGTH: 32 IN.

Identification: In summer, adult has an all black head with a broken white collar which separates it from the Red-throated and Arctic loons. Similar to the Yellow-billed Loon but has a straight black bill rather than the upturned yellow bill. Winter adults and young similar to other loons. Large size and noticeably heavy straight bill useful for identification in winter. In flight, looks more ponderous than the smaller Red-throated and Arctic loons, and has distinctly slower wingbeats. Loud, resonant yodeling call on breeding grounds is distinctive.

Status and Distribution:	SPRING	SUMMER	FALL	WINTER
Southeastern ★	C	U	C	U
Southcoastal ★	C	U	C	U
Southwestern ★	U	U	U	U
Central ★	C	C	C	—
Western ★	U	U	U	—
Northern	—	+	—	—

Habitat: Breeding — lakes in coniferous forests and heath in the Aleutian Islands. Nests on a mound of vegetation near water, often on small islands, sometimes on top of old muskrat houses. Prefers secluded lakes away from human activity. Highly territorial and usually only a single pair is found on the smaller lakes. In winter — inshore marine waters.

YELLOW-BILLED LOON

(Gavia adamsii)

LENGTH: 35 IN.

Identification: An adult in any plumage can be distinguished from the Common Loon by larger, whitish-yellow, chisel-shaped, slightly upturned bill. In the first fall, immatures of both species are similar, but the head pattern of the Yellow-billed Loon has a dark smudge behind the ears, the bill is usually held up at a slight angle, and the head and back often appear browner than in the Common Loon. Voice is similar to that of the Common Loon, although this species is described as less vocal.

Status and Distribution:	SPRING	SUMMER	FALL	WINTER
Southeastern	U	R	R	U
Southcoastal	U	R	R	U
Southwestern	R	—	R	R
Central	+	—	+	—
Western ★	U	R	R	—
Northern ★	U	U	U	—

Habitat: Breeding — tundra lakes, ponds and rivers. May visit inshore marine waters to feed. Nests in vegetation on small islands or on shore. In migration and winter — inshore and offshore marine waters.

YELLOW-BILLED LOON
Winter
(Dennis Paulson)

YELLOW-BILLED LOON
Summer
(E. Lieske)

ARCTIC LOON

(Gavia arctica)

LENGTH: 26 IN.

Identification: In summer, adult has a gray nape and black throat. White checkers on the back are separated into several large patches. In Common Loon and Yellow-billed Loon the checkers cover the entire back. In winter, similar to Common Loon but smaller in size with a more slender bill. Dark color of the cap reaches below the eye in a well-marked straight dark line. In contrast, the Common Loon has considerable white around the eyes and an irregular border between the cap and throat colors. Voice is a barking *caw wow* and a variety of wailing and honking notes.

Status and Distribution:	SPRING	SUMMER	FALL	WINTER
Southeastern	C	U	C	C
Southcoastal ★	C	U	C	C
Southwestern ★	C	C	C	R
Central ★	C	C	C	—
Western ★	C	C	C	—
Northern ★	C	C	C	—

Habitat: Breeding — lakes on tundra or in coniferous forests. Nests on projecting points or small islands. In migration and winter — inshore and offshore marine waters.

ARCTIC LOON
Summer
(Edgar Jones)

ARCTIC LOON
Winter
(Dennis Paulson)

RED-THROATED LOON
Winter
(Merrick Hersey)

RED-THROATED LOON

(Gavia stellata)

LENGTH: 25½ IN.

Identification: Summer adult has dark gray head, red throat patch, and plain brown back. Bill is slender, and carried slightly uptilted. All plumages at close range have the back speckled with white instead of the scaly or all dark appearance of the other loons. Head always pale gray contrasting little with the white throat. Voice is long series of quacking notes on breeding grounds, otherwise silent.

Status and Distribution:	SPRING	SUMMER	FALL	WINTER
Southeastern ★	C	C	C	U
Southcoastal ★	C	C	C	U
Southwestern ★	C	C	C	U
Central ★	U	U	U	—
Western ★	C	C	C	—
Northern ★	C	C	C	—

Habitat: Breeding — lakes, usually smaller and shallower than those inhabited by other loons. Nests on shores and islands of lakes. In migration and winter — inshore marine waters.

RED-THROATED LOON
Summer
(Kenneth Fink)

FAMILY *PODICIPEDIDAE*

GREBES

(4)

Grebes are thin-necked diving birds that are smaller than loons. Compared with loons they have relatively long necks and most rarely fly. Their legs are set well back on their bodies, they have flat lobes on their toes and a virtually nonexistent tail. Young, except Western, have striped heads. They feed primarily on fish.

RED-NECKED GREBE

(Podiceps grisegena)

LENGTH: 20 IN.

Identification: In breeding plumage, black crown, conspicuous white cheeks and throat and chestnut-red neck are characteristic. In winter, similar to other grebes with gray to brown upperparts and white underparts. Larger than Horned Grebe with longer yellowish bill and brownish neck. Slightly smaller and shorter necked than Western Grebe. Lacks strong contrast of black and white on head and neck of Western Grebe. More often seen in flight than other grebes. Only grebe with narrow white wing patch on both front and rear edge of each wing.

Status and Distribution:	SPRING	SUMMER	FALL	WINTER
Southeastern	C	U	C	C
Southcoastal ★	C	U	C	C
Southwestern ★	U	R	U	U
Central ★	C	C	C	—
Western ★	U	U	U	—
Northern ★	—	+	—	—

Habitat: Breeding — freshwater lakes, marshes and slow moving rivers. Nests float and are placed in vegetation along the margins of shallow lakes. In winter — inshore marine waters.

RED-NECKED GREBE
(Doug Murphy)

HORNED GREBE

(Podiceps auritus)

LENGTH: 13½ IN.

Identification: In breeding plumage, recognized by broad buffy ear tufts conspicuous against a black head and red neck. In winter, clear white cheeks, short neck and short slender bill separate it from other grebes.

HORNED GREBE
(Craig Harrison)

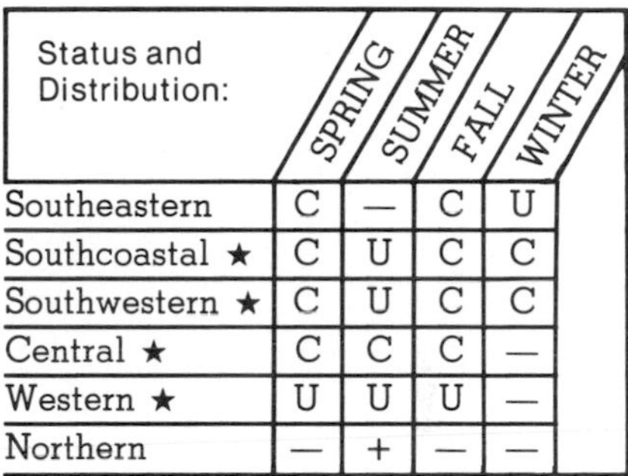

Status and Distribution:	SPRING	SUMMER	FALL	WINTER
Southeastern	C	—	C	U
Southcoastal ★	C	U	C	C
Southwestern ★	C	U	C	C
Central ★	C	C	C	—
Western ★	U	U	U	—
Northern	—	+	—	—

Habitat: Breeding — freshwater ponds, sloughs and lakes, usually in areas containing emergent vegetation. Nests are floating platforms of vegetation and mud anchored to growing vegetation in shallow lakes. In migration and winter — inshore marine waters.

WESTERN GREBE

(Aechmophorus occidentalis)

LENGTH: 26 IN.

Identification: Largest of North American grebes. Identified by long, very slender neck, contrasting black and white coloration and slender yellow bill.

Status and Distribution:	SPRING	SUMMER	FALL	WINTER
Southeastern	U	+	U	U
Southcoastal	—	—	+	+
Southwestern	—	—	—	+
Central	—	—	—	
Western	—	—	—	—
Northern	—	—	—	—

Habitat: Inshore marine waters mostly in the southern part of southeastern Alaska from mid-September through early May. Not known to breed in Alaska.

WESTERN GREBE
(Dennis Paulson)

PIED-BILLED GREBE
(Doug Murphy)

PIED-BILLED GREBE

(Podilymbus podiceps)

LENGTH: 13 IN.

Identification: Only grebe that is all brown in all plumages, with no indication of the angular head of the other species and with a much shorter, almost chickenlike white bill. In summer, the throat is black and the bill has a black band across it.

Habitat: Inshore marine waters and lakes.

Status and Distribution:	SPRING	SUMMER	FALL	WINTER
Southeastern	—	+	R	R
Southcoastal ★	+	+	+	+
Southwestern	—	—	—	—
Central	—	—	—	—
Western	—	—	—	—
Northern	—	—	—	—

FAMILY *DIOMEDEIDAE*
ALBATROSSES
(3)

Albatrosses are goose-sized seabirds with long, narrow, bowed wings that frequent the open ocean. They are much larger than gulls and fly low over the water with scarcely a wingbeat on windy days. Bill is strongly hooked at the tip and has tubular nostrils near its base. Albatrosses do not breed north of central and western Pacific islands.

SHORT-TAILED ALBATROSS
(Diomedea albatrus)
LENGTH: 35 IN.

Identification: Adult is distinguished from Laysan Albatross by an entirely white back. Immature is chocolate brown with a conspicuous pale bill and feet.

Habitat: Mostly offshore marine waters. Endangered species.

Status and Distribution:	SPRING	SUMMER	FALL	WINTER
Southeastern	+	—	—	—
Southcoastal	—	—	+	—
Southwestern	+	+	—	—
Central	—	—	—	—
Western	—	—	—	—
Northern	—	—	—	—

SHORT-TAILED ALBATROSS
(Craig Harrison)

BLACK-FOOTED ALBATROSS
(Diomedea nigripes)
LENGTH: 32 IN.
WINGSPAN: 7 FT.

Identification: Dark-bodied with dark feet and bill. Some older birds have white rumps and considerable white on the head.

Status and Distribution:	SPRING	SUMMER	FALL	WINTER
Southeastern	C	C	C	—
Southcoastal	C	C	C	R
Southwestern	C	C	C	—
Central	—	—	—	—
Western	R	R	R	—
Northern	—	—	—	—

Habitat: Mostly offshore marine waters. Most often seen from vessels crossing the Gulf of Alaska and near the Aleutian Islands.

BLACK-FOOTED ALBATROSS
(Dennis Paulson)

LAYSAN ALBATROSS
(Diomedea immutabilis)
LENGTH: 32 IN.
WINGSPAN: 6½ FT.

Identification: Huge, long-winged seabird with white body and black back and wings.

Status and Distribution:	SPRING	SUMMER	FALL	WINTER
Southeastern	R	—	—	—
Southcoastal	R	R	R	—
Southwestern	U	U	U	R
Central	—	—	—	—
Western	R	R	R	—
Northern	—	—	—	—

Habitat: Inshore and offshore marine waters. The western and central Aleutian Islands are a good area to view this species.

LAYSAN ALBATROSS
(Craig Harrison)

Notes: This species is not nearly as common as the Black-footed Albatross. Estimates of yearly populations in the southcoastal region are in the hundreds, whereas estimates for the Black-footed Albatross for the summer alone number in the thousands and possibly the tens of thousands.

FAMILY *PROCELLARIIDAE*

SHEARWATERS, PETRELS, FULMARS

(7 + 1)

These are gull-sized seabirds that resemble gulls but have longer, more slender wings and tubular nostrils. Sailing over the open sea with occasional rapid wingbeats, they are often seen skimming low over the waves on stiff, bowed wings. Northern Fulmar is the only member of this family that breeds in Alaska.

NORTHERN FULMAR

(Fulmarus glacialis)

LENGTH: 18 IN.

Identification: Color varies from light to dark. The lighter phase (gray back and wings, otherwise white) resembles an adult gull but the stubby large bill with large nostrils, held pointing downward, thick neck and stiff-winged flight distinguishes it from any gull. Darker phase (all dark gray) may be mistaken for dark shearwaters but is much heavier built, paler, and again with a thicker, down-pointing, yellow bill.

NORTHERN FULMAR
Light Phase
(Dennis Paulson)

Status and Distribution:	SPRING	SUMMER	FALL	WINTER
Southeastern	U	R	U	U
Southcoastal	C	C	C	U
Southwestern ★	C	C	C	U
Central	—	—	—	—
Western	U	C	U	—
Northern	—	R	—	—

Habitat: Inshore and offshore marine waters. Nests in colonies on sea cliffs on some of the outlying islands including the Semidi, Aleutian and Pribilof islands.

Notes: A fulmar usually feeds from the surface of the sea on small fish and squid. Often it follows ships or concentrates near canneries to feed on refuse.

NORTHERN FULMAR
Dark Phase
(Dennis Paulson)

PINK-FOOTED SHEARWATER

(Puffinus creatopus)

LENGTH: 19 IN.

Identification: One of 3 white-bellied shearwaters that might be seen offshore. Drab light brown above with an irregular line where the 2 colors meet. Considerable brown in the white wing linings. Pink bill.

Habitat: Inshore and offshore marine waters.

Status and Distribution:	SPRING	SUMMER	FALL	WINTER
Southeastern	R	R	R	—
Southcoastal	R	R	R	—
Southwestern	—	—	—	—
Central	—	—	—	—
Western	—	—	—	—
Northern	—	—	—	—

PINK-FOOTED SHEARWATER
(Dennis Paulson)

BULLER'S SHEARWATER
(Dennis Paulson)

FLESH-FOOTED SHEARWATER
(Puffinus carneipes)
LENGTH: 19½ IN.

Identification: Large, entirely chocolate brown with conspicuous pink bill and feet. Wing linings are dark, even darker than in most Short-tailed Shearwaters. A slow wingbeat is the best field mark at a distance.

Habitat: Inshore and offshore marine waters.

Status and Distribution:	SPRING	SUMMER	FALL	WINTER
Southeastern	—	—	—	—
Southcoastal	—	+	+	—
Southwestern	—	+	+	—
Central	—	—	—	—
Western	—	—	—	—
Northern	—	—	—	—

FLESH-FOOTED SHEARWATER
(Dennis Paulson)

BULLER'S SHEARWATER
(Puffinus bulleri)
LENGTH: 16½ IN.

Identification: Small, crisply gray above, with a black cap and tail and black M-pattern across the wings and back. Snowy white beneath, including the wing linings. The flash of the white wing linings is the best distant field mark. Wingbeat is much slower than that of the other small, white-bellied shearwater, the Manx.

Habitat: Offshore marine waters.

Notes: This species travels in flocks more than other shearwaters do.

Status and Distribution:	SPRING	SUMMER	FALL	WINTER
Southeastern	—	—	—	—
Southcoastal	+	R	+	—
Southwestern	—	—	—	—
Central	—	—	—	—
Western	—	—	—	—
Northern	—	—	-	—

SOOTY SHEARWATER

(Puffinus griseus)

LENGTH: 17 IN.

Identification: Appears dark at a distance. Often seen gliding over waves with narrow, rigidly held wings. Has dark bill and feet, most have whitish wing linings and uniformly dark head. Some have dark wing linings.

Habitat: Inshore and offshore marine waters. Approaches the coastline more often than other shearwaters.

Status and Distribution:	SPRING	SUMMER	FALL	WINTER
Southeastern	C	C	C	—
Southcoastal	C	C	C	—
Southwestern	C	C	C	+
Central	—	—	—	—
Western	—	—	—	—
Northern	—	—	—	—

Notes: In some years these birds are estimated to number in the millions in Alaska's offshore waters.

SHORT-TAILED SHEARWATER
(Doug Forsell)

Status and Distribution:	SPRING	SUMMER	FALL	WINTER
Southeastern	—	R	R	—
Southcoastal	U	C	U	+
Southwestern	C	C	C	+
Central	—	—	—	—
Western	C	C	C	—
Northern	—	R	R	—

SHORT-TAILED SHEARWATER

(Puffinus tenuirostris)

LENGTH: 14 IN.

Identification: Difficult to distinguish from Sooty Shearwater. *Usually* the underside of the wing is plain gray rather than whitish as in the Sooty Shearwater. Short-tailed Shearwater has a shorter, thinner bill than Sooty Shearwater but this may be difficult to see in the field. Throat is often whitish.

Habitat: Inshore and offshore marine waters. Most abundant near the Aleutian Islands and in the Bering Sea. Occurs less frequently along the coast of Alaska to Forrester Island in southeastern Alaska and north along the coast to Point Barrow. This species and the Northern Fulmar are the only shearwaters likely to be found in far northern waters.

Notes: This species, like the Sooty Shearwater, sometimes occurs in numbers estimated to be in the millions. Short-tailed Shearwater feeds on fish, squid, crustaceans and refuse thrown from ships.

SOOTY SHEARWATER
(Dennis Paulson)

MANX SHEARWATER
(John C. Pitcher)

MANX SHEARWATER

(Puffinus puffinus)
LENGTH: 14 IN.

Identification: Small bird, black above, white below, with pure white wing linings. Much more rapid wingbeat than other shearwaters.

Habitat: Inshore and offshore marine waters.

Status and Distribution:	SPRING	SUMMER	FALL	WINTER
Southeastern	—	—	—	—
Southcoastal	+	+	—	—
Southwestern	—	—	—	—
Central	—	—	—	—
Western	—	—	—	—
Northern	—	—	—	—

Notes: Manx Shearwater *(Puffinus puffinus)* is relegated to the Alaska Unsubstantiated List. This bird has been divided taxonomically by the American Ornithologists' Union into two species (Manx Shearwater *Puffinus puffinus* and Black-vented Shearwater *Puffinus opisthomelas*), both of which occur in the North Pacific Ocean. Despite the very different names, these two species can be very difficult to tell apart, and it is not known which one has occurred in Alaska, since Manx Shearwater was accorded a place on the Alaska List on the basis of sight records alone.

MOTTLED PETREL

(Pterodroma inexpectata)

LENGTH: 14 IN.

Identification: At close range a patchy pattern of gray above with a dark cap and forward edge of the wing, and mixed dark and white below is visible. Gray belly and dark line under the wing contrasts with white breast and undertail. Flight is much like that of other shearwaters but more rapid and often higher above the surface of the water. This species sometimes flies in great loops.

Status and Distribution:	SPRING	SUMMER	FALL	WINTER
Southeastern	U	U	U	—
Southcoastal	U	U	U	—
Southwestern	U	U	U	—
Central	—	—	—	—
Western	—	R	—	—
Northern	—	—	—	—

Habitat: Mostly offshore marine waters. Occasionally inshore waters in summer. Usually seen singly or in small groups on the open North Pacific.

MOTTLED PETREL
(John C. Pitcher)

FAMILY *HYDROBATIDAE*

STORM-PETRELS

(2)

Storm-Petrels are small blackbird-sized birds of the open sea with a forked or notched tail. They are often seen hovering or diving onto the ocean surface in search of food.

FORK-TAILED STORM-PETREL
(R. H. Day)

FORK-TAILED STORM-PETREL

(Oceanodroma furcata)

LENGTH: 8½ IN.

Identification: Pearl gray color distinguishes this species from Leach's Storm-Petrels, which are dark brown. Phalaropes, which fly steadily and are often seen in flocks, are the only other small, pale birds to be seen at sea.

Habitat: Inshore and offshore marine waters. Nests in colonies on offshore islands. Breeding pairs dig burrows in the soil or, more commonly, occupy rock crevices. Breeding locations include Saint Lazaria and Forrester islands in southeastern Alaska, the Aleutian Islands and Barren, Chiswell, Semidi and Shumagin islands.

Status and Distribution:	SPRING	SUMMER	FALL	WINTER
Southeastern ★	C	C	C	R
Southcoastal ★	C	C	C	R
Southwestern ★	C	C	C	R
Central	—	—	+	—
Western	—	U	U	—
Northern	—	—	—	—

Notes: Although this species congregates at food sources, it does not flock, each bird being independent in flight. Often attracted to boat lights at night. Commonly seen near shore, especially in fall.

LEACH'S STORM-PETREL
(Leonard Lee Rue III)

LEACH'S STORM-PETREL

(Oceanodroma leucorhoa)

LENGTH: 8 IN.

Identification: Dark brown above and below with a forked tail and conspicuous white rump patch.

Habitat: Inshore and offshore marine waters. Nests on islands in colonies with each nest placed at the end of a shallow burrow. Breeds on the Aleutian, Semidi and Shumagin islands; in the Sandman Reefs, south of the Alaska Peninsula; and on Saint Lazaria and Forrester islands, off southeastern Alaska.

Status and Distribution:	SPRING	SUMMER	FALL	WINTER
Southeastern ★	U	C	C	—
Southcoastal ★	R	R	R	—
Southwestern ★	U	C	C	—
Central	—	—	—	—
Western	—	—	—	—
Northern	—	—	—	—

Notes: Feeds nocturnally near its breeding grounds hence rarely seen at sea near shore.

FAMILY *PHALACROCORACIDAE*
CORMORANTS
(4)

Cormorants are large, dark, water birds with slender bills. All 4 of their toes are connected by webs. They hold their bills up at an angle and are longer tailed and broader winged than loons. Sometimes seen drying their wings by holding them open.

DOUBLE-CRESTED CORMORANT
(Phalacrocorax auritus)
LENGTH: 33 IN.

Identification: Distinguished from other cormorants by orange-yellow throat pouch and pale bill, and in breeding season by side-by-side crests on the head. Bulky neck is kinked in flight. Immatures have pale brownish breast. Often flies much higher than other cormorants, which tend to stay low over the water except at breeding colonies.

Status and Distribution:	SPRING	SUMMER	FALL	WINTER
Southeastern ★	U	U	U	U
Southcoastal ★	C	C	C	U
Southwestern ★	C	C	C	U
Central	—	+	—	—
Western	—	—	—	—
Northern	—	—	—	—

Habitat: Lakes, rivers, inshore marine waters. Nests in a variety of locations including cliff ledges, trees near either fresh or salt water or on the ground on small islands. Only cormorant to be seen on fresh water and in shallow estuaries.

DOUBLE-CRESTED CORMORANT
(Lee Post/Mike Lettis)

BRANDT'S CORMORANT
(David Hatler)

BRANDT'S CORMORANT

(Phalacrocorax penicillatus)

LENGTH: 34 IN.

Identification: Shaped more like a Pelagic Cormorant than Double-crested Cormorant with a long, slender neck and long, slender bill. Flies with a very slightly crooked or straight neck, and with the head moderately distinct from the neck. Bill looks heavier than that of the Pelagic or Red-faced cormorants. Shorter tail than other cormorants which is a good way to distinguish Brandt's Cormorant from smaller cormorants. At close range buffy feathers behind the naked dark throat pouch are visible. In breeding plumage, fine white plumes appear on the sides of neck and back, and throat pouch becomes bright blue. Immature is dark brown below, darker than young Double-crested Cormorants, but paler than young Pelagic and Red-faced cormorants.

Status and Distribution:	SPRING	SUMMER	FALL	WINTER
Southeastern ★	—	R	+	—
Southcoastal ★	—	R	—	—
Southwestern	—	—	—	—
Central	—	—	—	—
Western	—	—	—	—
Northern	—	—	—	—

Habitat: Inshore marine waters, rocky islands. Only known breeding colony in Alaska is on Seal Rocks, Hinchinbrook Entrance, Prince William Sound.

RED-FACED CORMORANT
(D.H.S. Wehle)

PELAGIC CORMORANT

(Phalacrocorax pelagicus)

LENGTH: 25½ IN.

Identification: Glossy greenish-black color is similar to that of the Red-faced Cormorant. Both Pelagic and Red-faced cormorants have white flank patches in breeding plumage and fore and aft crests on the head. Pelagic Cormorant has a dull red pouch and a small amount of dull red on its face. Immature is all dark, without the iridescence of the adult.

Status and Distribution:	SPRING	SUMMER	FALL	WINTER
Southeastern ★	C	U	C	C
Southcoastal ★	C	C	C	C
Southwestern ★	C	C	C	C
Central	—	—	—	—
Western ★	C	C	C	—
Northern	—	R	—	—

Habitat: Inshore marine waters, sea cliffs, rocky islands. Nests in colonies on small islands and narrow cliff ledges near the sea.

Notes: Dives deeper than other cormorants and swims underwater. Often approaches schools of small fish from below causing them to jump about at the surface and thus become easier to capture. Sometimes seen on floating logs and icebergs.

PELAGIC CORMORANT
(Dennis Paulson)

RED-FACED CORMORANT

(Phalacrocorax urile)

LENGTH: 29 IN.

Identification: Likely to be confused only with Pelagic Cormorant, the only other small cormorant in Alaska. In breeding season has bright red face patch and blue throat and much greater area of bare skin about the base of bill. In duller immature plumage, distinguished at close range by a heavier bill, which is usually pale and not black, and somewhat larger size than Pelagic Cormorant.

Habitat: Inshore marine waters. Nests in colonies on ledges of sea cliffs, small piles of rocks and on small shelves on volcanic cinder cones.

Status and Distribution:	SPRING	SUMMER	FALL	WINTER
Southeastern	—	—	—	+
Southcoastal ★	C	C	C	C
Southwestern ★	C	C	C	C
Central	—	—	—	—
Western	—	+	—	—
Northern	—	—	—	—

Notes: In North America this bird occurs only in Alaska.

FAMILY *ARDEIDAE*

HERONS, BITTERNS

(3 + 4)

These are wading birds with long necks and legs and rather long, straight, pointed bills.

GREAT BLUE HERON
(Doug Murphy)

GREAT BLUE HERON

(Ardea herodias)

LENGTH: 47 IN.
WINGSPAN: 6 FT.

Identification: Blue-gray and somewhat streaked. Likely to be confused only with Sandhill Crane which is plain gray and streakless. In flight, the heron carries its neck doubled back with its head against its shoulders; the crane carries its neck straight out. Heron is usually solitary; crane is often in pairs or flocks.

Status and Distribution:	SPRING	SUMMER	FALL	WINTER
Southeastern ★	U	U	U	U
Southcoastal ★	U	U	U	U
Southwestern	—	—	—	—
Central	—	+	—	—
Western	—	—	—	—
Northern	—	+	—	—

Habitat: Tidal sloughs, saltwater inlets and beaches, lower reaches of salmon spawning streams, shallow lakes, freshwater ponds and marshes. Nests in colonies in upper parts of tall trees and more rarely in bushes or on the ground. Sometimes perches in trees.

Notes: Expert at fishing; captures prey by remaining motionless or by a very slow stalk and a rapid strike with the bill.

BLACK-CROWNED NIGHT-HERON
(Uve Hublitz, Cornell Lab of Ornithology)

BLACK-CROWNED NIGHT-HERON

(Nycticorax nycticorax)

LENGTH: 23-28 IN.

Identification: Adult is distinctive with its black back and black cap. Gray wings, whitish underneath, and long white plumes on head in breeding plumage. Immature is brown with buffy spots on wings and back and streaks on head and underparts. Call is a loud, barking *Kwok!*

Habitat: Has occurred on Shemya and Atka islands in the Aleutians and on Saint Paul Island in the Pribilofs.

Status and Distribution:	SPRING	SUMMER	FALL	WINTER
Southeastern	—	—	—	—
Southcoastal	—	—	—	—
Southwestern	+	—	—	—
Central	—	—	—	—
Western	—	—	—	—
Northern	—	—	—	—

AMERICAN BITTERN
(Brian Milne)

AMERICAN BITTERN

(Botaurus lentiginosus)

LENGTH: 23½ IN.

Status and Distribution:	SPRING	SUMMER	FALL	WINTER
Southeastern ★	R	R	R	—
Southcoastal	—	—	—	—
Southwestern	—	—	—	—
Central	—	—	—	—
Western	—	—	—	—
Northern	—	—	—	—

Identification: Heavily striped with white and warm brown. Much more compact than larger Great Blue Heron but has same long, pointed bill, longish neck, long legs and habit of folding the neck in flight. Flying at a distance, bittern looks very pointed at the front end and appears all brown with darker flight feathers.

Habitat: Freshwater lakes and marshes with heavy aquatic vegetation. Nests have not been found in Alaska. Elsewhere nests consist of a platform of dead stalks in heavy vegetation. Found mostly along major mainland river systems of southeastern Alaska.

FAMILY *ANATIDAE*

SWANS, GEESE, DUCKS

(50)

This family of waterfowl is best described in the following groups:

Swans — Large waterfowl, in which the adults have an all white plumage and very long neck. Alaska swans do not pair until their third or fourth year but once paired, tend to remain together for life. The usual family seen in fall or winter includes 2 white parents and 3 to 5 gray young. Young assume pure white adult plumage early in their second year. Three species occur in Alaska.

Geese — Geese are smaller than swans and larger than ducks. They walk better than ducks and feed more frequently on land. Seven species occur in Alaska.

Surface-feeding Ducks — Includes birds from American Black Duck through American Wigeon. Surface-feeding, or puddle ducks, have feet set in the middle of their bodies and walk well, often nesting far from the water in meadows or woodland. They feed while walking or by tipping up in the water and "dabbling." These ducks leap from the water when taking flight. Most of them from Alaska winter in Pacific coast states. Fourteen species occur in Alaska.

Perching Ducks — Represented in Alaska by 1 species, the Wood Duck. This duck nests in holes in trees, has sharp claws and usually perches on branches near water.

Diving Ducks — Includes birds from Common Pochard through Black Scoter. They have feet set far back on their bodies and must balance in an awkward fashion when walking. They feed under water and can dive to depths of a hundred feet or more in search of food. Diving ducks patter across the water in a long take-off run before becoming airborne. Nineteen species occur in Alaska.

Stiff-tailed Ducks — Represented in Alaska by 1 species, the Ruddy Duck. They have stiff, elongated tail feathers and unusually large feet. They are nearly helpless on land and feed almost exclusively under water.

Mergansers — These are fish-eating ducks with slender bills equipped with sharp projections especially adapted for catching and holding fish. Four species occur in Alaska.

Plumages — In the swans and geese sexes are identical. In ducks, sexes are usually easily separated in winter and spring with the males being the more colorful. After nesting, ducks undergo an eclipse molt causing males to look much like females. This causes some confusion in identification; however, the distinctive speculum does not change providing a handy way to identify ducks in flight. The pictures in this book are winter-spring plumages.

TUNDRA SWAN

(Cygnus columbianus)

LENGTH: 52 IN.
WINGSPAN: 6-7 FT.

Identification: Bright yellow teardrop on otherwise black bill is typical of Tundra Swan although in some birds this spot is absent or too small to see.

Habitat: In summer — tundra. Nests usually on dry upland sites sometimes many yards from water, and occasionally on small islands. In migration — salt water, wetlands, lakes and rivers.

Notes: Recent inventories show more than 100,000 Tundra Swans in their principal wintering areas in California, Maryland, Virginia and North Carolina. Two-thirds of this population probably nest in Alaska with the birds south of Kotzebue wintering in the west and those from Kotzebue north making the long trek east.

Status and Distribution:	SPRING	SUMMER	FALL	WINTER
Southeastern	U	—	C	R
Southcoastal	C	R	C	R
Southwestern ★	C	C	C	R
Central ★	C	U	C	—
Western ★	C	C	C	—
Northern ★	U	U	U	—

Best places to watch for Tundra Swans include: Yukon-Kuskokwim Delta where nesting densities are highest; Naknek River near the King Salmon airport where large flocks gather in spring and fall; upper Cook Inlet including Potter Marsh and Portage; and wetlands near Cordova, Yakutat, Gustavus, Juneau and other southeast coastal areas particularly in October.

TUNDRA SWAN
(Dennis Paulson)

TRUMPETER SWAN

(Cygnus buccinator)

LENGTH: 65 IN.
WINGSPAN: 6-8 FT.

Identification: Difficult to distinguish from Tundra Swan. Has an all-black bill, lacking the yellow spot usually found on the bill of the Tundra Swan. Substantially larger than Tundra Swan and easily distinguished when the two are occasionally seen together during migration. Trumpeter Swan usually has an obvious pink area where upper and lower mandibles contact. Trumpeter's call is hornlike (often *ko-hoh*); tundra's is high-pitched, often quavering *(oo-oo-oo)* and is accentuated in the middle.

Status and Distribution:	SPRING	SUMMER	FALL	WINTER
Southeastern ★	U	R	U	R
Southcoastal ★	C	C	C	U
Southwestern	—	—	—	+
Central ★	U	U	U	—
Western ★	—	+	—	—
Northern ★	—	R	—	—

Habitat: Forest wetlands, lakes, marshes, rivers with dense vegetation. Nests in water by making a platform 6-12 feet in diameter from surrounding vegetation.

Notes: Trumpeter Swan is recognized as the largest of the 7 swans found worldwide and is probably the heaviest flying bird at 25 to 35, and occasionally 40, lbs. Eighty percent of world's population of trumpeters nests in Alaska, yet at 7,000 to 8,000 birds they are outnumbered 15 to 1 by smaller Tundra Swan.

Best places to see Trumpeter Swans in summer are Kenai National Wildlife Refuge, Minto Flats near Fairbanks, and along the highway east from Cordova. In winter they are often seen from the road at Eyak Lake in Cordova and Blind Slough in Petersburg.

TRUMPETER SWAN
(Tom Ulrich)

WHOOPER SWAN

(Cygnus cygnus)

LENGTH: 52 IN.
WINGSPAN: 6-7 FT.

Identification: Slightly smaller than Trumpeter Swan but otherwise resembles that species except for extensive yellow saddle covering half or more of upper bill in the adult.

Habitat: Mostly found in western and central Aleutian Islands where a few dozen winter. Not known to breed in Alaska.

Status and Distribution:	SPRING	SUMMER	FALL	WINTER
Southeastern	—	—	—	—
Southcoastal	—	—	+	—
Southwestern	R	R	R	U
Central	—	—	—	—
Western	R	R	—	—
Northern	—	—	—	—

WHOOPER SWAN
(A. J. Davis)

GREATER WHITE-FRONTED GOOSE
(Michael Hopiak, Cornell Lab of Ornithology)

GREATER WHITE-FRONTED GOOSE

(Anser albifrons)

LENGTH: 28½ IN.

Identification: Brown with white tail coverts. Shorter neck than similarly sized Canada Geese although the 2 species may closely resemble one another at a distance. Adult has a white patch on the front of the face. Immature lacks white patch but has yellow or orange legs and feet which no other Alaska geese have except much rarer Bean Goose and easily distinguished Emperor Goose. Young have very light black breast spotting while older birds become heavily spotted or blotched underneath.

Habitat: Breeding — Nests on flats or slight hummocks often bordering a stream or lake. In migration — coastal saltwater grass flats and inland open grassy fields.

Status and Distribution:	SPRING	SUMMER	FALL	WINTER
Southeastern	U	—	U	—
Southcoastal ★	C	R	C	+
Southwestern ★	C	C	C	+
Central ★	C	U	C	—
Western ★	C	C	C	—
Northern ★	C	C	C	—

Notes: Nests over most of Alaska north of Alaska Range. There are 2 separate populations; birds from Yukon River Delta go to California, birds from eastern and northern Alaska migrate southeast to Canadian prairies, the central flyway and eastern Mexico.

CANADA GOOSE
(Branta canadensis)

Identification: Most authorities agree there are 11 subspecies of Canada Geese in North America, of which 6 occur in Alaska. All have brown backs, white rump patches, long black necks and white cheeks. Size, range and habits separate these subspecies. Because they mate for life and the young accompany their parents on their first round trip migration, mixing among these subspecies is minimal. Larger subspecies make the familiar honk while smaller ones have a higher-pitched call.

Status and Distribution:	SPRING	SUMMER	FALL	WINTER
Southeastern ★	C	C	C	C
Southcoastal ★	C	C	C	U
Southwestern ★	U	R	C	+
Central ★	C	C	C	—
Western ★	C	C	C	—
Northern ★	C	C	C	—

Distribution and Habitat: Great subspecific diversity in breeding habitats and range makes a concise summary difficult. Each subspecies will be discussed separately.

VANCOUVER CANADA GOOSE — *B.c. fulva:* Dark goose, weighing up to 16 pounds. Nests from British Columbia throughout southeastern Alaska and perhaps to Prince William Sound. Nests are widely scattered and tend to be well hidden in the woods. Winters primarily within its breeding range in flocks up to 500, thus is essentially non-migratory. Tideflats near the Juneau airport are probably where it is most often seen; some individuals are present there almost all year.

DUSKY CANADA GOOSE — *B.c. occidentalis:* Superficially similar to but slightly smaller than Vancouver Canada Goose. Mostly nests in one great colony in grasslands of Copper River Delta and migrates to Willamette River Valley in Oregon.

LESSER CANADA GOOSE — *B.c. parvipes:* Medium-sized goose distributed in summer from Cook Inlet north through interior valleys. Most often seen at Potter Marsh near Anchorage, and Minto Flats near Fairbanks. Major staging areas are islands in the Yukon River, the Yukon Delta, and Cook Inlet. Winters in Pacific Coast states.

TAVERNER'S CANADA GOOSE —*B.c. taverneri:* The validity of taxonomic distinction and extent of breeding ranges of Taverner's Canada Goose and Lesser Canada Goose are controversial. However, scientists now believe *parvipes* nests generally in interior, forested areas while *taverneri* nests on the tundra. Up to 73,500 Taverner's Canada Geese have been counted staging for their fall migration in Cold Bay area.

ALEUTIAN CANADA GOOSE — *B.c. leucopareia:* Small goose with a broad white ring at the base of the neck. Rarest of all Canada Geese. Formerly nested over most of the Aleutian Islands but foxes introduced by fur farmers exterminated this subspecies on all islands except Buldir in western Aleutians and Chagulak Island in the eastcentral Aleutians. Closed hunting areas in California and Oregon, release of captive reared birds, and a decline of foxes in the Aleutians are allowing an increase in this rare bird. Winters in western Oregon, northwestern and central California. Movements of this subspecies within Alaska are not well known and Aleutian Canada Goose can be easily confused with more abundant Cackling Canada Goose, which can have a white neck ring.

CACKLING CANADA GOOSE — *B.c. minima:* Smallest of all Canada Geese. Not much larger than a Mallard. Nests in a loose colony along 100 miles of coastline between mouths of Kuskokwim and Yukon rivers. Winters in California.

CANADA GOOSE
Vancouver Subspecies

BRANT

(Branta bernicla)

LENGTH: 26 IN.

Identification: Very dark. Lacks white cheeks of Canada Geese. Adult has narrow, barred, white patch on the sides of the neck. In flight, looks dark with a conspicuous white posterior. Calls infrequently. Voice is a croaking sound very different from calls of other geese.

Status and Distribution:	SPRING	SUMMER	FALL	WINTER
Southeastern	U	R	R	R
Southcoastal	C	R	R	+
Southwestern	C	R	C	R
Central	+	—	—	—
Western ★	C	C	C	—
Northern ★	C	C	C	—

BRANT
(Dennis Paulson)

Habitat: Breeding — lowland, coastal tundra, usually just above high tide line. Perhaps half the population nests on the Yukon-Kuskokwim Delta on low, grassy flats dissected by numerous tidal streams. The rest nest farther north in coastal Alaska, Siberia and Canada. In migration—saltwater bays and estuaries.

Notes: Best place to see Brant is Yukon River Delta near Hooper Bay in early summer or at Izembek Bay near Cold Bay on the Alaska Peninsula in fall. At Izembek Bay in the fall the entire population spends a month or more fattening in the largest eel grass pasture in the world. In early November they fly en masse across the Gulf of Alaska, many reaching Mexico before making landfall.

SNOW GOOSE

(Chen caerulescens)

LENGTH: 28 IN.

Identification: Adult is pure white with black wing tips visible at a great distance. Immature is pale gray. This species is most vociferous of all waterfowl; call is a high-pitched yelp similar to bark of a small dog. The blue phase, very rare in Alaska, could be confused with the Emperor Goose (see photo).

Habitat: Breeding — low, grassy tundra. Nests in grassy areas on the tundra. In migration — may occur along almost all coastal areas of Alaska, except the Aleutian Islands, and in several locations in the interior including Yukon and Tanana river valleys.

Notes: Spectacular migration occurs from Wrangel Island in Siberia to Seward Peninsula early in September, thence to Yukon River Delta where flocks fatten on berries for a month. In October often seen at Pilot Point on north coast of the Alaska Peninsula, Cook Inlet, Cordova, Yakutat and on Stikine River Delta near Wrangell. Canadian birds visit Arctic National Wildlife Refuge in large numbers, foraging in the uplands before following Canada's Mackenzie River Valley south.

Status and Distribution:	SPRING	SUMMER	FALL	WINTER
Southeastern	U	—	U	—
Southcoastal	C	—	C	—
Southwestern	C	—	C	—
Central	C	+	C	—
Western ★	C	R	C	—
Northern ★	C	U	C	—

SNOW GOOSE
(Doug Murphy)

SNOW GOOSE
Blue Phase
(Doug Murphy)

BEAN GOOSE
(Kenneth Fink)

BEAN GOOSE

(Anser fabalis)

LENGTH: 28-36 IN.

Identification: Closely resembles Greater White-fronted Goose at a distance but is generally larger and more ponderous, darker and longer necked. Has no white around the bill. Has unspotted belly similar to young Greater White-fronted Geese. Bill is black with irregularly shaped orange ring around the middle.

Status and Distribution:	SPRING	SUMMER	FALL	WINTER
Southeastern	—	—	—	—
Southcoastal	—	—	—	—
Southwestern	R	—	—	—
Central	—	—	—	—
Western	+	—	—	—
Northern	—	—	—	—

Habitat: Asiatic goose found mostly in western and central Aleutian Islands during spring. Not known to breed in Alaska.

EMPEROR GOOSE

(Chen canagica)

LENGTH: 27 IN.

Identification: Adult is medium blue-gray, scaled with black and white, and identified by a white head and hind neck. From the rear in flight the white tail is prominent. Immature is dark in September but grows white feathers of adult plumage throughout the fall. In all plumages, only goose in Alaska with white *tail* and dark tail *coverts* (reverse is true of all other species).

Habitat: Breeding — low, wet tundra near the coast, often near lakes and ponds. Nests near water in grassy marsh habitat on an island, bank or in a large tussock. In winter — saltwater beaches.

Notes: Bulk of world's population nests in Yukon-Kuskokwim Delta. A few nest farther north to Kotzebue Sound; a few nest in eastern Siberia. Most Emperor Geese, including the Siberians, work their way down the coast of western Alaska in fall and most winter in the Aleutian Islands. Only rarely is an Emperor Goose seen east or south of Kodiak.

Status and Distribution:	SPRING	SUMMER	FALL	WINTER
Southeastern	+	—	—	—
Southcoastal	R	+	R	U
Southwestern ★	C	U	C	C
Central	—	—	—	—
Western ★	C	C	C	—
Northern	—	R	—	—

EMPEROR GOOSE
(G. V. Byrd)

ROSS' GOOSE

(Chen rossii)

LENGTH: 24 IN.

Identification: Petite version of the Snow Goose, very much like it at a distance. Bill is much smaller than Snow Goose and lacks the distinct black "lips". A bit of bluish-gray at the bill base is visible at extremely close range. Immature is pale gray but smaller and has a smaller bill than a Snow Goose.

Status and Distribution:	SPRING	SUMMER	FALL	WINTER
Southeastern	+	—	—	—
Southcoastal	—	—	—	—
Southwestern	—	—	—	—
Central	—	—	—	—
Western	—	—	—	—
Northern	—	+	—	—

Habitat: Has been found at the mouth of the Stikine River in southeastern Alaska and near Teshekpuk Lake on the Arctic coast. Not known to breed in Alaska.

ROSS' GOOSE
(Dennis Paulson)

AMERICAN BLACK DUCK

(Anas rubripes)

LENGTH: 22 IN.

Identification: Very dark, similar to Mallard in size and shape. Only duck found in Alaska in which sexes look the same. Wing linings white, contrasting greatly with overall color. Head conspicuously paler than body. Speculum darker blue than in Mallard, with a narrower white border.

Status and Distribution:	SPRING	SUMMER	FALL	WINTER
Southeastern	—	—	—	+
Southcoastal	+	—	+	—
Southwestern	—	—	—	—
Central	+	—	—	—
Western	—	—	—	—
Northern	—	—	—	—

Habitat: Has occurred near Fairbanks, Cordova and Gustavus. Not known to breed in Alaska.

AMERICAN BLACK DUCK
(Dennis Paulson)

MALLARD

(Anas platyrhynchos)

LENGTH: 20½-28 IN.

Identification: Male has green head and narrow white collar. Whitish outer sides of the tail, white wing linings, and white-bordered blue speculum on both male and female are good flight identifying marks. Voice of female is the familiar *quack*; male emits a quiet *reeb* or low *kwek*.

Habitat: Marshes, sloughs, lakes, rivers and most flooded land. Forages on land, especially upper tideland habitats. Seems to prefer fresh to salt water but will frequent estuarine areas, especially in winter. Nests on the ground, sometimes far from water and on rare occasions in trees.

Status and Distribution:	SPRING	SUMMER	FALL	WINTER
Southeastern ★	C	C	C	C
Southcoastal ★	C	C	C	C
Southwestern ★	C	C	C	C
Central ★	C	C	C	R
Western ★	C	C	C	—
Northern ★	R	R	—	—

Notes: Most widespread duck in the world. Most domestic ducks come from Mallard stock. Male has a little curled feather above the tail that often indicates the origin of domestic ducks which otherwise do not resemble Mallards.

MALLARD
Male, left; Female, right
(Dennis Paulson)

SPOT-BILLED DUCK
(E.R. Degginger, Bruce Coleman, Inc.)

SPOT-BILLED DUCK

(Anas poecilorhyncha)

LENGTH: 23-24 IN.

Identification: Dark bill with a yellow tip, dark cap and dark eyeline contrasts with the otherwise pale head. In flight look for blue speculum with a white area on the rear edge of the wings near the body, and white wing linings that contrast sharply with otherwise dark brown body and wings. The race that occurs in Alaska has a moustachial stripe. Sexes alike.

Habitat: Has been found on Adak Island and Kodiak Island. Breeds from northeast Asia to India.

Status and Distribution:	SPRING	SUMMER	FALL	WINTER
Southeastern	—	—	—	—
Southcoastal	—	—	—	—
Southwestern	+	—	+	—
Central	—	—	—	—
Western	—	—	—	—
Northern	—	—	—	—

GADWALL
Female, left; Male, right
(Dennis Paulson)

GADWALL

(Anas strepera)

LENGTH: 18½-23 IN.

Identification: At a distance a flock of Gadwalls appears drab. Adult male looks gray with a black posterior. All Gadwalls can be distinguished from other puddle ducks in flight by their white speculum. A female at close range looks much like a Mallard, with a dark bill with orange sides, but she is slightly smaller and more slender with a distinctly more slender bill and gray tail feathers. A female is difficult to distinguish unless she accompanies a male or exposes her wings.

Status and Distribution:	SPRING	SUMMER	FALL	WINTER
Southeastern ★	U	R	U	R
Southcoastal ★	C	U	C	U
Southwestern ★	U	U	U	U
Central	R	R	R	—
Western	—	+	+	—
Northern	—	+	—	—

Habitat: Sedge-grass marshes. Nests in heavy vegetation often several yards from water.

Notes: Nests in small numbers in Alaska. Spring and fall migrants are more abundant on grass flats of Copper River Delta than elsewhere. Hundreds winter in Prince William Sound, primarily at Port Wells and Port Fidalgo.

FALCATED TEAL
(Len Rue Jr.)

NORTHERN PINTAIL

(Anas acuta)

LENGTH: MALE, 25-29 IN.
FEMALE, 20½-22½ IN.

Identification: Male has long, slender neck, conspicuous white breast and brown head, and pointed tail. Female is plain brown, lacks eye stripe that characterizes most female dabblers, and has a gray bill. Both sexes at a distance and in flight present a slender, elegant appearance.

Status and Distribution:	SPRING	SUMMER	FALL	WINTER
Southeastern ★	C	U	C	U
Southcoastal ★	C	C	C	U
Southwestern ★	C	C	C	U
Central ★	C	C	C	+
Western ★	C	C	C	—
Northern ★	C	C	C	—

Habitat: Breeding — marshy, low country with shallow freshwater lakes, brackish estuaries and sluggish streams with marshy borders. Nests on the ground usually near fresh water in tall grass, occasionally some distance from water. In migration and winter — salt and brackish waters along the coast.

Notes: Most widely distributed and abundant puddle duck in Alaska, its major breeding ground.

NORTHERN PINTAIL
(Doug Murphy)

NORTHERN PINTAIL
Female
(Dennis Paulson)

FALCATED TEAL

(Anas falcata)

LENGTH: 19 IN.

Identification: Adult male is gray with conspicuously crested dark green and purple head. White spot on forehead, just above bill, distinctive at a distance. White throat is bordered behind with a black line. Speculum is dark, glossy green, and the basal wing feathers are long and sickle-shaped, hanging off the back. Female is similar to female Gadwall in size and shape but with a dark speculum and gray rather than orange bill.

Habitat: Most often seen in western and central Aleutian Islands. Breeds in central and eastern Siberia. Not known to breed in Alaska.

Status and Distribution:	SPRING	SUMMER	FALL	WINTER
Southeastern	—	—	—	—
Southcoastal	—	—	—	—
Southwestern	R	+	+	+
Central	—	—	—	—
Western	—	—	—	—
Northern	—	—	—	—

GREEN-WINGED TEAL
(Anas crecca)
LENGTH: 14 IN.

Identification: Small size, all dark color at a distance, and bright green speculum distinguish this species from other Alaskan ducks. Male has white vertical stripe before the wing, and creamy buff patches under the tail.

Habitat: Breeding — freshwater ponds, marshes and shallows of lakes surrounded by woods. Nests on the ground in long grass, usually near water. In migration and winter — brackish intertidal areas near the mouths of streams.

Notes: Smallest duck found in Alaska and one of the swiftest fliers.

Green-winged Teal breeding in the western and central Aleutians resembles Eurasian subspecies which has been recorded in the Pribilofs. Males of these subspecies have a horizontal white stripe above the wings and lack the vertical white stripe on side of body.

Status and Distribution:	SPRING	SUMMER	FALL	WINTER
Southeastern ★	C	U	C	U
Southcoastal ★	C	C	C	R
Southwestern ★	C	C	C	U
Central ★	C	C	C	—
Western ★	C	C	C	—
Northern ★	U	U	U	—

BAIKAL TEAL
(Anas formosa)
LENGTH: 18 IN.

Identification: Male is unmistakable with a striking face pattern. Otherwise male resembles Green-winged Teal but is a bit larger and has an all-dark undertail pattern. Female similar to female Green-winged Teal but has distinctive white spot at the base of the bill.

BAIKAL TEAL
(Tom Ulrich)

Status and Distribution:	SPRING	SUMMER	FALL	WINTER
Southeastern	—	—	—	—
Southcoastal	—	—	—	—
Southwestern	—	+	+	—
Central	—	—	—	—
Western	+	+	+	—
Northern	+	+	+	-

Habitat: Asiatic teal found along the coast and on islands in the Bering Sea and along Arctic Ocean coastline. Not known to breed in Alaska.

GREEN-WINGED TEAL
Male, left; Female, right
(Dennis Paulson)

GARGANEY
(Anas querquedula)
LENGTH: 15 IN.

Identification: Breeding male has reddish-purple head and broad white stripe over the eye. Female very similar to female Green-winged Teal but tends to be more grayish and shows a more conspicuous pale spot at the base of its bill. Uninterrupted eyeline helps separate it from female Baikal Teal.

Status and Distribution:	SPRING	SUMMER	FALL	WINTER
Southeastern	—	—	—	—
Southcoastal	—	—	+	—
Southwestern	R	+	R	—
Central	—	—	—	—
Western	—	—	—	—
Northern	—	—	—	—

GARGANEY
(Len Rue Jr.)

Habitat: Asiatic species that has occurred most often as a spring and fall migrant in the western and central Aleutian Islands. Not known to breed in Alaska.

BLUE-WINGED TEAL

(Anas discors)

LENGTH: 15 IN.

Identification: In the field small size, large white crescent in front of the eye of adult male, and blue forewing of both sexes are distinguishing. Blue forewing, conspicuous in flight, separates this species from all other ducks but Cinnamon Teal and Northern Shoveler. Northern Shoveler has a much larger bill. Adult male Cinnamon Teal is cinnamon red. Females and young Blue-winged and Cinnamon teals and Garganey cannot be safely separated in the field.

Habitat: Shallow muddy ponds, lake shores and sloughs overgrown with aquatic vegetation. Prefers fresh water; not often found in salt or brackish water.

Notes: Breeding records are not numerous for Alaska, partly because of lack of abundance and perhaps partly because of well-concealed nests.

Status and Distribution:	SPRING	SUMMER	FALL	WINTER
Southeastern ★	U	R	U	—
Southcoastal ★	R	R	R	+
Southwestern	+	—	+	—
Central ★	U	R	U	—
Western	—	—	—	—
Northern	—	+	—	—

BLUE-WINGED TEAL
(Dennis Paulson)

BLUE-WINGED TEAL
Female
(Dennis Paulson)

CINNAMON TEAL
(Dennis Paulson)

CINNAMON TEAL

(Anas cyanoptera)

LENGTH: 16 IN.

Identification: Male is all cinnamon red with blue shoulder patches. Female cannot be distinguished in the field from female Blue-winged Teals. In late summer, when male has molted into a plumage much like that of the female, these 2 species cannot be distinguished from one another.

Habitat: Intertidal wetlands, lakes. Not known to breed in Alaska.

Status and Distribution:	SPRING	SUMMER	FALL	WINTER
Southeastern	R	+	—	—
Southcoastal	+	—	—	—
Southwestern	—	—	—	—
Central	+	+	—	—
Western	—	—	—	—
Northern	—	—	—	—

CINNAMON TEAL
Female
(Kenneth Fink)

NORTHERN SHOVELER
(Mike Lettis)

NORTHERN SHOVELER

(Anas clypeata)

LENGTH: 18½ IN.

Identification: Long bill and light blue forewing patch are good field identification marks for both sexes at all seasons. In flight adult male can be recognized at long distances by white breast contrasting markedly with dark head and belly. Female is mottled brown, like other dabblers.

Status and Distribution:	SPRING	SUMMER	FALL	WINTER
Southeastern ★	U	R	U	R
Southcoastal ★	C	C	C	+
Southwestern	R	R	R	+
Central ★	C	C	C	—
Western ★	U	U	U	—
Northern ★	R	R	R	—

NORTHERN SHOVELER
Female
(Dennis Paulson)

Habitat: Breeding — shallow, often muddy, freshwater marshes, sloughs and lakes. Nests on ground, often but not necessarily close to water. In migration and winter — coastal saltwater mud flats and shallow freshwater areas.

Notes: Long bill has more comblike straining devices along the margin than bills of other waterfowl and is especially adapted to straining tiny food particles from open shallow waters. Also feeds on seeds, tubers of aquatic plants and a variety of small fish, crustaceans, mollusks and insects.

EURASIAN WIGEON
(Dennis Paulson)

EURASIAN WIGEON

(Anas penelope)

LENGTH: 18 IN.

Identification: Adult male can be distinguished from American Wigeon by a red-brown head topped with cream, and gray back and sides. Most females and immatures of the 2 species are too similar for separation in the field, but some Eurasian Wigeons have a reddish-tinged head. Head of the female American Wigeon is gray.

EURASIAN WIGEON
Female
(Dennis Paulson)

Status and Distribution:	SPRING	SUMMER	FALL	WINTER
Southeastern	R	+	—	+
Southcoastal	R	+	+	+
Southwestern	U	R	U	R
Central	R	+	—	—
Western	R	R	+	—
Northern	—	+	—	—

Habitat: This species is not known to breed in North America and is only an uncommon or rare visitor to scattered parts of Alaska. Most sightings have been of only 1 or a few birds and greatest numbers are seen in the Aleutian Islands. Habits are identical to those of American Wigeon and, when present, Eurasian Wigeon is almost always found with American Wigeon.

AMERICAN WIGEON
(Doug Murphy)

AMERICAN WIGEON
Female
(Sue Hills)

AMERICAN WIGEON

(Anas americana)

LENGTH: 20 IN.

Identification: At a distance the white crown, wing patch and side spot create a contrasting brown-and-white pattern on males. White forewing patches are conspicuous in flight, and the high-pitched whistles (like a flock of rubber ducks) can often be heard. At closer range, brown female has distinctly reddish body and contrasting gray head, unlike other dabblers which are more uniform. Small bill is blue gray.

Status and Distribution:	SPRING	SUMMER	FALL	WINTER
Southeastern ★	C	U	C	U
Southcoastal ★	C	C	C	U
Southwestern ★	C	C	C	R
Central ★	C	C	C	—
Western ★	C	C	C	—
Northern ★	U	U	U	—

Habitat: Breeding — freshwater marshes, sloughs, ponds and marshy edges of lakes. Unlike most dabbling ducks, females and young frequent open water in the habitat. Nests on the ground, sometimes a considerable distance from water. In migration and winter — shallow coastal bays.

Notes: American Wigeons have a habit of stealing plant materials brought to the surface by other waterfowl such as Canvasbacks, Redheads and Tundra Swans.

WOOD DUCK

(Aix sponsa)

LENGTH: 18 IN.

Identification: Male has striped, crested head, bright red at base of the bill and around the eye, dark red breast, finely barred sides, and iridescent blue wings. Female has a similar but shorter crest, is generally drab brown but with a conspicuous white patch around the eye and some iridescent blue on the wings. Wood Duck has a long tail, conspicuous in flight, and high, squeaky *whoo-eeek* call.

Status and Distribution:	SPRING	SUMMER	FALL	WINTER
Southeastern	+	+	—	—
Southcoastal	—	—	—	—
Southwestern	—	—	—	—
Central	—	—	—	—
Western	—	—	—	—
Northern	—	—	—	—

WOOD DUCK
Female
(Tom Ulrich)

Habitat: Has been found on Mendenhall River near Juneau, and in a slough along Stikine River in southeastern Alaska. Not known to breed in Alaska.

WOOD DUCK
(Tom Ulrich)

COMMON POCHARD
(Kenneth Fink)

COMMON POCHARD

(Aythya ferina)

LENGTH: 18 IN.

Identification: Resembles a hybrid between a Redhead and Canvasback, with the shape of the Redhead and the white body of the Canvasback. Bill of both sexes is dark with a blue-gray ring around the middle. Female is similar to a female Redhead and is difficult to distinguish by itself. Male Common Pochard is much paler than male Redhead.

Habitat: Has been found in western and central Aleutian Islands and in the Pribilof Islands. Not known to breed in Alaska.

Status and Distribution:	SPRING	SUMMER	FALL	WINTER
Southeastern	—	—	—	—
Southcoastal	+	—	—	—
Southwestern	R	+	+	—
Central	—	—	—	—
Western	—	—	—	—
Northern	—	—	—	—

CANVASBACK

(Aythya valisineria)

LENGTH: 22 IN.

Identification: Long bill and sloping forehead are unlike those of any other duck. Male's back, belly and inner half of the wing are white, and male shows more white in flight than most other ducks. At a distance, dark reddish head may look black as do breast and tail. Females are light brown and identified by head and bill shape. Both sexes have all black bills.

Status and Distribution:	SPRING	SUMMER	FALL	WINTER
Southeastern	R	+	R	+
Southcoastal ★	U	U	U	+
Southwestern	R	+	R	R
Central ★	U	U	U	—
Western	R	R	R	—
Northern	+	—	—	—

Habitat: Breeding — marshes, sloughs and deep water lakes with vegetated shorelines. Nests in marsh vegetation near open waters with sufficient depth for diving and abundant bottom vegetation. In migration — saltwater bays, large lakes and rivers.

CANVASBACK
Female
(Doug Murphy)

CANVASBACK
(Doug Murphy)

REDHEAD
(Tom Walker)

REDHEAD

(Aythya americana)

LENGTH: 20 IN.

Identification: Male is distinguished by round red-brown head and pale blue bill, gray back, and black breast and tail. Female is brownish with a light patch about the base of the bill, very similar to but paler than female Ring-necked Duck.

Habitat: Breeding — freshwater marshes and lakes. Most breed in eastern central Alaska in area of Tetlin Lakes and Yukon Flats. Nests in emergent vegetation over standing water or on a mass of plant material surrounded by water. In migration — saltwater bays, river deltas, freshwater lakes and marshes.

Notes: This species sometimes places its eggs in the nests of other species.

Status and Distribution:	SPRING	SUMMER	FALL	WINTER
Southeastern	R	+	R	+
Southcoastal ★	R	R	R	+
Southwestern	+	+	—	—
Central ★	U	R	U	—
Western	+	+	—	—
Northern	+	+	—	—

RING-NECKED DUCK

(Aythya collaris)

LENGTH: 16 IN.

Identification: Resembles the scaups in appearance, behavior and flight. Male is distinguished from male scaups by black back, gray sides, white vertical blaze behind the black breast, and at closer range, by whitish ring around the bill. Bill ring and characteristic triangular or pointed head shape distinguish the female. Ring-necked Duck looks short-bodied and long-necked compared with scaups. Both Ring-necked Ducks and Redheads have dark wings with gray stripes on the rear of each wing; scaups have a single white stripe on each wing.

Status and Distribution:	SPRING	SUMMER	FALL	WINTER
Southeastern ★	U	R	U	R
Southcoastal ★	R	R	R	R
Southwestern	+	+	—	—
Central ★	U	U	U	—
Western	—	+	—	—
Northern	+	+	—	—

Habitat: Mostly fresh water, sometimes found in saltwater bays during migration. Breeds in eastern central Alaska in such places as Tetlin Lakes and on the Yukon Flats, and in lower southeastern Alaska. A rare breeder in Alaska.

RING-NECKED DUCK
Female
(Dennis Paulson)

RING-NECKED DUCK
(Doug Murphy)

GREATER SCAUP
(Aythya marila)
LENGTH: 19 IN.

Identification: The 2 species of scaups are very similar in appearance and only experienced observers can distinguish between them, under good conditions. In good light and at close range, Greater Scaup adult male has a greenish gloss to the head; the head of the Lesser Scaup male is dark purple but this can vary. Head of the Greater Scaup is smoothly rounded, that of the Lesser Scaup is more puffy with almost a point toward the rear of the crown. White wing stripe of the Greater Scaup extends farther toward the wing tip, a field mark noticeable only in flight. A bluish bill and broad white stripe on the trailing edge of the wing in flight is characteristic of both species.

Status and Distribution:	SPRING	SUMMER	FALL	WINTER
Southeastern ★	C	U	C	C
Southcoastal ★	C	C	C	C
Southwestern ★	C	C	C	C
Central ★	C	C	C	—
Western ★	C	C	C	—
Northern ★	U	U	U	—

Habitat: Breeding — tundra or low forest closely adjacent to tundra. Freshwater lakes and ponds. Nests near water in dense vegetation. In winter — coastal saltwater bays.

GREATER SCAUP
Male, left; Female, right

LESSER SCAUP
(Doug Murphy)

LESSER SCAUP

(Aythya affinis)

LENGTH: 16 IN.

Identification: See Greater Scaup.

Habitat: Breeding — interior lakes and ponds, especially in the upper Yukon River Valley and its tributaries. Nests in dry grassy areas near lakeshores. In winter — saltwater bays but in smaller numbers than Greater Scaup.

Status and Distribution:	SPRING	SUMMER	FALL	WINTER
Southeastern ★	C	R	C	R
Southcoastal	R	+	R	R
Southwestern	—	—	—	+
Central ★	C	C	C	+
Western ★	R	R	R	—
Northern	—	+	—	—

LESSER SCAUP
Female
(Doug Murphy)

TUFTED DUCK

(Aythya fuligula)

LENGTH: 17 IN.

Identification: Adult male similar to Ring-necked Duck but has entirely white sides and usually a conspicuous tuft of feathers on back of the head. Female similar to a female scaup with a small head tuft, but rarely any white at the base of the bill as in female scaups. In flight Tufted Duck has a white wing stripe like Greater Scaup but male has much darker back.

Status and Distribution:	SPRING	SUMMER	FALL	WINTER
Southeastern	—	—	—	—
Southcoastal	+	—	+	+
Southwestern	R	R	R	R
Central	—	—	—	—
Western	+	+	—	—
Northern	—	—	+	—

TUFTED DUCK
(Dennis Paulson)

Habitat: A Eurasian species that occurs mostly in western and central Aleutian Islands where it has been found year round. Less numerous and less regular elsewhere, but has been found in eastern Aleutian Islands, Pribilof Islands, northern Bering Sea, southcoastal and northern Alaska. Not known to breed in Alaska.

TUFTED DUCK
Female
(Kenneth Fink)

COMMON GOLDENEYE

(Bucephala clangula)

LENGTH: 18 IN.

Identification: Adult male has round white spot behind bill. Head shape is distinctive and head is glossy, sometimes appearing greenish. Female Common Goldeneye is difficult to distinguish from female Barrow's Goldeneye but both are recognizable as goldeneyes by their gray body and contrasting brown puffy head. Female Common Goldeneye has yellow tip to the dark bill.

Status and Distribution:	SPRING	SUMMER	FALL	WINTER
Southeastern ★	C	U	C	C
Southcoastal ★	C	U	C	C
Southwestern ★	C	U	C	U
Central ★	C	C	C	+
Western	U	R	U	—
Northern	+	+	—	—

Habitat: Breeding — ponds and lakes with adjacent stands of trees. Nests in a cavity in a tree. Nesting largely confined to the valleys of Yukon and Kuskokwim rivers. However, because of the difficulty of separating female Common and Barrow's Goldeneyes during nesting, this breeding distribution is not certain. In winter — inshore marine waters.

COMMON GOLDENEYE
Female, left; Male, right

BARROW'S GOLDENEYE

BARROW'S GOLDENEYE

(Bucephala islandica)

LENGTH: 18 IN.

Identification: Adult male has large white crescent behind base of the bill. Male has more black on back than Common Goldeneye, a distinction which is noticeable from great distances. Female has gray body and puffy brown head. Females have an all yellow bill in winter and spring.

Status and Distribution:	SPRING	SUMMER	FALL	WINTER
Southeastern ★	C	U	C	C
Southcoastal ★	C	C	C	C
Southwestern ★	C	U	C	C
Central ★	C	C	C	—
Western	—	—	—	—
Northern	—	—	—	—

Habitat: Breeding — lakes and ponds, usually in wooded country. Nests in cavities in trees or if not available, may nest in holes among rocks or cliffs. In winter — inshore marine waters and lakes and rivers if there is open water.

BARROW'S GOLDENEYE
Female

BUFFLEHEAD

(Bucephala albeola)

LENGTH: 14 IN.

Identification: Male distinguished by large white patch on head, black back and white sides. Female identified by small size, puffy brown head with oval white spot behind each eye.

Status and Distribution:	SPRING	SUMMER	FALL	WINTER
Southeastern ★	C	U	C	C
Southcoastal ★	C	R	C	C
Southwestern ★	C	U	C	C
Central ★	C	C	C	+
Western ★	R	R	R	—
Northern	—	+	—	—

Habitat: Breeding — ponds and lakes in or near open woodland. Nests in cavities in trees, often in holes made by woodpeckers. In winter — inshore marine waters, fresh water if open.

BUFFLEHEAD

BUFFLEHEAD
Female

OLDSQUAW
Winter
Female, left; Male, right
(Jerry Hout)

OLDSQUAW

(Clangula hyemalis)

LENGTH: 20 IN.

Identification: Only sea duck with considerable white on the body and unpatterned dark wings. Male has long, pointed tail. Drastic plumage change between summer and winter, especially obvious in the male, is quite unusual among ducks and, of the Alaskan species, only the Ruddy Duck shares this characteristic. Oldsquaw is a noisy duck with a variety of calls, some of which are considered musical.

Status and Distribution:	SPRING	SUMMER	FALL	WINTER
Southeastern ★	C	U	C	C
Southcoastal ★	C	U	C	C
Southwestern ★	C	U	C	C
Central ★	C	U	C	—
Western ★	C	C	C	C
Northern ★	C	C	C	—

OLDSQUAW
Summer
(John C. Pitcher)

Habitat: Breeding — Arctic tundra near lakes or ponds and along the coast. Nests on the ground, often under low shrubs. In winter — inshore marine waters. Many Alaskan Oldsquaws winter in the Bering Sea, the Sea of Okhotsk and the Sea of Japan.

HARLEQUIN DUCK

(Histrionicus histrionicus)

LENGTH: 17 IN.

Identification: Male in nuptial plumage is mostly slate-blue with white spots and stripes and chestnut-colored flanks. Female is dusky brown with 3 round white spots on each side of the head, very much like a diminutive scoter with a very small bill. In flight the dark color, stripes on the male's back, and habit of flying just above the water's surface with very shallow wing-beats are good field marks.

Habitat: Breeding — cold, rapidly flowing streams, often but not always surrounded by forests. Nests on the ground, close to water and in areas protected by dense vegetation. Hole-nesting is not typical of this species in North America. In winter — inshore marine waters, rocky shores and reefs; often perches on rocks for preening and sleeping.

Status and Distribution:	SPRING	SUMMER	FALL	WINTER
Southeastern ★	C	C	C	C
Southcoastal ★	C	C	C	C
Southwestern ★	C	C	C	C
Central ★	U	U	U	—
Western ★	U	U	U	—
Northern ★	—	R	—	—

Notes: More abundant in Alaska than in any other part of its range. Male, with its brilliant plumage, is responsible for the name "harlequin" taken from the clown or harlequin of old English pantomime.

HARLEQUIN
Female, left; Male, right

STELLER'S EIDER
(Dennis Paulson)

STELLER'S EIDER
(Polysticta stelleri)
LENGTH: 18 IN.

Identification: Adult male has white head and large white shoulder patch. Male's chestnut-colored breast and belly is especially obvious in flight. Dark brown female is similar to other eiders, but female is more mottled than barred and the wing has a blue speculum bordered by a white stripe, similar to Mallard.

Status and Distribution:	SPRING	SUMMER	FALL	WINTER
Southeastern	+	—	—	+
Southcoastal	C	+	U	C
Southwestern	C	U	C	C
Central	—	—	—	—
Western ★	C	C	C	—
Northern ★	U	U	U	—

Habitat: Breeding — lowland tundra adjacent to the coast. Nests on small elevations near tidewater, also in flat mossy tundra. In winter — inshore marine waters around Kodiak Island and the south side of the Alaska Peninsula, and the eastern Aleutian Islands. In autumn huge flocks of Siberian-reared Steller's Eiders frequent Izembek and other Alaska Peninsula lagoons.

STELLER'S EIDER
Female
(Dennis Paulson)

COMMON EIDER
Female
(Edgar Jones)

COMMON EIDER

(Somateria mollissima)

LENGTH: 25 IN.

Identification: Largest wild duck in North America. Adult male is unique with white back and breast and black belly. Female is chunky, brown but paler than scoters, and obviously barred when seen at moderate or close range. Configuration where the head and bill meet is different for each eider species. In Common Eider the forehead feathers do not extend as far forward as do those on side of the bill.

Habitat: Breeding — low lying rocky marine shores with numerous islands. Nests on the ground, often in areas sheltered by rocks. In winter — inshore marine waters.

Status and Distribution:	SPRING	SUMMER	FALL	WINTER
Southeastern ★	R	R	R	R
Southcoastal ★	U	U	U	U
Southwestern ★	C	C	C	C
Central	—	—	—	—
Western ★	C	C	C	—
Northern ★	C	C	C	—

Notes: Flocks fly in long lines, often low over the water, and thousands may pass on peak migration days along the Arctic coast.

COMMON EIDER
(Jerry Hout)

KING EIDER
(Jim Hawkings)

KING EIDER

(Somateria spectabilis)

LENGTH: 22 IN.

Identification: At a distance male appears white in front and black behind, the only duck with this appearance. White shoulder patches are separated from white neck and breast by black back, very distinctive at great distances. Head of male has orange knoblike frontal shield outlined in black. Female and immature are difficult to distinguish from Common Eider but they have crescent-shaped rather than straight bars on the back and sides, and feathering on forehead extends farther forward than that on sides of the bill. In mixed flocks, female King Eiders appear richer-colored, more reddish brown than female Common Eiders.

Habitat: Breeding — ponds and lakes on Arctic tundra or lakes and streams not far from the coast. In Alaska King Eider breeds in small numbers along the Arctic coast from Point Hope to Demarcation Point. Nests on the ground near lakes or islands in lakes and sometimes on almost bare hillsides. In migration and winter — inshore marine waters.

Notes: During migration a million or more King Eiders pass close to such places as Hooper Bay, Cape Lisburne, Wainwright and Point Barrow in their annual flight from the Bristol Bay-to-Kodiak area to Canadian nest sites.

KING EIDER
Female
(Dennis Paulson)

Status and Distribution:	SPRING	SUMMER	FALL	WINTER
Southeastern	+	—	—	+
Southcoastal	U	—	U	U
Southwestern	C	R	C	C
Central	—	—	—	—
Western ★	C	U	C	+
Northern ★	C	U	C	—

SPECTACLED EIDER
(Henry Kyllingstad)

SPECTACLED EIDER

(Somateria fischeri)

LENGTH: 21 IN.

Identification: Both sexes identified by huge pale spectacles around the eyes. Male is much like a Common Eider at a distance but has a black instead of white breast. Female has feathering down the bill to the nostrils.

Habitat: Breeding — lowland tundra with small ponds. Nests in fairly high grass near ponds. Nests in a narrow coastal strip of Alaska from mouth of the Kuskokwim River north along Bering Sea coast to Arctic Ocean, and then east to Colville River Delta. A few nest in Siberia but this is a Bering Sea bird and largely an Alaskan species. Winter range is not known. An occasional winter bird has been sighted off Kodiak or near the tip of the Kenai Peninsula.

Status and Distribution:	SPRING	SUMMER	FALL	WINTER
Southeastern	+	—	—	—
Southcoastal	—	—	—	+
Southwestern	—		—	R
Central	—	—	—	—
Western ★	C	C	C	—
Northern ★	U	U	U	—

SPECTACLED EIDER
Female
(Jerry Hout)

WHITE-WINGED SCOTER
Male, left; Female, right

WHITE-WINGED SCOTER

(Melanitta fusca)

LENGTH: 21 IN.

Identification: Largest scoter. Identified in flight, and often in the water, by white wing patches of both sexes. A male on the water is easily recognizable by white crescent around the eye. A female without the wing patches visible is distinguished from female Surf Scoter by feathering on side of the bill, which extends almost as far forward as the nostrils.

Habitat: Breeding — most definite breeding records are near interior streams and lakes, chiefly in the upper Tanana and on the Yukon Flats. Nests on the ground under shrubs and trees sometimes several hundred yards from water. In winter — inshore marine waters.

Status and Distribution:	SPRING	SUMMER	FALL	WINTER
Southeastern	C	C	C	C
Southcoastal ★	C	C	C	C
Southwestern	C	C	C	C
Central ★	C	C	C	—
Western ★	U	U	U	—
Northern ★	U	U	U	—

Notes: If several White-winged Scoters nest on the same lake, as frequently happens in the Interior, one female will dominate, drive away the others, and gather all the young into one immense brood of 20 to 60 young. Males leave soon after incubation starts in early June and return to the sea coast.

SURF SCOTER
Female

SURF SCOTER

(Melanitta perspicillata)

LENGTH: 20 IN.

Identification: Adult male has solid black color and white patches on crown and nape. Immature female usually has 2 whitish spots on each side of the head like White-winged Scoter, but lacks white wing patch. In an adult female these spots tend to disappear and are often replaced by a pale nape patch much like that of the male. This nape patch is absent in White-winged Scoter. In a female the base of the bill is unfeathered, with as much bill visible behind the nostril as in front of it.

Habitat: Breeding — not well known but probably like other scoters, i.e., freshwater ponds, lakes, rivers with shrubby cover or woodland nearby. In winter — inshore marine waters.

Status and Distribution:	SPRING	SUMMER	FALL	WINTER
Southeastern	C	C	C	C
Southcoastal	C	C	C	C
Southwestern	C	U	C	C
Central ★	C	C	C	—
Western ★	C	C	C	—
Northern ★	U	U	U	—

SURF SCOTER

BLACK SCOTER
(Merrick Hersey)

BLACK SCOTER

(Melanitta nigra)

LENGTH: 19 IN.

Identification: Male solid black with base of bill bright yellow-orange. Female and immature are dark brown, with darker cap and pale cheeks and throat. Both sexes have a shorter, more typically ducklike bill than do other scoters. Primary feathers look quite pale in flight.

Habitat: Breeding — lakes, ponds or rivers in tundra or woodlands. Nests on the ground near water. In winter — inshore marine waters.

Status and Distribution:	SPRING	SUMMER	FALL	WINTER
Southeastern	U	U	U	U
Southcoastal	C	U	C	C
Southwestern ★	C	C	C	C
Central ★	R	R	R	—
Western ★	C	C	C	—
Northern	—	+	—	—

RUDDY DUCK

(Oxyura jamaicensis)

LENGTH: 15 IN.

Identification: Small diving duck with long tail, often held up at an angle. Chunky and short-necked, with a disproportionately large bill, very awkward on land and in the air. In breeding plumage, male has a cinnamon-red body, black cap, white cheeks, and bright sky-blue bill. In winter, bill turns dark and body plumage becomes brown. A female is always brown, with a brown cap and 2 dark stripes across each light cheek.

Habitat: Breeding — interior lakes, broods have been sighted at Tetlin Lakes and Minto Lakes in central Alaska. In migration and winter — inshore marine waters, lakes.

Status and Distribution:	SPRING	SUMMER	FALL	WINTER
Southeastern	+	—	+	+
Southcoastal	—	—	—	—
Southwestern	—	—	—	—
Central ★	+	+	—	—
Western	—	—	—	—
Northern	—	—	—	—

RUDDY DUCK
(Tom Ulrich)

HOODED MERGANSER
(Dennis Paulson)

HOODED MERGANSER

(Lophodytes cucullatus)

LENGTH: 18 IN.

Identification: From a distance male is black above, with dark reddish sides and white breast. White head patch appears narrow when the crest is down and very conspicuous when the crest is erect. Female and young are all brown with narrow merganser bills and puffy brown crests. Females of the other 2 species of mergansers are larger with more wispy crests and reddish-brown heads. Hooded Merganser flies very fast with rapid wingbeats and shows a more slender head and longer neck than other small ducks.

Status and Distribution:	SPRING	SUMMER	FALL	WINTER
Southeastern ★	U	U	U	U
Southcoastal ★	R	R	R	R
Southwestern	+	+	+	+
Central	R	R	R	+
Western	—	—	—	—
Northern	—	—	—	—

HOODED MERGANSER
Female
(Dennis Paulson)

Habitat: Breeding — wooded streams and, to a lesser degree, wooded shorelines of lakes. Nests in cavities in trees or on the top of snags. In Alaska — nests along the valleys of larger mainland rivers in southeastern Alaska where cottonwoods occur. In migration and winter — freshwater ponds and streams and occasionally saltwater bays.

SMEW
(Dennis Paulson)

SMEW

(Mergellus albellus)

LENGTH: 16 IN.

Identification: Small merganser with shorter bill than others of this group. Male almost entirely white with narrow, black markings on head and body and dark eye patch. Female has gray body, contrasting white cheeks and brown cap. Head in both sexes is puffy.

Status and Distribution:	SPRING	SUMMER	FALL	WINTER
Southeastern	—	—	—	—
Southcoastal	—	—	—	+
Southwestern	R	+	R	R
Central	—	—	—	—
Western	—	—	—	—
Northern	—	—	—	—

Habitat: Asiatic species found mostly in western and central Aleutian Islands during spring, fall and winter. Not known to breed in Alaska.

SMEW
Female
(Dennis Paulson)

COMMON MERGANSER

(Mergus merganser)

LENGTH: 22-27 IN.

Identification: Largest merganser. Adult male is white with black head and back. Only Common Goldeneye shares these characteristics at a distance, but the merganser has a long, slender, red bill and long, low silhouette. Female, like the female goldeneye, has a gray body and sharply set off brown head. In flight, Common Merganser appears very pointed in the front and has especially rapid shallow wingbeats.

Status and Distribution:	SPRING	SUMMER	FALL	WINTER
Southeastern ★	C	C	C	C
Southcoastal ★	C	C	C	C
Southwestern ★	C	C	C	C
Central ★	R	R	R	R
Western	—	+	—	—
Northern	—	—	—	—

COMMON MERGANSER
Female

Habitat: Breeding — forested areas where ponds are associated with upper portions of rivers and clear, freshwater lakes. Nests in hollow trees, in crevices of cliffs, and on the ground under cover. In migration and winter — prefers freshwater but if not available, then saltwater bays and inlets.

COMMON MERGANSER

RED-BREASTED MERGANSER
(Dennis Paulson)

RED-BREASTED MERGANSER

(Mergus serrator)

LENGTH: 23 IN.

Identification: Adult male has greenish-black, crested head and reddish breast band. Female and young similar to Common Merganser but the lighter reddish-brown of the head blends into the light throat, whereas head color is more sharply cut off in female Common Merganser.

Status and Distribution:	SPRING	SUMMER	FALL	WINTER
Southeastern ★	C	C	C	C
Southcoastal ★	C	C	C	C
Southwestern ★	C	C	C	C
Central ★	R	R	R	R
Western ★	C	C	C	—
Northern ★	R	R	R	—

Habitat: Breeding — lakes, ponds, rivers, often near sea coast. Occasionally may nest along the coast or on coastal islands. Nests on the ground under overhanging branches of trees among tree roots or in a pile of driftwood. In migration and winter — inshore marine waters.

RED-BREASTED MERGANSER
Female
(Dennis Paulson)

FAMILY *ACCIPITRIDAE*

HAWKS, EAGLES, HARRIERS, OSPREYS

(11)

These are birds of prey with hooked beaks and sharp, curved talons for catching and holding their prey. Eleven species occur in Alaska and they are divided into 4 groups:

(1) Accipiters or bird hawks are small to medium-sized hawks with short rounded wings and long tails. Two species are found in Alaska.

(2) Buteos and eagles are medium to large-sized hawks with broad wings and fairly short tails. They are often seen soaring. Seven species occur in Alaska.

(3) Harriers are medium-sized hawks with long wings, slim bodies and long tails. This group is represented in Alaska by 1 species.

(4) Ospreys are large hawklike birds of prey with powerful talons and spines on the soles of the feet to aid in capturing live fish, their main food supply.

NORTHERN GOSHAWK

(Accipiter gentilis)

LENGTH: 23 IN.
WINGSPAN: 3½-4 FT.

Identification: Long tail, short rounded wings, and habit of flying with short rapid wingbeats then sailing briefly identify this species as an accipiter. Much larger than Sharp-shinned Hawk, the only other accipiter found in Alaska. Adult has a blue-gray back, light stripe over its eye and gray underparts. Immature is brown above and white with brown streaks below. Immature has a light eyeline which distinguishes it from other large brown hawks, such as Red-tailed Hawk, when the whole bird is not clearly visible.

Status and Distribution:	SPRING	SUMMER	FALL	WINTER
Southeastern ★	U	U	U	U
Southcoastal ★	U	U	U	U
Southwestern ★	U	U	U	U
Central ★	U	U	U	U
Western	R	R	R	—
Northern	—	—	—	—

Habitat: Coastal and boreal forests, forest edges. Nests in heavy timber usually 30-40 feet up in a conifer.

Notes: Hunts for prey such as ptarmigan, rabbits and rodents by flying close to the ground usually near the edge of timber.

SHARP-SHINNED HAWK

(Accipiter striatus)

LENGTH: 12 IN.
WINGSPAN: 2 FT.

Identification: Small, with short rounded wings and long tail. Adult has a blue-gray back and rusty barred breast; immature has a brown back and streaked breast. Females are larger than males.

Status and Distribution:	SPRING	SUMMER	FALL	WINTER
Southeastern ★	C	U	C	U
Southcoastal ★	C	U	C	U
Southwestern	—	—	—	—
Central ★	C	C	C	+
Western ★	R	R	R	—
Northern	—	—	—	—

Habitat: Coastal and interior coniferous forests, shrubs, mixed deciduous-coniferous woodlands, forest edges. Nests in conifers usually 20-60 feet from the ground.

Notes: Difficult to see because of small size and habit of hunting close to the ground and perching in thick conifers.

NORTHERN GOSHAWK
(W. E. Ruth)

SHARP-SHINNED HAWK
(Gary Jones)

RED-TAILED HAWK
Immature Dark Phase
(Edgar Jones)

RED-TAILED HAWK
(Buteo jamaicensis)
LENGTH: 19-25 IN.
WINGSPAN: 4-4½ FT.

Identification: Large hawk with broad wings and broad, relatively short, rounded tail. Adult in coastal Alaska is reddish on upperside of the tail. Most adults and immatures show a dark belt of streaks across the abdomen. Breast and belly may be mostly white, reddish or dark brown to black. In eastern Alaska a form occurs (Harlan's Hawk) that is usually blackish with a whitish mottled tail. Less commonly this form is light underneath, with a whitish mottled tail. Individuals with intermediate plumage occur, even some with reddish tails. Most common buteo in forested Alaska.

Status and Distribution:	SPRING	SUMMER	FALL	WINTER
Southeastern ★	U	U	U	+
Southcoastal ★	R	R	R	+
Southwestern	—	—	—	—
Central ★	C	C	C	—
Western	—	+	—	—
Northern	+	—	—	—

Habitat: Coniferous forests and deciduous woodlands with open areas for hunting. Nests in trees or on cliffs.

Notes: Often soars in wide circles above trees or mountain ridges and perches on dead limbs or top branches of tall trees. Food consists of squirrels, rabbits, mice, lemmings and occasional birds.

RED-TAILED HAWK
Immature Light Phase
(Heinrich Springer)

RED-TAILED HAWK
Adult
(Henry Bunker)

SWAINSON'S HAWK
Light Phase
Adult
(Kenneth Fink)

SWAINSON'S HAWK

(Buteo swainsoni)

LENGTH: 22 IN.
WINGSPAN: 4-4½ FT.

Identification: More slender than Red-tailed Hawk with narrower, more pointed wings held up at a slight angle when soaring. Tail is always gray with narrow, dark bands, looking all dark at a distance. Light phase adult has a dark brown back and breast, white throat and belly — a different combination of light and dark underneath than any of the other buteos. Dark phase adult is all dark, including flight feathers. Dark phase Red-tailed and Rough-legged hawks have paler flight feathers. Immature is white below, with dark streaks all over.

Status and Distribution:	SPRING	SUMMER	FALL	WINTER
Southeastern	—	—	—	—
Southcoastal	+	—	+	—
Southwestern	—	—	—	—
Central ★	R	R	R	—
Western	—	—	—	—
Northern	—	—	—	—

Habitat: Open forests of the Interior. Nest locations are not well known in Alaska. Elsewhere they commonly nest in trees, usually deciduous, and sometimes on cliffs.

SWAINSON'S HAWK
Immature
(Dennis Paulson)

ROUGH-LEGGED HAWK
Light Phase
(Don Cunningham)

ROUGH-LEGGED HAWK

(Buteo lagopus)

LENGTH: 19-24 IN.
WINGSPAN: 4-4½ FT.

Identification: Large, with whitish tail with a dark terminal band, long rounded wings and a habit of hovering in the air over one spot. Plumage is variable, but most common variant is a dark back, light breast and lower belly, with some streaking of dark brown or black, and a solid, wide band of black across lower breast and upper belly. Head always pale, unlike Swainson's and Red-tailed hawks which usually have a dark head and light throat. Some Rough-legged Hawks are all dark but can be distinguished from other dark phase birds by the conspicuous light undersides of the primaries and the usually visible light-and-dark tail. Often a flash of white is also visible on upperside of the primaries.

Status and Distribution:	SPRING	SUMMER	FALL	WINTER
Southeastern	U	R	U	—
Southcoastal	R	+	R	+
Southwestern ★	U	C	U	—
Central ★	C	U	C	+
Western ★	U	C	U	—
Northern ★	C	C	C	—

Habitat: Upland tundra with cliffs and rocky outcrops. Nests on cliffs or trees.

GOLDEN EAGLE
Immature
(Nancy Ratner)

GOLDEN EAGLE

(Aquila chrysaetos)
LENGTH: 30-41 IN.
WINGSPAN: 6⅓-7⅔ FT.

Identification: Adult is difficult to distinguish from an immature Bald Eagle, but clues are golden back of the neck, and legs fully feathered to the toes. Immature has a white tail with a contrasting dark terminal band and a white area at base of the primary feathers in the spread wings. Golden Eagle has a smaller head than Bald Eagle and usually soars with wings held up at a slight angle.

Habitat: Upland tundra, mountain ridges. Nests on cliffs and in the tops of trees.

Status and Distribution:	SPRING	SUMMER	FALL	WINTER
Southeastern ★	R	R	R	R
Southcoastal ★	R	R	R	R
Southwestern ★	U	U	U	R
Central ★	C	C	C	+
Western ★	U	U	U	—
Northern ★	U	U	U	—

Notes: Prey consists of rabbits, marmots, squirrels, various rodents and birds. Usually seen soaring over mountain ridges in search of food.

GOLDEN EAGLE
Adult with young

WHITE-TAILED EAGLE

(Haliaeetus albicilla)
LENGTH: 27-35 IN.
WINGSPAN: 6-7½ FT.

Identification: Adult paler than adult Bald Eagle, with only the tail white. Immature all brown, often with whitish streaks on breast and dark wing linings. Most Bald Eagle immatures have pale wing linings. Distinguished from Golden Eagle by wedge-shaped tail.

Habitat: Asiatic bird which occurs primarily on islands in the southwestern region. Known to breed only on Attu Island, in western Aleutians.

Status and Distribution:	SPRING	SUMMER	FALL	WINTER
Southeastern	—	—	—	—
Southcoastal	—	—	—	—
Southwestern ★	R	R	R	R
Central	—	—	—	—
Western	—	—	—	—
Northern	—	—	—	—

WHITE-TAILED EAGLE
(Ed Greaves)

BALD EAGLE
Adult
(Michael Gordon)

BALD EAGLE

(Haliaeetus leucocephalus)
LENGTH: 30-43 IN.
WINGSPAN: 6½-8 FT.

Identification: Adult with white head and tail is unmistakable. Immature has a dusky head and tail which it retains for up to 4 years. Immature may be confused with a Golden Eagle, but Bald Eagle soars with the wings held flat and almost always has white in the wing linings (*not* base of the primaries, as in the Golden Eagle) or on the underparts.

Habitat: Coniferous forests, deciduous woodlands, rivers and streams, beaches and tidal flats, rocky shores and reefs. Nests in old growth timber along the coast and larger mainland rivers. In treeless areas, nests on cliffs or on the ground.

Notes: There are more Bald Eagles in Alaska than in all the other states combined. They are scavengers more than predators and subsist mainly on dead and dying fish. When fish are not available, they will kill birds, and sometimes small mammals. In the Aleutian Islands their main food supply is seabirds.

Status and Distribution:	SPRING	SUMMER	FALL	WINTER
Southeastern ★	C	C	C	C
Southcoastal ★	C	C	C	C
Southwestern ★	C	C	C	C
Central ★	U	U	U	R
Western ★	R	R	R	—
Northern	—	+	—	—

BALD EAGLE
Immature

STELLER'S SEA-EAGLE

(Haliaeetus pelagicus)
LENGTH: 27-36 IN.
WINGSPAN: 7-8 FT.

Identification: Similar to Bald and White-tailed eagles in size but has a larger bill and even more prominently wedge-shaped tail than White-tailed Eagle. Adult has white shoulders, thighs and tail which are distinctive. Immature is largely brown, with a mottled brown-and-white tail.

Status and Distribution:	SPRING	SUMMER	FALL	WINTER
Southeastern	—	—	—	—
Southcoastal	—	—	—	—
Southwestern	+	+	+	—
Central	—	—	—	—
Western	—	—	—	—
Northern	—	—	—	—

Habitat: Asiatic bird that has been reported from Kodiak Island, Unalaska in the Aleutian Islands and Saint Paul Island in the Pribilof Islands. Not known to breed in Alaska.

STELLER'S SEA-EAGLE
(John C. Pitcher)

NORTHERN HARRIER
Female
(Doug Murphy)

NORTHERN HARRIER

(Circus cyaneus)

LENGTH: 20 IN.
WINGSPAN: 3½-4½ FT.

Identification: Adult male is mostly gray turning to whitish on the spotted brown belly. Adult female is brown above and buffy below. Immatures of both sexes are brown above and rich reddish brown below. White rump patch in both sexes and in all plumages and wings held at an angle above the horizontal are diagnostic.

Habitat: Open country, especially tidal marshes and freshwater marshes; open mountain ridges of the Interior. Nests on the ground in wet marshy areas.

Status and Distribution:	SPRING	SUMMER	FALL	WINTER
Southeastern	U	R	U	R
Southcoastal ★	C	U	C	R
Southwestern ★	U	U	U	R
Central ★	U	U	U	+
Western ★	U	U	U	—
Northern ★	R	R	R	—

Notes: Differs considerably from all other birds of prey; is not deep chested as most hawks but has a long thin body with long, strong wings and a long, thin tail. Northern Harrier hunts close to the ground in search of mice and small birds. Roosts on the ground at night. During daylight it normally perches on the ground or on stumps or fence posts; only rarely does it perch in trees or bushes. Only hawk that always chooses a ground site for nesting.

OSPREY

(Pandion haliaetus)

LENGTH: 20-25 IN.
WINGSPAN: 4½-6 FT.

Identification: Fish-eating hawk, dark brown above and entirely white below, with a white head and dark eye stripe. In flight wings are arched, with the wrist at the highest point.

Habitat: Near lakes, rivers and sea coasts. Nests near water in trees or on cliffs. Occurs more frequently in Bristol Bay than elsewhere.

Notes: Usually hovers then plunges into the water feet first after fish.

Status and Distribution:	SPRING	SUMMER	FALL	WINTER
Southeastern ★	R	R	R	—
Southcoastal ★	R	R	R	—
Southwestern ★	R	R	R	—
Central ★	R	R	R	—
Western ★	R	R	R	—
Northern	—	+	—	—

OSPREY
(Dennis Paulson)

FAMILY *FALCONIDAE*

FALCONS

(5)

Falcons are fast-flying birds of prey that are characterized by long pointed wings and medium-to-long slender tails. Their pointed wings are designed for speed rather than for soaring as in the broad-winged buteos and eagles.

GYRFALCON
White Phase
(Fred Bruemmer)

GYRFALCON

(Falco rusticolus)

LENGTH: 20-25 IN.
WINGSPAN: 4 FT.

Identification: Largest falcon, with a streamlined body, pointed wings and long narrow tail. Three color phases exist — black, gray and white. Gray phase is most common in Alaska. More uniformly colored than Peregrine Falcon and lacks the dark hood of that species. Has broader wings and shallower wingbeat than Peregrine Falcon. Flies with short rapid wingbeats and usually does not soar for long periods.

Habitat: Open country. Nests on cliff ledges.

Status and Distribution:	SPRING	SUMMER	FALL	WINTER
Southeastern	U	—	U	R
Southcoastal ★	R	R	R	R
Southwestern ★	U	U	U	U
Central ★	U	U	U	R
Western ★	U	U	U	U
Northern ★	U	U	U	—

Notes: Primarily a bird hunter that feeds on ptarmigan and seabirds. When birds are unavailable, preys on small mammals.

PEREGRINE FALCON
(Edgar Jones)

PEREGRINE FALCON

(Falco peregrinus)

LENGTH: 15-21 IN.
WINGSPAN: 3¼-3¾ FT.

Identification: Crow-sized falcon commonly referred to as the duck hawk. Head pattern characterized by broad to narrow black mustaches. Pointed wings, narrow tail and quick wingbeats identify it as a falcon. Adult has a slaty-colored back, often a dark cap, and a light barred breast. Immature is brown above, with heavy streaking on white underparts. Birds of the Aleutian Islands and southcoastal areas of Alaska are darker than Arctic-breeding birds.

Habitat: Open country especially shores and marshes frequented by waterfowl and shorebirds, cliffs on islands, along the coast and in the mountains. Nests on cliff ledges.

Status and Distribution:	SPRING	SUMMER	FALL	WINTER
Southeastern ★	U	U	U	R
Southcoastal ★	U	R	U	R
Southwestern ★	C	U	C	U
Central ★	R	R	R	—
Western ★	R	R	R	—
Northern ★	R	R	R	—

Notes: One of the swiftest birds in the world. Has been clocked at speeds up to 180 miles per hour, when diving after prey.

MERLIN
(Doug Herr)

MERLIN

(Falco columbarius)

LENGTH: 12 IN.
WINGSPAN: 2 FT.

Identification: Because of small size, may be confused only with Sharp-shinned Hawk or American Kestrel. Pointed wings and steady wingbeat separate Merlin from Sharp-shinned Hawk. Lack of reddish in the tail and lack of conspicuous black face markings distinguish it from American Kestrel. Tail is barred dark and light, quite different from reddish tail of the kestrel, and flight is more rapid and powerful.

Status and Distribution:	SPRING	SUMMER	FALL	WINTER
Southeastern ★	U	R	U	+
Southcoastal ★	R	R	R	R
Southwestern ★	U	U	U	+
Central ★	U	U	U	+
Western ★	R	R	R	—
Northern	R	R	—	—

Habitat: Open coastal and interior forests particularly near tidal marshes and interior muskegs. Nests on cliff ledges, in a tree hollow or on the ground.

AMERICAN KESTREL

(Falco sparverius)

LENGTH: 9-12 IN.
WINGSPAN: 1¾-2 FT.

Identification: Only small falcon in Alaska with conspicuous reddish color in the tail and on the back. Black-and-white face pattern. Habitually hovers with wings beating rapidly, and, when perched, occasionally flicks tail.

Status and Distribution:	SPRING	SUMMER	FALL	WINTER
Southeastern	C	+	C	+
Southcoastal	R	—	R	+
Southwestern	—	—	—	—
Central ★	C	C	C	—
Western	—	—	—	—
Northern	+	—	—	—

Habitat: Forest edges and openings. Nests in tree cavities.

Notes: Diet consists of insects, mice and occasionally small birds.

AMERICAN KESTREL
(Frank Jackson)

EURASIAN KESTREL

(Falco tinnunculus)

LENGTH: 12-15 IN.

WINGSPAN: 2¼-2½ FT.

Identification: Noticeably larger than American Kestrel. Male distinguished from male American Kestrel by gray tail and head and chestnut-colored upper wing coverts. American Kestrel has reddish tail and gray upper wing coverts. Both adult and immature Eurasian Kestrels have one dark vertical bar on face; American Kestrel has two vertical bars. Merlins are smaller, slate-blue above (male) or brown above (female). Eurasian Kestrel has spotted chestnut-colored upperparts (male) or rusty, barred underparts (female).

Habitat: Has been found on Attu and Shemya islands in western Aleutians. Breeds in Eurasia and Africa.

Status and Distribution:	SPRING	SUMMER	FALL	WINTER
Southeastern	—	—	—	—
Southcoastal	—	—	—	—
Southwestern	+	—	+	—
Central	—	—	—	—
Western	—	—	—	—
Northern	—	—	—	—

EURASIAN KESTREL
Female
(Hans Reinhard, Bruce Coleman, Inc.)

FAMILY *PHASIANIDAE*

GROUSE, PTARMIGANS

(7)

Members of this family are chickenlike birds that forage for food on the ground or in trees when the ground is snow covered. They are distinguished by the presence of feathers over the nostrils, lower legs and, in ptarmigans, the entire foot.

BLUE GROUSE

(Dendragapus obscurus)

LENGTH: 15½-21 IN.

Identification: Adult male is slate-colored with a yellow comb and a long black tail tipped with pale gray. Female is browner and more heavily barred than male and is only a little over two-thirds as large, but she has the same distinctive tail tip. Tail pattern is diagnostic for each Alaska grouse species (except between Rock and Willow ptarmigan which both have black tails).

Habitat: Coniferous forests, muskegs and alpine meadows near treeline. Nests on the ground often near a tree, log or rock.

Notes: Male in courtship is well known for its booming or hooting notes given while sitting in a conifer. Locating one is difficult due to ventriloquial quality of the voice and grouse's habit of changing the direction of hooting every few minutes.

Status and Distribution:	SPRING	SUMMER	FALL	WINTER
Southeastern ★	C	C	C	C
Southcoastal	+	—	—	—
Southwestern	—	—	—	—
Central	—	—	—	—
Western	—	—	—	—
Northern	—	—	—	—

BLUE GROUSE
Female
(Jack Gustafson)

BLUE GROUSE
(Loyal Johnson)

SPRUCE GROUSE
Female
(Will Troyer)

SPRUCE GROUSE

(Dendragapus canadensis)

LENGTH: 16 IN.

Identification: Male gray, with a sharply defined black breast and some white spotting on the sides. Red comb over the eye is often visible. Female is rusty-brown and thickly barred, more heavily barred below than female Blue Grouse. A rusty-orange band at tip of the dark tail is characteristic; however, this band is missing in birds found in southeastern Alaska, which have a row of conspicuous white spots at base of the black tail instead.

Habitat: Coniferous forests and mixed deciduous-spruce woodlands, muskegs, forest edges and openings. Inhabits white spruce-paper birch woodlands, black spruce bogs and in lower southeastern Alaska, Sitka spruce-hemlock forests. Nests on the ground at base of a tree or under a log.

Notes: Individual birds spend most of their life in one area of only a few acres. However, in September and October they may travel several miles to get grit along roads, streams and lakes. They need a large amount of grit to make the digestive change from a fall diet of berries and leaves to a winter diet of fibrous needles.

Status and Distribution:	SPRING	SUMMER	FALL	WINTER
Southeastern ★	R	R	R	R
Southcoastal ★	U	U	U	U
Southwestern ★	R	R	R	R
Central ★	C	C	C	C
Western ★	R	R	R	R
Northern	—	—	—	—

SPRUCE GROUSE
(James Simmen)

RUFFED GROUSE
(Edgar Jones)

RUFFED GROUSE

(Bonasa umbellus)

LENGTH: 17½ IN.

Identification: Two color phases exist: a reddish-brown phase with back and tail brown, and a gray phase with a gray tail. Gray phase is more common in Alaska. Dark band near the tip of the fan-shaped tail is diagnostic.

Habitat: Deciduous woodlands — stands of aspen and birch mostly on drier south facing slopes, willow and alder thickets along streams and rivers. Nests on the ground under dense cover usually near the base of a tree. In central Alaska occurs in Yukon, Tanana and Kuskokwim valleys and along Taku and Stikine rivers in southeastern Alaska.

Notes: Males establish territory and begin courtship by making a drumming sound that suggests the starting of a motor in the distance. This sound is produced by quick forward and upward strokes of the wings while standing erect.

Status and Distribution:	SPRING	SUMMER	FALL	WINTER
Southeastern ★	+	+	+	—
Southcoastal	—	—		
Southwestern	—	—	—	—
Central ★	C	C	C	C
Western	—	—	—	—
Northern	—	—	—	—

SHARP-TAILED GROUSE
(Mark McDermott)

SHARP-TAILED GROUSE

(Tympanuchus phasianellus)

LENGTH: 15-20 IN.

Identification: Medium-sized with a short, stiff, dun-colored tail that shows white in flight. The V-marked underparts are diagnostic.

Status and Distribution:	SPRING	SUMMER	FALL	WINTER
Southeastern	—	—	—	—
Southcoastal	—	—	—	—
Southwestern	—	—	—	—
Central ★	U	U	U	U
Western	—	—	—	—
Northern	—	—	—	—

Habitat: Muskegs in interior coniferous forests, willow and stunted spruce thickets, forest edges in more open areas than preferred by the forest grouse. Nests on the ground in brush or grass.

Notes: In the spring courtship ritual, males taxi like wind-up airplanes on display grounds. At dawn cocks gather on their dancing ground with dominant males in the center and subordinate males at the edge. They then follow a routine of feet drumming, and circling, accompanied by tail rasping and popping sounds generated by their bulging air sacs.

ROCK PTARMIGAN
Winter
(Tom Walker)

ROCK PTARMIGAN
Summer
(Rick McIntyre)

Status and Distribution:	SPRING	SUMMER	FALL	WINTER
Southeastern ★	C	C	C	C
Southcoastal ★	C	C	C	C
Southwestern ★	C	C	C	C
Central ★	C	C	C	C
Western ★	C	C	C	C
Northern ★	U	U	U	U

ROCK PTARMIGAN

(Lagopus mutus)

LENGTH: 14 IN.

Identification: In white winter plumage Rock Ptarmigan may be separated from the other 2 species by a black bar through the eye of the male. Black tail distinguishes it from White-tailed Ptarmigan. In other plumages Rock Ptarmigan is difficult to separate from Willow Ptarmigan, although it is somewhat smaller than the willow. Voice of the courting male Rock Ptarmigan is a growling *kurr kurr.*

Habitat: Upland and coastal (Aleutian Islands) tundra, especially rocky mountain ridges, shrub thickets. Nests on the ground usually under shrubs.

Notes: Breeding Rock Ptarmigan frequent higher and more rocky ground than Willow Ptarmigan. In winter most males frequent the lower edge of the breeding grounds and females move to shrubby openings on low, forested hills. Winter flocks wander from place to place in search of food. They feed and search for food during most of the daylight hours. Rock Ptarmigan must eat the equivalent of one-tenth to one-fifth of their body weight each day.

WHITE-TAILED PTARMIGAN
Summer
(Lynn Erckmann)

WHITE-TAILED PTARMIGAN

(Lagopus leucurus)

LENGTH: 13 IN.

Identification: Smallest ptarmigan. Has all white tail in all plumages. Other ptarmigan have a black tail, although the long, white tail coverts may obscure much of it. In summer, back feathers are more finely barred and color tone is grayish instead of brown. Voice consists of cackling notes, clucks and soft hoots.

Habitat: Upland tundra, especially high mountain ridges, shrub thickets. Nests on the ground on mossy mountain ledges or against big boulders to catch the sun's warmth. In summer, hens with broods stay high on the breeding grounds near moist areas where they feed on young plant growth around edges of melting snow patches. Rock slides and boulder fields offer protection for chicks. In late fall White-tailed Ptarmigan usually move lower and spend the winter on slopes or in high valleys among the alders, willows and birches that project above the snow.

Status and Distribution:	SPRING	SUMMER	FALL	WINTER
Southeastern ★	U	U	U	U
Southcoastal ★	R	R	R	R
Southwestern	—	—	—	—
Central ★	U	U	U	U
Western	—	—	—	—
Northern	—	—	—	—

WHITE-TAILED PTARMIGAN
Winter
(Paul Arneson)

WILLOW PTARMIGAN

(Lagopus lagopus)

LENGTH: 16 IN.

Identification: In winter lacks the black eye bar of male Rock Ptarmigan and the white tail of White-tailed Ptarmigan. In summer Willow and Rock ptarmigans are difficult to separate, but both sexes of Willow Ptarmigan are usually more reddish than Rock Ptarmigan and have slightly heavier bills. The male willow molts head and neck plumage in spring and body plumage some months later. Usually the Willow Ptarmigan is found among willows and heavily vegetated tundra and slopes; the Rock Ptarmigan prefers the higher, more barren and rocky slopes. Male has a deep raucous call that sounds much like *go back go back.*

Habitat: Willow shrub thickets, tundra, muskeg. Nests on the ground, usually in wetter places with more luxuriant vegetation than the other 2 species of ptarmigan.

Notes: Willow Ptarmigan was selected as the official state bird in a vote taken by school children just before Alaska became a state. Male Willow Ptarmigan often help to care for their chicks, a habit unique among North American grouse and ptarmigan. If the female is killed, the male will take over all family responsibilities.

WILLOW PTARMIGAN
Winter
(Don Cornelius)

Status and Distribution:	SPRING	SUMMER	FALL	WINTER
Southeastern ★	U	U	U	U
Southcoastal ★	U	U	U	U
Southwestern ★	C	C	C	C
Central ★	C	C	C	C
Western ★	C	C	C	C
Northern ★	C	C	C	C

WILLOW PTARMIGAN
Summer

WILLOW PTARMIGAN
Female
Summer

FAMILY *GRUIDAE*

CRANES

(1 + 1)

These are large, long-legged, long-necked wading birds. Cranes are among the tallest birds in the world.

SANDHILL CRANE

(Grus canadensis)

LENGTH: 34-48 IN.
WINGSPAN: 6-7 FT.

Identification: Long-legged, long-necked gray bird with a bold red crown in the adult. Flies with extended neck and with wings jerking upward with each beat. Flocks flying at a distance could be mistaken for geese if long legs and very long necks were not obvious. The somewhat similar Great Blue Heron is solitary, relatively silent, flies with neck retracted, and has more slender body and very different stance. Crane and heron are rarely seen in same habitat.

Status and Distribution:	SPRING	SUMMER	FALL	WINTER
Southeastern ★	C	R	C	—
Southcoastal ★	C	R	C	—
Southwestern ★	C	C	C	—
Central ★	C	U	C	—
Western ★	C	C	C	—
Northern ★	U	U	U	—

Habitat: Breeding — lowland tundra marshes. Nests on the ground in grassy marshes. In migration — tidal flats, muskegs. Winters in southern California, Texas and Mexico.

Notes: Often observed flying in V or line formation at fairly high altitude. Courtship ritual involves elaborate head bowing, leaping into the air and wing flapping.

SANDHILL CRANE
(Doug Murphy)

FAMILY *RALLIDAE*

RAILS, GALLINULES, COOTS

(2 + 1)

Small to medium-sized marsh and water birds, with short tails and wings, and large feet. Coots have lobes on the sides of their toes.

SORA

(Porzana carolina)

LENGTH: 8½ IN.

Identification: Only rail in Alaska. Has striped brown back, gray underparts with barred sides, black face patch and bright yellow bill. Call is a descending whinny.

Habitat: Freshwater marshes and ponds. Nests have not been found in Alaska. Elsewhere — a basket of woven marsh grass attached to vegetation over water or on the ground near marsh or pond. Found mostly along mainland river systems of southeastern Alaska.

Notes: This small bird skulks in marsh vegetation and is unlikely to be seen.

Status and Distribution:	SPRING	SUMMER	FALL	WINTER
Southeastern ★	R	R	R	—
Southcoastal	—	—	—	—
Southwestern	—	—	—	—
Central	—	+	—	—
Western	—	—	—	—
Northern	—	—	—	—

SORA
(Don Cunningham)

AMERICAN COOT
(Michael Hopiak, Cornell Lab of Ornithology)

AMERICAN COOT

(Fulica americana)

LENGTH: 15 IN.

Identification: All dark gray with a white bill. Has lobed rather than webbed feet.

Habitat: Lakes, ponds, marshes. Intertidal ponds and sloughs.

Status and Distribution:	SPRING	SUMMER	FALL	WINTER
Southeastern	+	—	R	R
Southcoastal	+	+	+	—
Southwestern	—	—	+	—
Central ★	R	R	R	—
Western	—	+	—	—
Northern	—	+	—	—

FAMILY *HAEMATOPODIDAE*

OYSTERCATCHERS

(1)

This family contains large, dumpy, short-legged shorebirds with long red bills that are flattened laterally.

AMERICAN BLACK OYSTERCATCHER

(Haematopus bachmani)

LENGTH: 17 IN.

Identification: Crow-sized, all black shorebird with bright red bill and pinkish legs and feet. Rounded wings beat rapidly and are kept below the level of the body in flight, all of which distinguishes the oystercatcher from a crow at a distance. Call is a loud, whistled *wheee-whee-whee-whee.*

Habitat: Rocky shores, reefs and islands. Nests in beach gravel, often near grass line.

Status and Distribution:	SPRING	SUMMER	FALL	WINTER
Southeastern ★	C	C	C	R
Southcoastal ★	C	C	C	U
Southwestern ★	C	C	C	C
Central	—	—	—	—
Western	—	—	—	—
Northern	—	—	—	—

AMERICAN BLACK OYSTERCATCHER
(Don Cornelius)

FAMILY *CHARADRIIDAE*
PLOVERS
(7 + 1)

Plovers are plump-bodied shorebirds with thick pigeonlike bills, short legs and large eyes. Plovers characteristically run short distances and then stop.

COMMON RINGED PLOVER
(Charadrius hiaticula)
LENGTH: 7½ IN.

Identification: Difficult to distinguish from Semipalmated Plover but in summer plumage the black breast band is considerably wider, and head markings are more contrasting. Has webbing between the bases of 2 toes whereas in semipalmated webbing occurs between all 3 toes.

Habitat: Asiatic species that has occurred as a spring migrant and breeder on Saint Lawrence Island in the Bering Sea and as a casual migrant in the Aleutian Islands.

Status and Distribution:	SPRING	SUMMER	FALL	WINTER
Southeastern	—	—	—	—
Southcoastal	—	—	—	—
Southwestern	+	—	+	—
Central	—	—	—	—
Western ★	+	+	—	—
Northern	—	—	—	—

COMMON RINGED PLOVER
(E. Lieske)

EURASIAN DOTTEREL
(E. Lieske)

EURASIAN DOTTEREL

(Charadrius morinellus)

LENGTH: 8½ IN.

Identification: In summer has white stripe over the eye meeting at nape, white throat and narrow white band across the breast. Breast is gray, belly chestnut and black. In winter is sandy brown, but the head pattern and particularly the white breast band are diagnostic. From above in flight much like Lesser Golden-Plover but smaller and unpatterned. Call is a musical twitter or trill.

Habitat: Asiatic shorebird most often seen in summer on mountains of Bering Strait islands and Seward Peninsula in western Alaska. Although it no doubt breeds in these mountains, no nests have been found.

Status and Distribution:	SPRING	SUMMER	FALL	WINTER
Southeastern	—	—	—	—
Southcoastal	—	—	+	—
Southwestern	—	—	+	—
Central	—	+	—	—
Western ★	R	R	—	—
Northern ★	—	+	—	—

SEMIPALMATED PLOVER

SEMIPALMATED PLOVER

(Charadrius semipalmatus)

LENGTH: 7 IN.

Identification: Small, with a single black breast band, duller in the fall. Legs and base of the bill are orange. In areas bordering the Bering Sea, potentially confused with Common Ringed Plover. Call is plaintive *chu-wi.*

Status and Distribution:	SPRING	SUMMER	FALL	WINTER
Southeastern ★	C	C	C	—
Southcoastal ★	C	C	C	—
Southwestern ★	C	C	C	—
Central ★	C	C	C	—
Western ★	C	C	C	—
Northern ★	U	U	U	—

Habitat: Breeding — gravelly or sandy beaches of lakes, ponds, rivers and glacial moraines. Nests on the ground in sand, gravel or moss. In migration — lakes, ponds, rivers, glacial moraines and tidal flats.

KILLDEER

(Charadrius vociferus)

LENGTH: 10 IN.

Identification: Two black breast bands are diagnostic. In flight, tail looks longer than in other shorebirds, and its reddish base is conspicuous at close range. Call is raucous cry of *kill-dee, kill-dee.*

Status and Distribution:	SPRING	SUMMER	FALL	WINTER
Southeastern ★	U	U	U	R
Southcoastal ★	R	R	R	—
Southwestern	+	+	—	—
Central ★	R	R	R	—
Western	+	+	—	—
Northern	+	+	—	—

Habitat: Marshes, tidal sloughs, lake shores, rivers, ponds, grasslands. Nests on gravel shores, or in fields or pastures.

MONGOLIAN PLOVER
(John C. Pitcher)

MONGOLIAN PLOVER

(Charadrius mongolus)

LENGTH: 7½ IN.

Identification: In breeding plumage has conspicuous rusty breast band and rust color in the light head stripe. In winter much duller, like a washed-out Semipalmated Plover but larger. In flight shows a narrower wing stripe and less conspicuous tail pattern than Semipalmated or Common Ringed plovers. Call is a short trill.

Status and Distribution:	SPRING	SUMMER	FALL	WINTER
Southeastern	—	—	—	—
Southcoastal	—	+	—	—
Southwestern	R	+	R	—
Central	—	—	—	—
Western ★	R	+	+	—
Northern	—	+	+	—

Habitat: Most often seen in spring in western Aleutian Islands and on Saint Lawrence Island. Has been recorded nesting on the mainland coast of western Alaska. Asiatic bird.

KILLDEER
(Merrick Hersey)

LESSER GOLDEN-PLOVER
Immature

LESSER GOLDEN-PLOVER
(Pluvialis dominica)
LENGTH: 10 IN.

Identification: Always appears darker than similar but slightly larger Black-bellied Plover. In summer and winter back is golden brown; in breeding plumage entire underside of male golden plover is black while undertail coverts of Black-bellied Plover are white. Female of both species may have much white underneath, even in full breeding plumage. Lesser Golden-Plover appears all dark in flight in any plumage with uniformly dark wings, rump and tail, while Black-bellied Plover has conspicuous white wing stripes and white tail and rump. Fast flier. Call a whistled *queedle.*

Habitat: Breeding — tundra on drier hillsides. Nests on tundra in moss. In migration — tidal flats, usually the drier upper portions, and tundra.

Status and Distribution:	SPRING	SUMMER	FALL	WINTER
Southeastern	U	—	U	+
Southcoastal	C	+	C	—
Southwestern	C	—	C	—
Central ★	C	C	C	—
Western ★	C	C	C	—
Northern ★	C	C	C	—

LESSER GOLDEN-PLOVER
(Doug Murphy)

BLACK-BELLIED PLOVER

(Pluvialis squatarola)

LENGTH: 12 IN.

Identification: Likely to be confused only with Lesser Golden-Plover. In winter, plumage shows contrasting black axillar feathers under the wing base like no other shorebird. Noisy; common call is plaintive whistled *whee-e-ee.*

Status and Distribution:	SPRING	SUMMER	FALL	WINTER
Southeastern	C	—	C	—
Southcoastal	C	U	C	—
Southwestern	C	—	C	—
Central	R	R	R	—
Western ★	C	U	C	—
Northern ★	U	U	U	—

Habitat: Breeding — tundra, usually drier ridges within wet tundra areas. Nests on ground in tundra. In migration — tidal flats, saltwater and freshwater shores.

BLACK-BELLIED PLOVER
Immature

BLACK-BELLIED PLOVER

FAMILY *SCOLOPACIDAE*

SANDPIPERS

(50 + 5)

Members of this family vary considerably in size, shape and color. Their bill is more slender than the plovers', soft and rather flexible. Unlike plovers, sandpipers typically move slowly and continuously when foraging, probing or picking from the surface as they go. These shorebirds typically inhabit lakeshores, intertidal areas or other moist places. They usually lay 4 eggs in shallow depressions in the ground. Before and after the breeding season most are gregarious and can be seen in large flocks, often several species together.

BLACK-TAILED GODWIT

(Limosa limosa)

LENGTH: 16 IN.

Identification: In summer similar to Hudsonian Godwit but with an immaculate cinnamon head and breast, paler flanks which are barred with bold black bars. Hudsonian Godwit has dark cinnamon breast and belly, pale head. In all seasons Black-tailed Godwit has white wing linings, rather than black as in the Hudsonian Godwit. Only godwit with a straight bill.

Habitat: This Asiatic shorebird has been found in western and central Aleutian Islands and on Bering Sea islands. Not known to breed in Alaska.

Status and Distribution:	SPRING	SUMMER	FALL	WINTER
Southeastern	—	—	—	—
Southcoastal	—	—	—	—
Southwestern	+	+	—	—
Central	—	—	—	—
Western	+	—	—	—
Northern	—	—	—	—

BLACK-TAILED GODWIT
(John C. Pitcher)

HUDSONIAN GODWIT

(Limosa haemastica)

LENGTH: 15 IN.

Identification: Large shorebird with long, slender, slightly upturned bill. In summer the underparts are extensively dark cinnamon, narrowly barred with black; the back is brown. In winter entirely pale brownish-gray. Shows a vivid pattern in flight with a conspicuous white wing stripe, black underwings and white-based, black-tipped tail. Similarly sized Bar-tailed Godwit is drab in comparison.

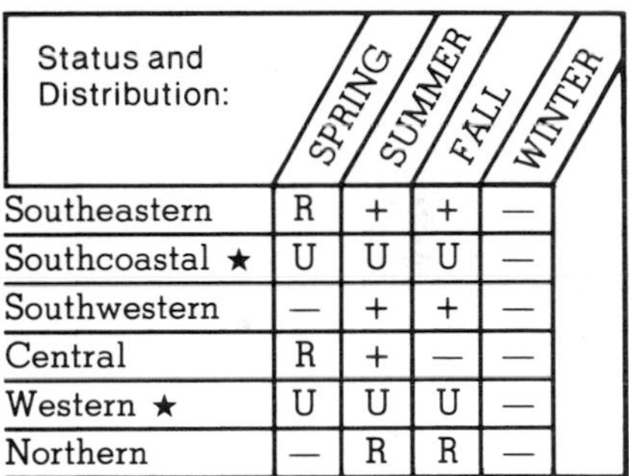

Status and Distribution:	SPRING	SUMMER	FALL	WINTER
Southeastern	R	+	+	—
Southcoastal ★	U	U	U	—
Southwestern	—	+	+	—
Central	R	+	—	—
Western ★	U	U	U	—
Northern	—	R	R	—

Habitat: Breeding — sedge-grass marshes, wet tundra, taiga bogs. In migration — tidal flats and beaches.

HUDSONIAN GODWIT
(Larger Bird)
(Dennis Paulson)

MARBLED GODWIT

(Limosa fedoa)

LENGTH: 16-20 IN.

Identification: Largest godwit in Alaska. Resembles a larger, entirely tawny brown version of the summer-plumaged Bar-tailed Godwit. At all seasons is evenly buff-colored ventrally. In flight, wings are conspicuously cinnamon. Immature Bar-tailed Godwit in fall has paler breast and belly and lighter tail than any Marbled Godwit. Call is a loud *kerreck.*

Habitat: Tidal flats. No nests have been found in Alaska.

Status and Distribution:	SPRING	SUMMER	FALL	WINTER
Southeastern	R	+	—	—
Southcoastal	R	—	+	—
Southwestern ★	R	R	—	—
Central	—	—	—	—
Western	—	—	—	—
Northern	—	—	—	—

MARBLED GODWIT
(Kenneth Fink)

BAR-TAILED GODWIT
Female, left; Male, right
(Cheryl Boise)

BAR-TAILED GODWIT

(Limosa lapponica)

LENGTH: 16 IN.

Identification: Has long, slightly upturned bill. Male is rich rufous below in breeding plumage, female is duller with more white. In all plumages looks rather plain above in flight, with poorly defined wing stripe and rump and tail slightly lighter than the back. Field guides portray European subspecies which has a much more constrasting rump and tail than does the Alaska one.

Habitat: Breeding — wet lowland tundra. Nests on the ground in moss. In migration — tidal flats.

Status and Distribution:	SPRING	SUMMER	FALL	WINTER
Southeastern	+	—	+	—
Southcoastal	R	—	R	—
Southwestern	C	—	C	—
Central	—	—	—	—
Western ★	C	C	C	—
Northern ★	U	U	U	—

FAR EASTERN CURLEW

(Numenius madagascariensis)

LENGTH: 20-26 IN.

Identification: Considerably larger than other two curlews, with plain brown back, wings and tail, and boldly streaked, beige underparts. Head is finely streaked, without the conspicuous stripes of other curlews.

Habitat: Asiatic bird found mostly in spring and summer on Aleutian Islands and Pribilof Islands. Not known to breed in Alaska.

Status and Distribution:	SPRING	SUMMER	FALL	WINTER
Southeastern	—	—	—	—
Southcoastal	—	—	—	—
Southwestern	+	+	—	—
Central	—	—	—	—
Western	+	—	—	—
Northern	—	—	—	—

WHIMBREL

(Numenius phaeopus)

LENGTH: 17 IN.

Identification: At a distance appears entirely plain brown. At close range a long downcurved bill and striped crown are visible. May be confused only with Bristle-thighed Curlew, or with the much rarer, larger curlews with unstriped heads. Whimbels from Siberia occur regularly in southwestern and western Alaska. They have a conspicuous white back and dark-spotted white rump. Call is a loud, repeated, whistled *pi-pi-pi-pip.*

Status and Distribution:	SPRING	SUMMER	FALL	WINTER
Southeastern	U	—	U	—
Southcoastal	C	U	C	—
Southwestern	C	C	C	—
Central ★	C	C	U	—
Western ★	C	C	U	—
Northern ★	U	U	—	—

WHIMBREL
(Heinrich Springer)

Habitat: Breeding — tundra. Nests in a depression or on a mound of vegetation in the tundra. In migration — tidal flats and beaches. In migration this large shorebird is quite conspicuous among the smaller sandpipers. However, on the tundra Whimbrel blends well with its surroundings and is often difficult to see.

FAR EASTERN CURLEW
(John C. Pitcher)

BRISTLE-THIGHED CURLEW
(Henry Kyllingstad)

BRISTLE-THIGHED CURLEW

(Numenius tahitiensis)

LENGTH: 17 IN.

Identification: Similar to Whimbrel, with long, downcurved bill, large size and conspicuous head stripe. Tawnier all over than Whimbrel, pale salmon-colored on the rump and tail. Breast is finely *streaked;* breast of Whimbrel is always marked with fine chevrons instead. Flight call is a slurred whistle.

Habitat: Breeding — flat, dry tundra on exposed ridges. Nests in depressions on the tundra. In migration — drier coastal tundra, tidal flats and beaches.

Status and Distribution:	SPRING	SUMMER	FALL	WINTER
Southeastern	+	—	—	—
Southcoastal	+	—	+	—
Southwestern	R	—	R	—
Central	+	—	—	—
Western ★	U	U	U	—
Northern	R	R	—	—

Notes: Alaska is the only known nesting place for this species.

UPLAND SANDPIPER

UPLAND SANDPIPER

(Bartramia longicauda)

LENGTH: 11½ IN.

Identification: Large, buffy, with a long neck, small head and straight bill that is shorter than the head. Blackish lower back and longish tail, both visible in flight. Flies with wings held low like a Spotted Sandpiper. Often holds wings up for a moment on alighting. Voice on the breeding grounds is a long mournful rolling whistle; flight call similar to Whimbrel's.

Status and Distribution:	SPRING	SUMMER	FALL	WINTER
Southeastern	+	—	+	—
Southcoastal	+	—	+	—
Southwestern	—	—	—	—
Central ★	U	U	U	—
Western	—	—	—	—
Northern	—	—	—	—

Habitat: Open grassy fields and sparsely vegetated uplands. Never associated with water. Frequently perches on small trees or fence posts. Occurs primarily in interior Alaska, in areas such as Mount McKinley National Park and open grassy ridges north of Fairbanks.

SPOTTED REDSHANK

(Tringa erythropus)

LENGTH: 12 IN.

Identification: Shaped like Greater Yellowlegs but with slightly shorter neck and legs. Has bright red or red-orange legs in all plumages. In summer mostly black, with white spotting above; in winter gray above and white below, plainer than a yellowlegs. In flight similar to a yellowlegs but white of the rump extends up the back in a point, similar to the pattern of a dowitcher. Call is a loud, whistled *tew-it.*

Status and Distribution:	SPRING	SUMMER	FALL	WINTER
Southeastern	—	—	—	—
Southcoastal	—	—	—	—
Southwestern	+	—	R	—
Central	—	—	—	—
Western	—	—	—	—
Northern	—	—	—	—

Habitat: Asiatic migrant that has occurred in the western and central Aleutian Islands, primarily in fall, and as a fall migrant in the Pribilof Islands. Not known to breed in Alaska.

SPOTTED REDSHANK
Nonbreeding
(Kenneth Fink)

COMMON GREENSHANK
(John C. Pitcher)

COMMON GREENSHANK

(Tringa nebularia)

LENGTH: 12 IN.

Identification: Similar to Greater Yellowlegs but legs are greenish, not yellow, and in flight the white of the rump extends in a point up the back. Has very white tail, not densely barred like that of the yellowlegs. Leg color distinguishes this species from Spotted Redshank in winter plumage. Call is similar to Greater Yellowlegs.

Habitat: Asiatic shorebird seen mostly in western Aleutian Islands. Not known to breed in Alaska.

Status and Distribution:	SPRING	SUMMER	FALL	WINTER
Southeastern	—	—	—	—
Southcoastal	—	—	—	—
Southwestern	R	+	+	—
Central	—	—	—	—
Western	—	—	—	—
Northern	—	—	—	—

GREATER YELLOWLEGS

(Tringa melanoleuca)

LENGTH: 14 IN.

Identification: Yellowlegs are slim, gray and white, with long bright yellow legs. In flight they show a white rump and gray-and-white barred tail and no wing stripe. Greater and Lesser yellowlegs often appear together and can be distinguished by size. When separate, size can be confusing. Greater Yellowlegs have a longer, heavier and very slightly upturned bill. Voice is usually 3 or 4 note whistle sounding like *whew-whew-whew.* Display song is a repeated whistle *whee-oodle.*

Status and Distribution:	SPRING	SUMMER	FALL	WINTER
Southeastern ★	C	C	C	—
Southcoastal ★	C	C	C	—
Southwestern ★	C	C	C	—
Central ★	R	R	R	—
Western ★	R	R	R	—
Northern	—	+	—	—

Habitat: Breeding — muskegs, fresh-water marshes. Breeds from the lower Yukon River Valley to the Alaska Peninsula and south and east around the coast into southeastern Alaska. Nests on the ground in moss. In migration — tidal flats, lakes, ponds.

GREATER YELLOWLEGS
Immature
(Jim Hawkings)

LESSER YELLOWLEGS
Immature

LESSER YELLOWLEGS

(Tringa flavipes)

LENGTH: 11 IN.

Identification: Smaller version of Greater Yellowlegs with shorter, slighter, straight bill. Voice is 1 or 2 notes like *tew tew.* Display song is *wheedle-bree.*

Status and Distribution:	SPRING	SUMMER	FALL	WINTER
Southeastern ★	C	R	C	—
Southcoastal ★	C	C	C	—
Southwestern	R	—	R	—
Central ★	C	C	C	—
Western ★	U	U	U	—
Northern ★	—	+	—	—

Habitat: Breeding — muskeg, freshwater marshes. Breeds primarily from Kobuk River Valley through Yukon-Kuskokwim area to Kenai Peninsula and Yakutat Bay. In migration — tidal flats, lakes, ponds.

Notes: Noisy. When approached, yellowlegs usually begin calling. During nesting season they often stand on the topmost twig of a small tree and if disturbed, they will dive at the intruder while uttering shrill alarm notes.

SOLITARY SANDPIPER

(Tringa solitaria)

LENGTH: 8 IN.

Identification: Shaped like yellowlegs. Dark olive-brown above, with conspicuous eye ring, and shorter, greenish legs. In flight shows blackish underwings, dark rump and tail. Tail has flashy white sides barred with black. Often flies high in the air when flushed. Call is a high-pitched whistle *wheet-wheet-wheet-wheet.*

Status and Distribution:	SPRING	SUMMER	FALL	WINTER
Southeastern ★	U	R	U	—
Southcoastal ★	U	R	U	—
Southwestern ★	—	R	—	—
Central ★	U	U	U	—
Western ★	+	R	—	—
Northern ★	+	+	—	—

Habitat: Breeding — muskegs, freshwater marshes, lakes, ponds. Nests in deserted nests of other birds such as robins and thrushes. In migration — muddy shorelines of ponds and streams in wooded areas. Rarely occurs on salt water.

Notes: Usually solitary or with 1 or 2 others.

SOLITARY SANDPIPER

GREEN SANDPIPER
(R.J. Chandler)

GREEN SANDPIPER

(Tringa ocrophus)

LENGTH: 9½ IN.

Identification: Dark above; dark streaking on breast; white eye ring, rump patch and belly; dark underwings. Similar to Solitary Sandpiper in plumage, flight pattern and voice. Best distinguished in flight by a conspicuous white rump patch and white tail barred with black. (Solitary has a dark rump and tail. Tail has white sides barred with black.) Best distinguished from Wood Sandpiper by its dark underwings; Wood Sandpiper has white underwings. Common Sandpiper has dark rump, white wing stripes and whitish underwings.

Habitat: Has been found on Attu Island in western Aleutians, and on Saint Lawrence Island. Breeds in northern Eurasia.

Status and Distribution	SPRING	SUMMER	FALL	WINTER
Southeastern	—	—	—	—
Southcoastal	—	—	—	—
Southwestern	+	—	—	—
Central	—	—	—	—
Western	+	—	—	—
Northern	—	—	—	—

WOOD SANDPIPER
(John C. Pitcher)

WOOD SANDPIPER

(Tringa glareola)
LENGTH: 8 IN.

Identification: Built like a Solitary Sandpiper, but warm brown dorsally, not olive. Legs are duller yellow than those of the yellowlegs. Wings are light underneath, more like yellowlegs than Solitary Sandpiper. Resembles a pale Solitary Sandpiper with bold white rump. Flight call is a 3-note whistle.

Habitat: Tundra, tidal flats. Asiatic sandpiper frequently observed in recent years in southwestern and western Alaska. Now considered an uncommon to fairly common spring migrant in western and central Aleutian Islands where it has been seen in groups of 2 to 5 and occasionally in flocks of 20 to 45. Nesting has been recorded in western and central Aleutian Islands.

Status and Distribution:	SPRING	SUMMER	FALL	WINTER
Southeastern	—	—	—	—
Southcoastal	—	—	—	—
Southwestern ★	U	R	R	—
Central	—	—	—	—
Western	R	+	—	—
Northern	—	+	—	—

TEREK SANDPIPER

(Xenus cinereus)

LENGTH: 9 IN.

Identification: Larger than Spotted and Common sandpipers. Plain gray above and white below with short yellow legs and conspicuously upturned, long bill (only small shorebird with such a bill). In summer shows a pair of black stripes down the back. In flight plain above but with white patches on the rear edge of each wing. Bobs like Spotted and Common sandpipers. Call is a fluted *tutututututu.*

Status and Distribution:	SPRING	SUMMER	FALL	WINTER
Southeastern	—	—	—	—
Southcoastal	—	+	+	—
Southwestern	R	+	+	—
Central	—	—	—	—
Western	R	—	+	—
Northern	—	—	—	—

Habitat: Asiatic migrant found mostly in western Aleutian Islands and along the Bering Sea coast and islands. Not known to breed in Alaska.

TEREK SANDPIPER
(Rick Austin)

COMMON SANDPIPER

(Actitis hypoleucos)

LENGTH: 8 IN.

Identification: In spring or summer easily distinguished from very similar Spotted Sandpiper by plain, unspotted underparts, streaked breast, greenish-gray legs and feet (Spotted Sandpiper's are flesh-pink), and all dark bill. In fall these species are very similar. Common has a proportionately longer tail, at rest wings reach to base of tail whereas the spotted's reach to mid-tail. In flight the common's tail is outlined in white whereas the spotted's tail contains dark bands extending into the white. Spotted Sandpiper is unknown on Bering Sea islands.

Status and Distribution:	SPRING	SUMMER	FALL	WINTER
Southeastern	—	—	—	—
Southcoastal	—	—	—	—
Southwestern	R	—	R	—
Central	—	—	—	—
Western	R	—	—	—
Northern	—	—	—	—

Habitat: Asiatic migrant in western and central Aleutian Islands, Pribilof Islands and Saint Lawrence Island. Not known to breed in Alaska.

COMMON SANDPIPER
(Kenneth Fink)

SPOTTED SANDPIPER
Nonbreeding
(Kenneth Fink)

SPOTTED SANDPIPER

(Actitis macularia)

LENGTH: 7½ IN.

Identification: Breeding adult unmistakable with large black spots on white underparts. In autumn spots disappear and plumage is brown above and white below, with a dark mark on the side at the bend of the wing. In all plumages has a narrow wing stripe and dark tail. Teeters almost constantly. Has shallow wing strokes in flight. Call is series of high-pitched whistles, much like Solitary Sandpiper, but dropping toward the end of the series.

Habitat: Shores of rivers, streams, lakes and saltwater beaches. Nests near water in gravel or grass.

Notes: One of Alaska's most widely distributed breeding birds. When flushed, flies out over the water with short jerky wingbeats, only to swing back to shore a short distance away.

Status and Distribution:	SPRING	SUMMER	FALL	WINTER
Southeastern ★	C	C	C	—
Southcoastal ★	C	C	C	+
Southwestern ★	U	U	U	—
Central ★	C	C	C	—
Western ★	U	U	U	—
Northern ★	U	U	U	—

SPOTTED SANDPIPER
Breeding

GRAY-TAILED TATTLER
(John C. Pitcher)

GRAY-TAILED TATTLER

(Heteroscelus brevipes)

LENGTH: 9½ IN.

Identification: Very similar to Wandering Tattler. In winter and juvenile plumage the two tattlers are so similar they should be separated by voice. In summer Gray-tailed Tattler is distinguished by much less prominently barred underparts, the center of the belly and undertail being immaculate. Bars are lighter and narrower than in Wandering Tattler. Call is double whistle *too-weet.*

Habitat: Asiatic migrant found mostly in the Aleutian Islands and Bering Sea islands. Not known to breed in Alaska.

Status and Distribution:	SPRING	SUMMER	FALL	WINTER
Southeastern	—	—	—	—
Southcoastal	—	—	+	—
Southwestern	R	—	R	—
Central	—	—	—	—
Western	R	—	+	—
Northern	+	+	—	—

WANDERING TATTLER
Breeding
(Gilbert Staender)

WANDERING TATTLER
Immature
(Dennis Paulson)

WANDERING TATTLER

(Heteroscelus incanus)

LENGTH: 11 IN.

Identification: Uniform dark gray on upperparts, wings and tail distinguish this species from others found along rocky coasts. In breeding plumage has heavily barred underparts, unlike most other shorebirds. Noisy; call is a ringing series of whistled notes that can be easily heard over pounding surf or rushing water.

Status and Distribution:	SPRING	SUMMER	FALL	WINTER
Southeastern	U	R	U	—
Southcoastal ★	C	U	C	—
Southwestern ★	U	R	U	—
Central ★	U	U	U	—
Western ★	U	U	U	—
Northern ★	+	+	+	—

Habitat: Breeding — gravel bars of mountain streams. Nests in gravel near streams. In migration — rocky saltwater beaches.

Notes: Usually found alone or with 1 or 2 others. Almost exclusively an Alaskan breeding bird. Elsewhere has been reported from only 1 small area in Yukon Territory.

RUDDY TURNSTONE

(Arenaria interpres)

LENGTH: 9 IN.

Identification: In spring and summer is striking black, white and russet. In autumn adult and immature are brownish, but still show enough of their peculiar breast and wing pattern to be distinctive. A very dull Ruddy Turnstone can be separated from Black Turnstone by oranger legs, white throat, browner back and the double-rounded line where breast and belly colors meet. In flight both turnstones show a vivid calico pattern above. Voice is a chattering call, slower and lower-pitched than Black Turnstone.

Status and Distribution:	SPRING	SUMMER	FALL	WINTER
Southeastern	U	—	U	—
Southcoastal	C	R	U	—
Southwestern	C	U	C	—
Central	R	+	—	—
Western ★	C	C	C	—
Northern ★	U	U	U	—

Habitat: Breeding — drier tundra areas, dunes. Nests in a depression on the ground. In migration — rocky shores, tidal flats and beaches.

RUDDY TURNSTONE
(Jerry Hout)

BLACK TURNSTONE

(Arenaria melanocephala)

LENGTH: 9 IN.

Identification: Chunky, short-legged shorebird with blackish chest and white lower breast and belly. Black-and-white wing and back pattern can be seen in flight. Breast coloration meets that of the belly in a straight line, and legs vary from dull dark yellowish to black. Voice is a high and shrill chattering call.

Status and Distribution:	SPRING	SUMMER	FALL	WINTER
Southeastern	C	R	C	R
Southcoastal	C	U	C	R
Southwestern ★	C	U	C	R
Central	—	+	+	—
Western ★	C	C	C	—
Northern	+	—	—	—

BLACK TURNSTONE
Breeding
(Jerry Hout)

Habitat: Breeding — wet tundra. Nests on the ground in grassy areas near ponds. In migration and winter — rocky shores, tidal flats and beaches.

BLACK TURNSTONE
Nonbreeding
(Jim Hawkings)

WILSON'S PHALAROPE
Female
(Doug Murphy)

WILSON'S PHALAROPE
(Phalaropus tricolor)
LENGTH: 9 IN.

Identification: Larger and more slender than Red-necked and Red phalaropes, with a long, slender bill. In summer females are gray above, with a black and rusty neck stripe and rusty back stripes, appearing overall considerably paler than Red-necked Phalaropes. Male is a duller version of the same pattern. In these and in the plain winter-plumaged bird, breast and belly are immaculate white. In flight the impression is of a yellowlegs, with dark wings and white rump and tail, but with a whiter breast and much shorter greenish legs.

Status and Distribution:	SPRING	SUMMER	FALL	WINTER
Southeastern	+	+	—	—
Southcoastal	+	—	—	—
Southwestern	—	—	—	—
Central	+	+	—	—
Western	+	—	—	—
Northern	+	+	—	—

Habitat: Freshwater marshes and ponds, usually those with open water surrounded by shallow vegetated areas. Not known to breed in Alaska. Feeds on land much more readily than other phalaropes and not likely to be seen on the ocean.

WILSON'S PHALAROPE
(Doug Murphy)

RED-NECKED PHALAROPE

(Phalaropus lobatus)

LENGTH: 7 IN.

Identification: Breeding female is gray above with a patch of rufous on the neck and a white throat. Male is browner and more variable but similar in pattern, always with a white eye line. In winter all are dark gray above and white below, the back heavily marked with pale lines. Call is a *tic, tic.*

Habitat: Breeding — wet tundra, freshwater marshes, ponds and lakes. Nests on the ground in wet grassy areas near water. In migration — inshore and offshore marine waters, tidal ponds and sloughs, lakes and ponds.

Status and Distribution:	SPRING	SUMMER	FALL	WINTER
Southeastern	C	U	C	R
Southcoastal ★	C	C	C	+
Southwestern ★	C	C	C	—
Central ★	C	C	C	—
Western ★	C	C	C	—
Northern ★	C	C	C	—

Notes: Phalaropes differ from other shorebirds by having lobes or scalloped margins on their toes which enable them to swim with ease. Females are more brilliantly colored than the males and do all the courting. Males incubate and take care of the young.

RED-NECKED PHALAROPE
Breeding

RED-NECKED PHALAROPE
Nonbreeding
(Dennis Paulson)

RED-NECKED PHALAROPE
Female
Breeding
(Dennis Paulson)

RED PHALAROPE
Female
Breeding
(Jim Erckmann)

RED PHALAROPE

(Phalaropus fulicaria)

LENGTH: 8 IN.

Identification: Breeding female is brown above and rich reddish below, with a black crown, white face and yellow bill. Male is very variable, from just duller than the female but with a brownish streaked crown to virtually white beneath. In winter both sexes are pale gray above and white below. Young are darker-backed, looking more like Red-necked Phalaropes, but are larger, with a thicker bill. In fall, Red Phalarope looks paler than Red-necked Phalarope, without the conspicuous back stripes. Both have vivid white wing stripes and a dark mark through the eye. Call note resembles *tic tic.*

Habitat: Breeding — wet tundra near ponds and lakes. Nests on the ground in tundra. In migration — inshore and offshore marine waters, preferably offshore.

Status and Distribution:	SPRING	SUMMER	FALL	WINTER
Southeastern	R	—	R	—
Southcoastal	C	R	C	—
Southwestern	C	U	C	—
Central	+	+	—	—
Western ★	C	C	C	—
Northern ★	C	C	C	—

RED PHALAROPE
Breeding
(Jim Erckmann)

RED PHALAROPE
Nonbreeding
(Dennis Paulson)

COMMON SNIPE

Gallinago gallinago)

LENGTH: 11 IN.

Identification: Extremely long, slender bill distinguishes Common Snipe from almost all other Alaskan birds. Only dowitchers have comparable bills, and in any plumage they lack the stripes on the crown and back of Common Snipe. In flight the short, dark tail (orange at close range) and lack of white on wings and lower back separate Common Snipe from the dowitchers.

Habitat: Breeding — muskegs, freshwater marshes. Nests on the ground usually in grass. In migration and winter — sedgegrass meadows at the head of tidal flats and freshwater marshes.

Status and Distribution:	SPRING	SUMMER	FALL	WINTER
Southeastern ★	C	C	C	U
Southcoastal ★	C	C	C	R
Southwestern ★	C	C	C	+
Central ★	C	C	C	—
Western ★	C	C	C	—
Northern ★	C	C	C	—

Notes: High circling courtship flight is unusual. During this flight the bird makes a loud winnowing sound like *who who who who who who who,* increasing and then decreasing in intensity. The sound is made by stiffened tail feathers held at right angles to the body as the bird dives downward after each ascent. The wings are reported to produce the pulsations of sound.

COMMON SNIPE
(Jerrold Olson)

SHORT-BILLED DOWITCHER

(Limnodromus griseus)

LENGTH: 11½ IN.

Identification: Medium-sized with a long straight bill. White on the lower back and rump, conspicuous in flight, penetrates forward in a point, unlike white rumps of many other shorebirds which are cut straight across. Field identification of the 2 species of dowitchers is difficult. They are best distinguished by voice. Common call of the Short-billed Dowitcher is a low mellow *tu-tu-tu* much like that of Lesser Yellowlegs; call of the Long-billed Dowitcher is a high single or sometimes repeated *peep.*

SHORT-BILLED DOWITCHER

Habitat: Breeding — muskegs. Nesting locations are not well known. One nest was found in a muskeg and consisted of a small hollow in the moss. In migration — tidal flats and ponds, especially the muddy portions.

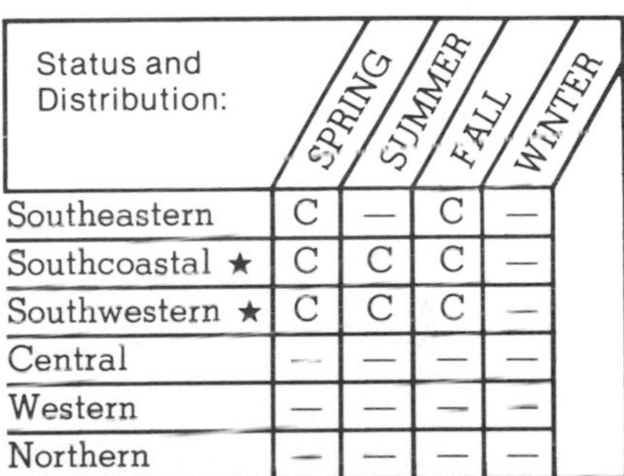

Status and Distribution:	SPRING	SUMMER	FALL	WINTER
Southeastern	C	—	C	—
Southcoastal ★	C	C	C	—
Southwestern ★	C	C	C	—
Central	—	—	—	—
Western	—	—	—	—
Northern	—	—	—	—

LONG-BILLED DOWITCHER

(Limnodromus scolopaceus)

LENGTH: 11½ IN.

Identification: In the breeding Long-billed the sides of breast are barred rather than spotted as in the Short-billed Dowitcher.

Habitat: Breeding — wet tundra. Nests on the ground in wet marshy areas. In migration — tidal flats and ponds, especially muddy areas.

Status and Distribution:	SPRING	SUMMER	FALL	WINTER
Southeastern	U	—	U	—
Southcoastal	C	—	C	—
Southwestern	U	—	U	—
Central ★	C	U	U	—
Western ★	C	C	C	—
Northern ★	C	C	C	—

LONG-BILLED DOWITCHER
(Doug Murphy)

SURFBIRD
Immature

SURFBIRD

(Aphriza virgata)

LENGTH: 10 IN.

Identification: Chunky, short-legged and short-billed. In breeding plumage breast is heavily spotted and streaked, back is reddish brown. Shape, behavior, habitat and flight pattern are diagnostic. In winter plain gray, lighter than Black Turnstone with which it is often associated. Also larger and thicker-billed than the turnstones. In flight appears all dark with a thin white wing stripe and white rump and tail base contrasting with black tail tip. Unlike turnstones and tattlers, it is usually silent.

Status and Distribution:	SPRING	SUMMER	FALL	WINTER
Southeastern	U	R	U	R
Southcoastal ★	C	U	C	U
Southwestern ★	R	R	R	R
Central ★	U	U	U	—
Western ★	R	R	R	—
Northern	—	—	—	—

SURFBIRD
Breeding
(Doug Murphy)

Habitat: Breeding — alpine tundra along mountain ridges. Nests on the ground in rocky area interspersed with small clumps of vegetation. In migration and winter — rocky shores and rockier portions of tidal flats.

GREAT KNOT

(Calidris tenuirostris)

LENGTH: 11½ IN.

Identification: Shaped much like Red Knot but is a bit larger and more heavily marked in all plumages. In summer back is marked with rufous, breast heavily blotched with black and sides covered with bold black heart-shaped or arrowhead-shaped spots. In winter breast is lightly spotted and the crown streaked. Legs are greenish as in Red Knot, and flight pattern is similar except that the paler rump contrasts considerably with the tail in Great Knot.

Habitat: Asiatic shorebird that has been found in western and central Aleutian Islands and on the Bering Sea coast and islands. Not known to breed in Alaska.

Status and Distribution:	SPRING	SUMMER	FALL	WINTER
Southeastern	—	—	—	—
Southcoastal	—	—	—	—
Southwestern	+	—	—	—
Central	—	—	—	—
Western	+	—	—	—
Northern	—	—	—	—

GREAT KNOT
(John C. Pitcher)

RED KNOT
(Kenneth Fink)

RED KNOT

(Calidris canutus)

LENGTH: 10½ IN.

Identification: Chunky, short-legged sandpiper of medium size that feeds on mud flats. In spring breast is brick red, the back mottled; in fall upperparts are light gray and underparts white. In spring only dowitchers and Red Phalaropes have plain reddish underparts, and Red Knot's short, straight black bill separates it from those species. When knots and dowitchers have their bills hidden, which is often, the slightly lighter breast color and white undertail coverts in Red Knot are diagnostic. In fall Red Knot is the only bird so evenly gray with a straight bill rather short for its body size. Flight pattern, with white wing stripe and pale rump and tail, separates it from all shorebirds but Black-bellied Plover which is larger and has conspicuous black axillar feathers. Knots are relatively silent; their 2-noted whistled song is given from high in the air.

Status and Distribution:	SPRING	SUMMER	FALL	WINTER
Southeastern	R	—	—	—
Southcoastal	C	—	R	—
Southwestern	+	+	R	—
Central	+	—	—	—
Western ★	U	U	R	—
Northern ★	R	R	R	—

Habitat: Breeding — gravelly ridges in alpine tundra. Nests on the ground in shallow depressions in gravel or rubble. In migration — tidal flats. Locally abundant on tidal flats of Copper and Bering river deltas in the spring where flocks of over 40,000 have been seen.

SANDERLING

(Calidris alba)

LENGTH: 8 IN.

Identification: Small, with a short, heavy black bill, black legs and a conspicuous white wing stripe in flight. In spring is bright buffy, much more uniformly reddish above than other small sandpipers. In fall migration is palest of small sandpipers, with pale gray back and snowy white underparts. The bend of its wing is conspicuously dark at this time. Call is a sharp *wick-wick.*

Status and Distribution:	SPRING	SUMMER	FALL	WINTER
Southeastern	U	R	U	R
Southcoastal	U	U	U	R
Southwestern	U	—	U	R
Central	R	—	R	—
Western	U	R	U	—
Northern ★	U	R	U	—

SANDERLING
Immature

Habitat: Breeding — primarily in Canadian arctic islands and Greenland; very rarely in Alaska at Point Barrow. In migration and winter — sandy beaches, tidal flats and rocky beaches.

SANDERLING
Immature

SEMIPALMATED SANDPIPER
Immature

SEMIPALMATED SANDPIPER

(Calidris pusilla)

LENGTH: 6½ IN.

Status and Distribution:	SPRING	SUMMER	FALL	WINTER
Southeastern	U	—	U	—
Southcoastal	U	R	U	—
Southwestern	R	—	R	—
Central ★	C	+	U	—
Western ★	U	R	U	—
Northern ★	C	C	U	—

Identification: One of 3 common very small sandpipers — with the Western and Least sandpipers — that may be confused with each other. Semipalmated and Western sandpipers have black legs, easily seen at close range. Semipalmated has a short, thick bill; western a longer, thinner bill with a slight droop at the tip. In breeding plumage semipalmated is mottled with brown above; western with gray and reddish. In drab fall plumage these species are more similar but birds with any reddish remaining (often on the scapulars) are westerns. Call of semipalmated is shorter and lower than western. Trills given on breeding ground are simple and unmusical, song flight is relatively low and short.

Habitat: Breeding — wet tundra, sand dunes. Nests on the ground in tundra or short-grass of sand dunes. In migration — tidal flats and beaches, lake shores.

Notes: Smaller Alaskan sandpipers are called peeps. In mixed flocks of peeps, comparing size can aid identification.

SEMIPALMATED SANDPIPER
Breeding
(Lynn Erckmann)

WESTERN SANDPIPER
Immature

WESTERN SANDPIPER

(Calidris mauri)

LENGTH: 6½ IN.

Identification: Among Alaskan peeps, Western Sandpiper is distinguished from Least Sandpiper by black legs (not yellowish-green) and longer bill, reddish-marked head and back in spring and summer, and paler back and less-marked breast in fall. Compared with Semipalmated Sandpiper, western shows much more rusty color on the crown and upperparts in breeding plumage. Is the only peep with distinct, arrowhead-shaped flank spots in breeding plumage. In autumn, separation of the 2 species is difficult. Call is a thin, high *jeet.* Breeding song is more varied than that of Semipalmated Sandpiper, rising and falling in pitch.

Habitat: Breeding — drier areas of the tundra. Nests on the ground in short tundra vegetation. In migration — tidal flats and beaches.

WESTERN SANDPIPER
Breeding

Status and Distribution:	SPRING	SUMMER	FALL	WINTER
Southeastern	C	R	C	—
Southcoastal	C	U	C	—
Southwestern	C	R	C	—
Central ★	R	+	R	—
Western ★	C	C	C	—
Northern ★	U	U	U	—

RUFOUS-NECKED STINT
(John C. Pitcher)

RUFOUS-NECKED STINT

(Calidris ruficollis)

LENGTH: 5 IN.

Identification: In summer has a bright rufous head and breast. In winter plumage is very similar to Little Stint, Western and Semipalmated sandpipers.

Habitat: Breeding — wet tundra. Nests in a depression in the tundra. In migration — tidal flats. Asiatic species.

Status and Distribution:	SPRING	SUMMER	FALL	WINTER
Southeastern	—	—	+	—
Southcoastal	+	+	+	—
Southwestern	R	+	R	—
Central	—	—	—	—
Western ★	R	R	—	—
Northern ★	R	R	R	—

LITTLE STINT
(J.P. Meyers, VIREO)

LITTLE STINT

(Calidris minuta)

LENGTH: 5 IN.

Identification: Small sandpiper with black legs and short bill tapering to a fine point. Very similar to Rufous-necked Stint. In breeding plumage the orange feather edges on back and coverts, rusty face and white throat help separate Little Stint from Rufous-necked Stint which has rufous feather edges on back, bright chestnut-colored face, throat and upper breast. In winter plumage grayish above and white below making it very difficult to distinguish from Rufous-necked Stint.

Status and Distribution:	SPRING	SUMMER	FALL	WINTER
Southeastern	—	—	—	—
Southcoastal	—	—	—	—
Southwestern	—	—	+	—
Central	—	—	—	—
Western	+	—	—	—
Northern	+	—	—	—

Habitat: Has been found at Point Barrow; the Pribilof Islands; Gambell, Saint Lawrence Island; and Buldir Island in western Aleutian Islands. Breeds in northern Eurasia.

LITTLE STINT
Immature
(R.J. Chandler)

TEMMINCK'S STINT
Immature
(Dennis Paulson)

TEMMINCK'S STINT

(Calidris temminckii)

LENGTH: 5½ IN.

Identification: In summer a gray peep with irregular black spots on back forming no pattern, and with short, yellowish or greenish legs. A peep with yellowish legs in the Bering Sea area might be either a Temminck's Stint, Least Sandpiper or Long-toed Stint, none of which is common. In winter very plain gray above and white below, the plainest of the peeps or stints. Outer tail feathers are pure white rather than the gray of other peeps. Call is short, high-pitched trill.

Habitat: Asiatic shorebird that has been seen mostly as a migrant in western Aleutian Islands, Pribilof Islands and in the Bering Strait area. Not known to breed in Alaska.

Status and Distribution:	SPRING	SUMMER	FALL	WINTER
Southeastern	—	—	—	—
Southcoastal	—	—	—	—
Southwestern	R	+	R	—
Central	—	—	—	—
Western	R	+	R	—
Northern	—	—	—	—

TEMMINCK'S STINT
(John C. Pitcher)

LONG-TOED STINT
(John C. Pitcher)

LONG-TOED STINT

(Calidris subminuta)

LENGTH: 5¾ IN.

Identification: Looks enough like Least Sandpiper to be usually indistinguishable in the field, although Least Sandpiper is less likely to be observed in the western Aleutian Islands and Bering Sea islands. Toes conspicuously longer than those of other peeps are visible under close observation. Crown, ear, and finely streaked breast band are washed with pale cinnamon in comparison with much browner Least Sandpiper. Call is a low, short, trilled *chrrup*.

Status and Distribution:	SPRING	SUMMER	FALL	WINTER
Southeastern	—	—	—	—
Southcoastal	—	—	—	—
Southwestern	R	—	R	—
Central	—	—	—	—
Western	R	—	—	—
Northern	—	—	—	—

Habitat: Asiatic shorebird that has been seen mostly as a migrant in the Aleutian Islands, Pribilof Islands and in the Bering Strait area. Not known to breed in Alaska although may nest in years when enough birds are present to stimulate breeding activity.

WHITE-RUMPED SANDPIPER

(Calidris fuscicollis)

LENGTH: 7½ IN.

Identification: Like Baird's, larger than other peeps and has longer wings. More rufous in summer and grayer in winter than Baird's Sandpiper and colored somewhat like a Western Sandpiper. In flight white rump contrasts with darker tail. Call is a very high mouselike squeak.

Status and Distribution:	SPRING	SUMMER	FALL	WINTER
Southeastern	—	—	—	—
Southcoastal	+	—	+	—
Southwestern	—	—	—	—
Central	R	—	—	—
Western	—	—	—	—
Northern ★	R	R	—	—

Habitat: Breeding — wet grassy tundra. Nests on the ground in tundra moss. In migration — tidal flats and beaches.

Notes: Like Pectoral and Curlew sandpipers only the female incubates the eggs and rears the young. Most other shorebirds share these duties.

WHITE-RUMPED SANDPIPER
Female
Breeding
(Gary Jones)

LEAST SANDPIPER
Breeding
(Jim Hawkings)

LEAST SANDPIPER

(Calidris minutilla)

LENGTH: 5½ IN.

Identification: Yellowish rather than black legs distinguish this smallest sandpiper. Least Sandpipers are browner than Semipalmated Sandpipers in the fall and browner than Western Sandpipers in any plumage. Brown-breasted rather than gray-breasted as in the other 2 small peeps. Call is a thin, rising *pree-eet.*

Habitat: Breeding — sedge-grass marshes near tidal flats, freshwater marshes, muskegs. Nests on the ground in both wet and dry grassy areas. In migration — tidal flats, lakes, ponds, marshes.

Notes: Often feeds among marsh vegetation and on mud flats. Rarely occurs in large flocks.

Status and Distribution:	SPRING	SUMMER	FALL	WINTER
Southeastern ★	C	U	C	—
Southcoastal ★	C	C	C	—
Southwestern ★	C	C	C	—
Central ★	C	U	U	—
Western ★	U	U	U	—
Northern ★	U	U	R	—

BAIRD'S SANDPIPER
Breeding
(Jim Erckmann)

BAIRD'S SANDPIPER

(Calidris bairdii)

LENGTH: 7 IN.

Identification: Almost the size of a Sanderling. Wing tips extend beyond the tail tip when folded, as the wings are relatively longer than in the smaller species. In all plumages Baird's have black legs and an overall buffy appearance, not as bright or uniform as a Sanderling and with pale feather edges on the back presenting a somewhat scaly appearance. This is especially pronounced in young heading south in autumn. Call is a louder, deeper version of Least Sandpiper's. Breeding song is a loud, long trill, *durreee, durreee* given from high in the air.

Status and Distribution:	SPRING	SUMMER	FALL	WINTER
Southeastern	U	—	U	—
Southcoastal	U	—	U	—
Southwestern	R	—	U	—
Central ★	U	U	U	—
Western ★	U	U	U	—
Northern ★	C	C	C	—

Habitat: Breeding — tundra, preferably drier portions. Nests on dry tundra. In migration — lakes, ponds, tidal flats and beaches often in drier areas.

Notes: Rarely occurs in flocks of more than a few individuals.

BAIRD'S SANDPIPER
Immature

PECTORAL SANDPIPER

(Calidris melanotos)

LENGTH: 9 IN.

Identification: Brown with yellowish legs, obvious light streaks on the back, and a heavily streaked brown breast with streaks sharply cut off from white of the belly. Male is somewhat larger than a female. Appears long-necked and alert compared with other small to medium-sized sandpipers. Call, when flushed, is rolling, somewhat like that of Baird's Sandpiper.

Habitat: Breeding — grassy areas in wet tundra. Nests on the ground within tundra vegetation. In migration — sedge-grass areas of tidal flats, grassy marshes, grassy edges of lakes and ponds.

Status and Distribution:	SPRING	SUMMER	FALL	WINTER
Southeastern	C	R	C	—
Southcoastal	C	+	C	—
Southwestern	R	R	C	—
Central	C	U	U	—
Western ★	C	C	C	—
Northern ★	C	C	C	—

Notes: Their "hooting" mating call given in low flights across the tundra is unique among American shorebirds. To call they fill their esophagus with air until breast and throat are inflated to at least twice normal size.

SHARP-TAILED SANDPIPER

(Calidris acuminata)

LENGTH: 8½ IN.

Identification: Breeding plumaged adult has bold spotting on orange breast, rusty cap and upperparts. Immature has buffy breast only lightly streaked and not set off from the white belly as in Pectoral Sandpiper. The back and especially the cap are ruddy-colored.

Habitat: Nests and eggs have not been found in Alaska even though it is almost certain to breed here. In migration — grassy areas of tidal flats, marshes, lakes and ponds.

Status and Distribution:	SPRING	SUMMER	FALL	WINTER
Southeastern	+	—	+	—
Southcoastal	—	—	R	—
Southwestern	+	—	U	—
Central	—	—	—	—
Western ★	+	+	U	—
Northern	+	—	+	—

Notes: Quite similar in appearance and behavior to more common Pectoral Sandpiper in immature plumage and probably has gone unnoticed in many areas.

SHARP-TAILED SANDPIPER
Immature
(R. H. Day)

ROCK SANDPIPER
Breeding
(Jim Erckmann)

ROCK SANDPIPER

(Calidris ptilocnemis)

LENGTH: 9 IN.

Identification: In summer rust-colored on the crown and back, like a Dunlin, but darker and with a similar black patch on the breast rather than the belly. In winter medium gray between the shades of Surfbird and Black Turnstone, with a slender, Dunlinlike bill and yellowish legs. In flight rather plain looking with a narrow white wing stripe. Darker color, yellowish legs and bill base, and spotted sides distinguish Rock Sandpiper from similar Dunlin. Relatively silent in migration; summer song of Rock Sandpiper is loud and given high in the air over a rather large territory.

Status and Distribution:	SPRING	SUMMER	FALL	WINTER
Southeastern	C	—	C	C
Southcoastal	C	—	C	C
Southwestern ★	C	C	C	C
Central	—	—	—	—
Western ★	C	C	C	—
Northern	—	—	—	—

ROCK SANDPIPER
Nonbreeding
(John Sarvis)

Habitat: Breeding — tundra. Nests on the ground in mossy or rocky tundra. In migration and winter — tidal flats and beaches usually in more rocky areas.

Notes: Of shorebirds commonly inhabiting rocky areas, this one is the smallest.

STILT SANDPIPER
Breeding
(Dennis Paulson)

STILT SANDPIPER

(Calidris himantopus)

LENGTH: 8 IN.

Identification: Summer adults have a chestnut cheek patch and heavily barred underparts; winter birds are streaked gray above and mostly white below, rather like a winter-plumaged Dunlin but with much longer legs. In flight the wings lack stripes and tail and rump are white, as in yellowlegs and Wilson's Phalarope. Bill is slightly drooped like that of Dunlin. Call is a short, single note, rarely heard.

Habitat: Breeding — nests of this eastern sandpiper have not been found in Alaska. Elsewhere nesting occurs on wet tundra. In migration — tidal flats, lake shores, ponds and sloughs.

Status and Distribution:	SPRING	SUMMER	FALL	WINTER
Southeastern	+	—	+	—
Southcoastal	—	—	+	—
Southwestern	+	—	—	—
Central	R	—	—	—
Western	+	—	—	—
Northern ★	R	R	R	—

DUNLIN

(Calidris alpina)

LENGTH: 8 IN.

Identification: Medium-sized sandpiper with a longish bill, noticeably downcurved near the tip. In spring and summer rich reddish above and white below, with a large black patch on the belly. In winter unpatterned grayish brown above and on the breast, and white below. One of the most drab shorebirds in winter. In flight similar to most peeps with a narrow white wing stripe and white sides to the rump. Call, often given in flight, is a high, rasping *cheezp.* Breeding song is a musical rising and falling trill delivered from the air over a smaller area than that of the Rock Sandpiper.

Habitat: Breeding — wet grassy tundra and coastal sedge-grass marshes. Nests on the ground in grassy areas. In migration and winter — tidal flats and muddy and sandy beaches. Sometimes associated with Rock Sandpipers in rocky areas.

Status and Distribution:	SPRING	SUMMER	FALL	WINTER
Southeastern	C	—	C	U
Southcoastal ★	C	R	C	U
Southwestern ★	C	C	C	U
Central	+	+	+	—
Western ★	C	C	C	—
Northern ★	U	U	U	—

DUNLIN
Breeding

DUNLIN
Immature

CURLEW SANDPIPER

(Calidris ferruginea)

LENGTH: 8½ IN.

Identification: Long, evenly downcurved bill is best field mark. Summer plumage is bright rufous above and below. In winter is gray, rather clear-breasted, and shows a white rump in flight. Curlew Sandpiper is a bit longer-legged (the feet extending beyond the tail in flight), and longer-necked than a Dunlin, giving it a more elegant appearance. Call is a soft, whistled *chirrup.*

Habitat: Dry tundra adjacent to the coast. Asiatic sandpiper that has been found breeding in northern Alaska at Barrow. Elsewhere only a casual migrant.

Status and Distribution:	SPRING	SUMMER	FALL	WINTER
Southeastern	—	—	—	—
Southcoastal	+	—	—	—
Southwestern	+	—	+	—
Central	—	—	—	—
Western	+	—	—	—
Northern ★	R	R	+	—

SPOONBILL SANDPIPER
(John C. Pitcher)

CURLEW SANDPIPER
(John C. Pitcher)

SPOONBILL SANDPIPER

(Eurynorhynchus pygmeus)

LENGTH: 6½ IN.

Identification: Broad spoon-shaped bill tip is diagnostic but may be difficult to see in side view. In summer and winter much like Rufous-necked Sandpiper with which it occurs in Siberia, but in winter may be recognized by more white on the forehead and a more prominent white wing bar.

Habitat: Asiatic sandpiper found in northern Alaska at Wainwright and in the western Aleutian Islands on Buldir Island. Not known to breed in Alaska.

Status and Distribution:	SPRING	SUMMER	FALL	WINTER
Southeastern	—	—	—	—
Southcoastal	—	—	—	—
Southwestern	+	—	—	—
Central	—	—	—	—
Western	—	—	—	—
Northern	—	—	+	—

Notes: Spoonbill Sandpiper is now considered accidental in Alaska.

BROAD-BILLED SANDPIPER
Immature
(R.H. Day)

BROAD-BILLED SANDPIPER

(Limicola falcinellus)

LENGTH: 6¾ IN.

Identification: The thick longish black bill that is slightly decurved, two white lines over the eye and conspicuous white "V" on the back help separate the broad-billed from other sandpipers in any plumage.

Habitat: Has been found on Adak and Shemya islands in the western Aleutians. Breeds in northern Europe and Asia.

Status and Distribution:	SPRING	SUMMER	FALL	WINTER
Southeastern	—	—	—	—
Southcoastal	—	—	—	—
Southwestern	—	—	+	—
Central	—	—	—	—
Western	—	—	—	—
Northern	—	—	—	—

BUFF-BREASTED SANDPIPER

(Tryngites subruficollis)

LENGTH: 8½ IN.

Identification: Slender and small-headed, similar to but much smaller than an Upland Sandpiper, with a brown back and warm buffy underparts. No other shorebird is unmarked buff from throat to undertail. Legs are bright yellow, wing linings are white, contrasting strongly with the belly. Usually silent.

Status and Distribution:	SPRING	SUMMER	FALL	WINTER
Southeastern	+	—	+	—
Southcoastal	—	—	+	—
Southwestern	—	—	+	—
Central	R	—	+	—
Western	+	—	+	—
Northern ★	R	R	R	—

Habitat: Breeding — dry tundra ridges. Nests on the ground in dry areas. In migration — drier areas of tidal flats, sandy beaches, grassy fields and meadows.

Notes: Impressive display on the breeding grounds with 1 or both wings raised to show the white linings.

BUFF-BREASTED SANDPIPER
(Dick Wood)

RUFF
(Rick Austin)

RUFF

(Philomachus pugnax)

LENGTH: 11½ IN.

Identification: Male is considerably larger than female. In spring breeding-plumaged male has huge erectile ruffs of white, brown or black. Fall male and female are warm brown, similar to Pectoral or Sharp-tailed sandpipers but with the back scaled, not striped, the breast buffy and the belly white. Legs are yellowish and the bill short and straight with a pale base. In flight resembles a large Pectoral Sandpiper with conspicuous white patches at the base of the tail. Feet project beyond tail in flight.

Status and Distribution:	SPRING	SUMMER	FALL	WINTER
Southeastern	+	—	+	—
Southcoastal	—	—	+	—
Southwestern	R	—	R	—
Central	—	—	—	—
Western	R	—	R	—
Northern ★	—	+	+	—

Habitat: Asiatic shorebird that has been found mostly in western and central Aleutian Islands, on the Bering Sea islands and on the Chukchi Sea coast. Only 1 nest has been found, in northern Alaska.

FAMILY *LARIDAE*

JAEGERS, GULLS, TERNS

(26 + 2)

Jaegers are gull-like predatory seabirds with strongly hooked bills and sharp claws. Their wings are narrow and pointed, dark with white patches near the tip. They fly in a fast, falconlike manner, forcing gulls and terns to drop or disgorge just-caught fish. The agility of the jaegers during these maneuvers is breathtaking. Adults of the 3 jaegers have characteristic projecting central tail feathers.

Gulls and terns are long-winged birds that inhabit oceans, lakes and rivers. Plumages are mostly white below and gray above, often with black on the wing tips or head. The back and wings together are called the mantle. Most are colonial nesters and usually lay 2 to 3 eggs. Gulls are excellent scavengers and feed on almost anything edible by picking their food up from the water surface or ground. The bill is slightly hooked and the tail is usually square or rounded (except Sabine's Gull, which is shallowly forked). Terns dive into the water to pursue food. They have sharp-pointed bills and deeply forked tails.

POMARINE JAEGER
(Gary Jones)

POMARINE JAEGER

(Stercorarius pomarinus)

LENGTH: 22 IN.

Identification: At a distance recognized by purposeful flight and black wing linings, with a flash of white visible near the wing tip at closer range. Central tail feathers project from 1 to 4 inches and are blunt and usually twisted. Most adults are light beneath, with variable amounts of barring, but some are virtually all black. Immature jaegers can be very difficult to identify. Immature pomarine is barred all over and lacks the longer tail feathers.

Status and Distribution:	SPRING	SUMMER	FALL	WINTER
Southeastern	R	—	U	—
Southcoastal	C	R	C	—
Southwestern	C	U	C	—
Central	—	+	—	—
Western ★	C	R	C	—
Northern ★	U	U	U	—

Habitat: Breeding — low wet tundra in areas interspersed with lakes and ponds. Nests on the ground in slight depressions. In migration — inshore and offshore marine waters.

Notes: Largest of the jaegers; usually chases large or medium-sized gulls.

PARASITIC JAEGER

(Stercorarius parasiticus)

LENGTH: 17 IN.

Identification: Distinguished from the Pomarine Jaeger by pointed central tail feathers, shorter than those of adult Long-tailed Jaeger. Adult is dark brown above and often has a breast band, as in the pomarine, but lacks bars of that species. Some birds are all dark as in the pomarine. First year birds of the 3 jaeger species are very difficult to separate in the field.

Status and Distribution:	SPRING	SUMMER	FALL	WINTER
Southeastern ★	U	U	U	—
Southcoastal ★	U	C	C	—
Southwestern ★	C	C	C	—
Central ★	—	R	—	—
Western ★	C	C	C	—
Northern ★	C	C	C	—

PARASITIC JAEGER
Light Phase
(Jim Hawkings)

Habitat: Breeding — wet tundra, tidal flats and beaches, coastal marshes. Nests on the ground in depressions. In migration — tundra, tidal flats, beaches, coastal marshes, inshore and offshore marine waters.

PARASITIC JAEGER
Dark Phase
(Mike Lettis)

LONG-TAILED JAEGER
(Doug Murphy)

LONG-TAILED JAEGER

(Stercorarius longicaudus)

LENGTH: 21 IN.

Identification: Adult has long, streaming central tail feathers. In molt, adult with only partly developed tail feathers resembles Parasitic Jaeger but has a gray-brown rather than brown back, no breast band, and bluish-gray instead of black legs. Dark phase birds are extremely rare. First year immature is difficult to separate from other jaegers but shows less white in the spread wing and is slightly smaller and paler than Parasitic Jaeger in similar plumage. Long-tailed Jaeger has light, airy flight.

Habitat: Breeding — wet coastal tundra and drier upland tundra of the interior. Nests on the ground. In migration — inshore and offshore marine waters.

Status and Distribution:	SPRING	SUMMER	FALL	WINTER
Southeastern	—	R	R	—
Southcoastal ★	R	R	R	+
Southwestern ★	U	U	U	—
Central ★	C	C	C	—
Western ★	C	C	C	—
Northern ★	C	C	C	—

SOUTH POLAR SKUA

(Catharacta maccormicki)

LENGTH: 21 IN.

Identification: All dark at a distance with very broad black wings that show a conspicuous white patch near the tip. At close range some show a golden nape. Heavier-bodied and stockier than Pomarine Jaeger.

Habitat: Inshore and offshore marine waters, prefers offshore waters. Not known to breed in Alaska.

Status and Distribution:	SPRING	SUMMER	FALL	WINTER
Southeastern	—	—	—	—
Southcoastal	—	R	R	—
Southwestern	—	R	+	—
Central	—	—	—	—
Western	—	—	—	—
Northern	—	—	+	—

SOUTH POLAR SKUA
(Dennis Paulson)

GLAUCOUS GULL
(E. Lieske)

GLAUCOUS GULL

(Larus hyperboreus)

LENGTH: 27 IN.

Identification: Very large with pure white primaries and no dark color on the wing tips. Eye is yellow. As in other large gulls, bill is yellow with a red spot, feet pink. Immature at a distance looks uniform pale buff (first year) or white (second year) with flesh color on the basal two-thirds of the bill. At close range immature appears finely barred and spotted with pale markings.

Habitat: Breeding — cliffs near the coast, islands, tundra. Nests in colonies on cliff ledges and on the ground in slightly elevated portions of the tundra, or on islands in tundra lakes. In migration and winter — tidal flats and beaches, inshore marine waters.

Status and Distribution:	SPRING	SUMMER	FALL	WINTER
Southeastern	R	—	—	R
Southcoastal	R	R	R	R
Southwestern ★	U	U	U	U
Central	R	R	R	—
Western ★	C	C	C	—
Northern ★	C	C	C	—

Notes: Often preys on eggs and young of other birds. Will mob other birds forcing them to disgorge food.

GLAUCOUS-WINGED GULL

GLAUCOUS-WINGED GULL

(Larus glaucescens)

LENGTH: 26 IN.

Identification: Much like Glaucous Gull, adult has gray wing tips with white spots, visible from above or below. Eyes are usually brown but may vary to much paler, although never clear pale yellow. First year immature is buffy, somewhat darker than young Glaucous Gull, and with all black bill. Second and third year immatures become increasingly like adults, which mature in the fourth or fifth year. Intermediate-plumaged birds vary widely and can be difficult to identify. In addition, species of larger gulls hybridize, which also makes identification difficult.

Status and Distribution:	SPRING	SUMMER	FALL	WINTER
Southeastern ★	C	C	C	C
Southcoastal ★	C	C	C	C
Southwestern ★	C	C	C	C
Central	—	R	R	—
Western ★	C	C	C	—
Northern	—	—	—	—

Habitat: Breeding — tidal flats and beaches, inshore marine waters, islands and cliffs. Nests in colonies on flat low islands, cliff ledges and on rocky beaches. In migration and winter — various habitats including coastal communities, garbage dumps, around canneries, salmon streams, inshore and offshore marine waters, tidal flats and beaches.

SLATY-BACKED GULL
(Doug Forsell)

SLATY-BACKED GULL

(Larus schistisagus)

LENGTH: 27 IN.

Identification: Large gull of Herring-Glaucous-winged group of gulls. Entirely dark gray mantle in the adult. No other Bering Sea gull has a dark back, although Western Gull that may occur occasionally in southern Alaska looks virtually identical. Immature similar to dark immature Herring Gull.

Status and Distribution:	SPRING	SUMMER	FALL	WINTER
Southeastern	—	—	—	—
Southcoastal	—	—	+	+
Southwestern	R	R	R	+
Central	—	—	—	—
Western	R	R	R	—
Northern	R	R	R	—

Habitat: Asiatic gull seen mostly along the inshore marine waters of western and northern Alaska and in the Aleutian Islands. Not known to breed in Alaska.

HERRING GULL

HERRING GULL

(Larus argentatus)

LENGTH: 24 IN.

Identification: Adult Herring Gull much like Glaucous Gull, with red-spotted yellow bill and flesh-colored legs, but wing tips are jet black from above and below, with a few white spots at very tips of the feathers. Eye is pale, cold yellow, giving bird a reptilian look. First year bird is dusky gray-brown with a dark bill and eye. Head is pale but wings are much darker than in Glaucous and Glaucous-winged gulls. Second and third year birds are gray on the back, with dark wing tips, a dark tail and light rump.

Habitat: Breeding — lakes, rivers, islands, tidal flats and beaches. Nests on the ground in hollows, on sand, gravel, rocks and grassy fields, cliff ledges and trees. In migration and winter — lakes, rivers, tidal flats and beaches, garbage dumps, inshore marine waters.

Status and Distribution:	SPRING	SUMMER	FALL	WINTER
Southeastern ★	C	C	C	C
Southcoastal ★	C	U	C	U
Southwestern	R	R	R	R
Central ★	U	U	U	—
Western ★	R	R	R	—
Northern ★	—	+	+	—

Notes: Tend to occur more inland than other gulls. Scavengers. Like crows, will break open clam shells by dropping them on rocks from the air.

THAYER'S GULL

(Larus thayeri)

LENGTH: 24 IN.

Identification: Distinctly smaller bill than the larger gulls. Mantle varies from as light as that of Herring Gull to somewhat darker, eye is usually brown but may be almost as light as that of Herring Gull, and wing tips have more or less black on them. Usually more white in the wing tip than in Herring Gull. Best field mark is nature of the wing tip coloration, black above and gray below. In all plumages wing tips are colored like Herring Gull above and Glaucous-winged Gull below. This can be seen in flight or at rest.

Status and Distribution:	SPRING	SUMMER	FALL	WINTER
Southeastern	C	+	C	U
Southcoastal	R	R	R	R
Southwestern	+	—	+	+
Central	—	—	—	—
Western	—	—	—	—
Northern	—	—	R	—

Habitat: In migration and winter — similar to Herring Gulls. Not known to breed in Alaska.

THAYER'S GULL
(Dennis Paulson)

CALIFORNIA GULL

(Larus californicus)

LENGTH: 21½ IN.

Identification: Medium gray mantle (darker than Herring, Glaucous-winged or Ring-billed gulls) and black wing tips, more extensive than those of Herring Gull. Greenish legs. Yellow bill marked with both a red spot and a black spot near the tip. Eyes are dark. Immature is much like young Herring Gull but smaller, with a more slender bill that is flesh-colored for the basal two-thirds.

Status and Distribution:	SPRING	SUMMER	FALL	WINTER
Southeastern	+	R	+	—
Southcoastal	—	—	+	—
Southwestern	—	—	—	—
Central	—	—	—	—
Western	—	—	—	—
Northern	—	—	—	—

Habitat: Found mostly in southern part of southeastern Alaska along inshore marine waters and coastal beaches. Not known to breed in Alaska.

CALIFORNIA GULL
(Dennis Paulson)

RING-BILLED GULL
(Doug Murphy)

RING-BILLED GULL

(Larus delawarensis)

LENGTH: 19½ IN.

Identification: Very pale gray mantle and strongly contrasting black wing tips. Mantle is distinctly paler than in either California or Mew gulls, and wings are snowy white beneath. Bill is yellow, with a black ring near the tip, and legs are yellow. Immature is paler than young California or Mew gulls with a narrow black band near the tail tip. In Mew and California gulls and still larger species, the tail band is broader.

Status and Distribution:	SPRING	SUMMER	FALL	WINTER
Southeastern	R	R	R	R
Southcoastal	R	R	R	R
Southwestern	—	+	+	—
Central	+	—	—	—
Western	—	—	—	—
Northern	—	—	—	—

Habitat: Inshore marine waters, tidal flats and beaches. Not known to breed in Alaska.

BLACK-TAILED GULL

(Larus crassirostris)

LENGTH: 18 IN.

Identification: Adult has dark mantle and black wing tips that usually lack any white spots at their tips (present in other large adult gulls found in Alaska). Broad black subterminal band across white tail is very distinctive. Has yellow legs, and yellow bill with black ring and red tip. Immatures are mottled brown with pale forehead and throat and blackish wings and tail. Immatures have flesh-colored legs and bill with black tip.

Habitat: Has been found on Attu Island in western Aleutians and at sea off Amchitka Island in westcentral Aleutians. Breeds from northern Asia to eastern China.

Status and Distribution:	SPRING	SUMMER	FALL	WINTER
Southeastern	—	—	—	—
Southcoastal	—	—	—	—
Southwestern	+	+	—	—
Central	—	—	—	—
Western	—	—	—	—
Northern	—	—	—	—

BLACK-TAILED GULL
(Esao Hashimoto, ANIMALS ANIMALS)

MEW GULL

MEW GULL

(Larus canus)

LENGTH: 17 IN.

Identification: Smallest of commonly seen white-headed gulls, half the bulk of Glaucous-winged Gull with which it is often seen. Narrow wings and rapid wingbeat allow distant identification; at closer range, delicate yellowish bill and greenish-yellow legs are diagnostic. Mantle darker than in larger species, underwing often looks dark. Brown eye. White spots in the black wing tips are larger and more prominent than in other gulls of this type, and often appear as a white band across the wing tip. First year immature is grayish- brown with a dark terminal tail band and a short, ploverlike bill.

Status and Distribution:	SPRING	SUMMER	FALL	WINTER
Southeastern ★	C	C	C	C
Southcoastal ★	C	C	C	C
Southwestern ★	C	C	C	C
Central ★	C	C	C	—
Western ★	C	C	C	—
Northern ★	R	R	R	—

Habitat: Breeding — tundra, lakes, rivers, streams, islands. Nests on tundra, in trees, on stumps, cavities in sand by water. In migration and winter — inshore and offshore marine waters, tidal flats and beaches, lakes, rivers, rocky shores and reefs.

COMMON BLACK-HEADED GULL

(Larus ridibundus)

LENGTH: 14½ IN.

Identification: Adults similar to Bonaparte's Gull but larger with a longer dark red bill. Has dark red, not pink, feet. Best distant field mark is dark gray lower surface of wing tips (white in Bonaparte's Gull). Immature is like immature Bonaparte's Gull but bill is yellow with a black tip rather than black.

Status and Distribution:	SPRING	SUMMER	FALL	WINTER
Southeastern	—	—	—	—
Southcoastal	—	+	+	—
Southwestern	R	R	+	—
Central	—	—	—	—
Western	R	—	—	—
Northern	—	+	—	—

Habitat: Asiatic gull found in all coastal regions of Alaska except southeastern. Most often seen in western and central Aleutian Islands and Pribilof Islands. Not known to breed in Alaska.

COMMON BLACK-HEADED GULL
(Dennis Paulson)

FRANKLIN'S GULL
(John C. Pitcher)

FRANKLIN'S GULL

(Larus pipixcan)

LENGTH: 14½ IN.

Identification: Summer adult has black head, reddish bill and dark gray wings with a white band across the tip. Larger than Bonaparte's Gull and much darker looking above. Winter bird loses black on the head except for a dark patch on the hind neck. Immature is brownish-gray above with dark nape patch and narrow black band at tail tip. Alaskan records are of breeding-plumaged adults.

Status and Distribution:	SPRING	SUMMER	FALL	WINTER
Southeastern	—	—	—	—
Southcoastal	+	+	—	—
Southwestern	—	+	—	—
Central	—	—	—	—
Western	—	—	—	—
Northern	—	—	—	—

Habitat: Inshore marine waters, offshore islands. Not known to breed in Alaska.

BONAPARTE'S GULL

(Larus philadelphia)

LENGTH: 13 IN.

Identification: Largely white wing tips that flash conspicuously in flight at considerable distances and ternlike flight are diagnostic. Summer adult has black head which turns mostly white in autumn and winter except for a conspicuous black ear spot. First year bird is similar to winter adult but has a dark band at the end of tail and brown markings on wings.

Status and Distribution:	SPRING	SUMMER	FALL	WINTER
Southeastern ★	C	C	C	+
Southcoastal ★	C	C	C	+
Southwestern ★	C	C	C	—
Central ★	U	U	U	—
Western ★	C	C	C	—
Northern	—	+	—	—

Habitat: Breeding — coniferous woods near lakes and ponds. Nests in low conifers. In migration and winter — tidal flats, beaches, inshore marine waters, lakes, salmon streams.

BONAPARTE'S GULL
(Doug Murphy)

IVORY GULL

(Pagophila eburnea)

LENGTH: 16 IN.

Identification: Snowy white, with black legs and dark, yellow-tipped bill. Immature is heavily marked on the wings and tail tip with small black spots, and has a dark smudge on the face.

Status and Distribution:	SPRING	SUMMER	FALL	WINTER
Southeastern	—	+	+	—
Southcoastal	+	—	—	—
Southwestern	R	—	R	U
Central	—	—	—	—
Western	U	—	U	U
Northern	U	R	U	—

Habitat: Inshore and offshore marine waters, pack and drift ice of Chukchi, Bering and Beaufort seas, coastal areas. Not known to breed in Alaska.

Notes: With the long wings, flight is similar to a tern. Less inclined to land on water than other gulls, although does rest on the ice. Feeds on carrion and offal as much as live food.

IVORY GULL
(Jim Hawkings)

BLACK-LEGGED KITTIWAKE

(Rissa tridactyla)

LENGTH: 17 IN.

Identification: Adult has black wing tips that look as if they had been dipped in ink, a yellow bill and black legs. First year bird is white below with a dark band across the back of the neck (shared by winter adults), a dark ear spot, dark tail tip, black bill and legs, and an M-shaped mark across the mantle. Wingbeats are short and choppy.

Habitat: Breeding — sea cliffs, inshore marine waters. Nests on cliff ledges. In migration and winter — inshore and offshore marine waters, tidal flats, beaches, rocky shores, reefs.

Status and Distribution:	SPRING	SUMMER	FALL	WINTER
Southeastern ★	U	U	U	U
Southcoastal ★	C	C	C	U
Southwestern ★	C	C	C	U
Central	—	—	+	—
Western ★	C	C	C	—
Northern	—	C	C	—

Notes: Mostly birds of the ocean, often far offshore. Rarely ventures inland. Feeds mostly on small fish captured in a ternlike manner by diving while on the wing.

BLACK-LEGGED KITTIWAKE
(Tom Walker)

RED-LEGGED KITTIWAKE
(Jo Keller)

RED-LEGGED KITTIWAKE

(Rissa brevirostris)

LENGTH: 15 IN.

Identification: Red legs and feet. Shorter and heavier bill than Black-legged Kittiwake. Mantle is darker above than in Black-legged Kittiwake. Wing linings are conspicuously dark, a good distant field mark. First year bird lacks dark diagonal bar across the wing coverts and black tip on the tail of immature Black-legged Kittiwake.

Habitat: Breeding — Pribilof Islands, Buldir and Bogoslof islands in the Aleutian Islands. Nests on cliff ledges and points. In migration and winter — inshore and offshore marine waters.

Notes: Tends to feed even more offshore than Black-legged Kittiwake.

Status and Distribution:	SPRING	SUMMER	FALL	WINTER
Southeastern	—	—	—	—
Southcoastal	—	+	+	R
Southwestern ★	U	C	U	U
Central	—	+	—	—
Western	—	R	—	—
Northern	—	—	—	—

ROSS' GULL
(John C. Pitcher)

ROSS' GULL

(Rhodostethia rosea)

LENGTH: 13½ IN.

Identification: Small, with a wedge-shaped tail, an entirely gray mantle and darker gray wing linings. Breeding adult has a rosy tinge to the body and a dark neck ring. Immature has a mantle pattern similar to a young kittiwake.

Status and Distribution:	SPRING	SUMMER	FALL	WINTER
Southeastern	—	—	—	—
Southcoastal	—	—	—	—
Southwestern	+	—	+	+
Central	—	—	—	—
Western	R	+	R	—
Northern	+	+	C	—

Habitat: Inshore and offshore marine waters. Best place to see this bird is Point Barrow vicinity in fall. Not known to breed in Alaska.

SABINE'S GULL

(Xema sabini)

LENGTH: 13½ IN.

Identification: Only gull with forked tail. Black bill has yellow tip. Adult has dark gray hood and bold black-and-white pattern on spread wings. Black primaries and white wedge on midwing are unique. Immature is brown on back with the adult's wing pattern.

Status and Distribution:	SPRING	SUMMER	FALL	WINTER
Southeastern	R	—	R	—
Southcoastal	U	R	U	—
Southwestern ★	U	U	U	—
Central	—	+	—	—
Western ★	C	C	C	—
Northern ★	C	C	C	—

COMMON TERN
(John C. Pitcher)

SABINE'S GULL
(Dick Wood)

Habitat: Breeding — wet tundra, lakes, ponds, tidal flats. Nests on the tundra near lakes and ponds. In migration — inshore and offshore marine waters, tidal flats and beaches.

COMMON TERN

(Sterna hirundo)

LENGTH: 14½ IN.

Identification: North American Common Tern has an orange-red bill with black tip and is pure white beneath rather than gray like Arctic Tern, but this Common Tern is less likely to be seen in Alaska than strays from the Old World which have entirely black bills and brown feet in breeding plumage. Immature and non-breeding bird are more difficult to distinguish from Arctic Terns, but the neck and bill are longer, giving them a more pointed look in front, with more of the bird projecting in front of the wings. Common Tern has more obvious black posterior borders on each wing than does Arctic Tern.

Status and Distribution:	SPRING	SUMMER	FALL	WINTER
Southeastern	—	—	—	—
Southcoastal	—	—	—	—
Southwestern	R	R	+	—
Central	—	—	—	—
Western	+	—	—	—
Northern	—	—	—	—

Habitat: Seen most frequently in western and central Aleutian Islands and in Pribilof Islands during spring and summer. Not known to breed in Alaska.

ARCTIC TERN
(Lee Post)

ARCTIC TERN

(Sterna paradisaea)

LENGTH: 15 IN.

Identification: Long, pointed wings, forked tail, black cap, bright red bill and feet allow easy identification.

Status and Distribution:	SPRING	SUMMER	FALL	WINTER
Southeastern ★	C	C	C	—
Southcoastal ★	C	C	C	—
Southwestern ★	C	U	C	—
Central ★	U	U	U	—
Western ★	C	C	C	—
Northern ★	U	U	U	—

Habitat: Breeding — tidal flats, beaches, glacial moraines, rivers, lakes, marshes. Nests in colonies or scattered pairs on sand, gravel, moss or in rocks. In migration — inshore and offshore marine waters, tidal flats, beaches, rivers, lakes.

Notes: May be observed hovering over water in search of small fish which probably make up most of its diet. Have one of the longest migrations of any species. Some individuals that breed in the arctic have been found wintering in the antarctic, a 20,000-mile round trip.

ALEUTIAN TERN

(Sterna aleutica)

LENGTH: 15 IN.

Identification: Adult darker above and below than Arctic Tern with a dark bill and feet, and white forehead. Gray back and belly contrast strongly with white tail, unlike Arctic Tern in which the back and tail look about the same. Unique call notes include a loud, ploverlike whistle, and loud chirpings, both totally unlike the nasal, bickering *keearr* of Arctic Tern.

Status and Distribution:	SPRING	SUMMER	FALL	WINTER
Southeastern ★	+	+	—	—
Southcoastal ★	U	U	U	—
Southwestern ★	U	U	U	—
Central	—	—	—	—
Western ★	U	U	U	—
Northern	—	—	—	—

Habitat: Breeding — coastal areas, marshes, islands, rivers, lagoons, inshore marine waters. Nests on ground in matted dry grass. In migration — offshore marine waters.

Notes: In North America this tern only nests in Alaska.

ALEUTIAN TERN
(R. T. Wallen)

CASPIAN TERN
(J. Surman, Cornell Lab of Ornithology)

CASPIAN TERN

(Sterna caspia)

LENGTH: 19-23 IN.

Identification: Large tern, larger than a Mew Gull, with large red bill, short crested black cap, slightly forked tail, and black on the undersides of the wing tips. Immatures have white streaking on the cap.

Habitat: Has been found in southeastern Alaska at Ketchikan, Juneau, Sitka, at the mouth of the Stikine River, and in south-coastal Alaska at Homer.

Status and Distribution:	SPRING	SUMMER	FALL	WINTER
Southeastern	+	+	—	—
Southcoastal	—	+	—	—
Southwestern	—	—	—	—
Central	—	—	—	—
Western	—	—	—	—
Northern	—	—		—

BLACK TERN

(Chlidonias niger)

LENGTH: 9½ IN.

Identification: In summer head and underparts black, and mantle and tail gray. Immature and winter-plumaged adult are much grayer above than Arctic Tern and smaller and shorter-tailed than any of the other Alaskan terns. Gray tail is diagnostic.

Status and Distribution:	SPRING	SUMMER	FALL	WINTER
Southeastern	—	—	+	—
Southcoastal	—	+	—	—
Southwestern	—	—	—	—
Central	+	—	—	—
Western	—	—	—	—
Northern	—	+	—	—

Habitat: Primarily freshwater marshes. Not known to breed in Alaska.

BLACK TERN
(John C. Pitcher)

FAMILY *ALCIDAE*
ALCIDS
(16)

Members of this family are seabirds that come to shore only to breed. They nest in colonies and lay only 1 or 2 eggs. They have small narrow wings that are used for swimming underwater and for flight. When on land, alcids stand almost erect and penguinlike. All are short-necked and heavy-bodied and have webbed feet placed far back on the body to facilitate diving. Most are black and white, some have brightly colored bills.

COMMON MURRE
Winter
(Lee Post)

COMMON MURRE
(Uria aalge)
LENGTH: 16½ IN.

Identification: Looks black above and white below on the water or in flight. Actually, Common Murre is very dark brown above but this is only distinguishable in good light at medium or close range. In breeding plumage entire head and upper breast are dark; in winter throat and breast are white. Bill is long, pointed and quite slender, and lacks the pale bill mark of Thick-billed Murre. Breast and belly coloration meet at an obtuse angle. In winter has white cheeks and a distinct dark line extending behind the eye.

Status and Distribution:	SPRING	SUMMER	FALL	WINTER
Southeastern ★	C	C	C	C
Southcoastal ★	C	C	C	C
Southwestern ★	C	C	C	C
Central	—	—	—	+
Western ★	C	C	C	C
Northern	—	+	—	—

COMMON MURRE
Summer
(Jerry Hout)

Habitat: Breeding — coastal sea cliffs and islands, inshore marine waters. Nests in colonies on the ground on cliff ledges and on the flat tops of cliffs. In winter — inshore and offshore marine waters.

THICK-BILLED MURRE
(Mark Rauzon)

THICK-BILLED MURRE

(Uria lomvia)

LENGTH: 18 IN.

Identification: Black above, white below. In breeding plumage entire head and upper breast are black; in winter throat and breast are white. Bill is shorter and more curved than in Common Murre and has a pale line along the upper mandible visible only at close range. White of the belly in summer penetrates forward at an acute angle into the black breast. In winter the dark cap extends below eye level both before and behind the eye.

Status and Distribution:	SPRING	SUMMER	FALL	WINTER
Southeastern	—	—	—	R
Southcoastal ★	R	R	R	R
Southwestern ★	C	C	C	C
Central	—	—	—	—
Western ★	C	C	C	—
Northern	R	R	R	—

Habitat: Breeding — coastal sea cliffs and islands, inshore marine waters. Nests in colonies on the ground on cliff ledges and on the flat tops of cliffs. In winter — inshore and offshore marine waters.

DOVEKIE

(Alle alle)

LENGTH: 8 IN.

Identification: Sharply black and white with an entirely black head and breast in summer. In winter white of the throat extends up in a half-collar almost around the neck. Otherwise looks much like a Least Auklet.

Status and Distribution:	SPRING	SUMMER	FALL	WINTER
Southeastern	—	—	—	—
Southcoastal	—	—	—	—
Southwestern	—	+	—	—
Central	—	—	—	—
Western ★	R	R	R	—
Northern	—	+	—	—

Habitat: Considered a rare probable breeder on the islands in Bering Strait.

DOVEKIE
(Fred Bruemmer)

BLACK GUILLEMOT
(Fred Bruemmer)

BLACK GUILLEMOT

(Cepphus grylle)

LENGTH: 13 IN.

Identification: Both Black Guillemot and Pigeon Guillemot are black, plump-bodied and pigeon-billed. Mouth lining and feet are bright red and a conspicuous white shoulder patch covers much of the wing base. Much larger White-winged Scoter has a smaller white patch on the rear edge of the wing. Black Guillemot has an immaculate shoulder patch; Pigeon Guillemot's has a black wedge. Black Guillemot has white wing linings, an excellent field mark in flight. Winter adult is pale, very whitish at a distance, with the same distinguishing marks. Immature of both species, commonly seen in late summer, has dark bars across white wing patches and may be much darker than winter adult.

Status and Distribution:	SPRING	SUMMER	FALL	WINTER
Southeastern	—	—	—	—
Southcoastal	—	—	—	—
Southwestern	R	—	—	R
Central	—	—	+	—
Western ★	U	U	U	U
Northern ★	U	U	U	U

Habitat: Breeding — Chukchi and Beaufort sea coasts. Nests in burrows and beach flotsam. In winter — inshore and offshore marine waters, leads and edge of the ice pack.

Notes: Distribution of the 2 guillemot species overlaps in the Bering Strait area.

PIGEON GUILLEMOT
Summer
(Bill Donaldson)

PIGEON GUILLEMOT
Winter
(John Sarvis)

PIGEON GUILLEMOT

(Cepphus columba)

LENGTH: 13 IN.

Identification: See Black Guillemot.

Habitat: Breeding — inshore marine waters, cliffs, islands. Nests in cliff crevices and between boulders above high tide line. In winter — inshore and offshore marine waters.

Status and Distribution:	SPRING	SUMMER	FALL	WINTER
Southeastern ★	C	C	C	C
Southcoastal ★	C	C	C	C
Southwestern ★	C	C	C	C
Central	—	—	—	—
Western ★	C	C	C	—
Northern	—	—	—	—

MARBLED MURRELET

(Brachyramphus marmoratus)

LENGTH: 9½ IN.

Identification: Marbled and Kittlitz's murrelets are smallest of the common alcids along Alaska's southern coast. In summer brown mottled with white (Marbled Murrelet somewhat darker than Kittlitz's Murrelet) because of the need for camouflage at interior nesting sites. In winter both murrelets black above and white below, like tiny murres but with a white stripe on either side of the back. Black cap of Marbled Murrelet extends below the eyes; entire face of Kittlitz's Murrelet is white to above the eyes. Marbled Murrelet has a longer bill than Kittlitz's Murrelet. Small size, slender appearance for an alcid, and distinct rocking from side to side while in buzzy flight are distinctive of both murrelets. Flight is very rapid, wings long and pointed. Almost always seen in pairs and probably stay mated for life.

Status and Distribution:	SPRING	SUMMER	FALL	WINTER
Southeastern ★	C	C	C	C
Southcoastal ★	C	C	C	C
Southwestern ★	U	U	U	U
Central	—	—	—	—
Western	—	+	—	—
Northern	—	—	—	—

Habitat: Breeding — inshore marine waters. Little is known of the Marbled Murrelet's nesting habits. One nest was found high in a Douglas fir in California and another was found on the ground in the Barren Islands between the Kenai Peninsula and Kodiak. In winter — inshore and offshore marine waters.

MARBLED MURRELET
Summer

MARBLED MURRELET
Winter

KITTLITZ'S MURRELET
(Brachyramphus brevirostris)
LENGTH: 9 IN.

Identification: Difficult to distinguish from Marbled Murrelet. Best distinguished when flushed from water: Kittlitz's has a white tail, marbled has dark tail. Call is deep squawk; marbled's call is soft whistle. See Marbled Murrelet.

Habitat: Breeding — inshore marine waters and adjacent mountains, sea cliffs. Little is known about the nesting habits but 1 egg is usually laid on bare rock above timberline and/or on unvegetated glacial moraines and on grassy ledges of island sea cliffs. In winter — inshore and offshore marine waters.

Status and Distribution:	SPRING	SUMMER	FALL	WINTER
Southeastern ★	U	U	U	U
Southcoastal ★	C	C	C	U
Southwestern ★	U	U	U	R
Central	—	—	—	—
Western ★	U	U	U	—
Northern	R	R	R	—

KITTLITZ'S MURRELET
(David G. Roseneau)

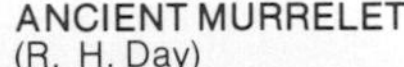

ANCIENT MURRELET
(R. H. Day)

ANCIENT MURRELET

(Synthliboramphus antiquus)

LENGTH: 10 IN.

Identification: Breeding bird has a white stripe over the eye and a black throat patch. In all plumages black cap contrasts with gray back, and there is no white scapular line as in Marbled and Kittlitz's murrelets. Has broader wings and lacks the very fast, rocking flight of other murrelets.

Habitat: Breeding — inshore marine waters and islands including Aleutian Islands, Shumagin Islands, Semidi Islands and Forrester Island. Nests in colonies and lays eggs in crevices or burrows. In winter — inshore and offshore marine waters.

Notes: In migration often occurs in flocks rather than pairs. Young leave the nest from 1 to 4 nights after hatching. In response to parents' calls, they scramble down to the sea and are led offshore. Prefers the open ocean and is usually not found in sheltered inshore waters inhabited by other murrelets.

Status and Distribution:	SPRING	SUMMER	FALL	WINTER
Southeastern ★	U	U	U	U
Southcoastal ★	U	U	U	U
Southwestern ★	C	C	C	C
Central	—	—	—	—
Western	—	R	—	—
Northern	—	—	—	—

CASSIN'S AUKLET

(Ptychoramphus aleuticus)

LENGTH: 7½ IN.

Identification: Small, stocky, looking entirely gray-brown at a distance but with a white center on the belly. On the water appears all dark. At close range a tiny white spot over the eye and a pale area at base of the lower mandible are visible.

Status and Distribution:	SPRING	SUMMER	FALL	WINTER
Southeastern ★	R	U	R	U
Southcoastal	R	R	R	—
Southwestern ★	C	C	C	C
Central	—	—	—	—
Western	—	—	—	—
Northern	—	—	—	—

Habitat: Breeding — inshore coastal waters and islands. Breeds in scattered colonies from Buldir Island in the western Aleutian Islands to Forrester Island in southeastern Alaska. Largest colonies are found in the Sandman Reefs and Shumagin Islands, south of the Alaska Peninsula, and at Forrester Island. Nests are similar to Ancient Murrelets' but the burrows tend to be deeper. In winter — inshore and offshore marine waters.

CASSIN'S AUKLET
(W. E. Townsend)

PARAKEET AUKLET
(Tom Walker)

PARAKEET AUKLET

(Cyclorrhynchus psittacula)

LENGTH: 10 IN.

Identification: Chunkier than a murrelet, looks black and white at a distance. Head and throat are black in summer; throat is white in winter. At close range the enlarged bright red bill is obvious.

Status and Distribution:	SPRING	SUMMER	FALL	WINTER
Southeastern	R	+	—	—
Southcoastal ★	U	U	U	+
Southwestern ★	C	C	C	U
Central	—	—	—	—
Western ★	C	C	C	—
Northern	—	—	+	—

Habitat: Breeding — inshore marine waters and islands, especially in Aleutian, Shumagin and Pribilof islands. Nests under loose boulders and in crevices in sea cliffs. In winter — inshore and offshore marine waters.

Notes: Less colonial in nesting habits than other auklets. Tends to occur in scattered pairs. On occasion gathers in flocks.

CRESTED AUKLET

(Aethia cristatella)

LENGTH: 9½ IN.

Identification: All dark appearance with stubby orange bill and crest that curves forward over it. Immature is difficult to distinguish from Cassin's Auklet.

Status and Distribution:	SPRING	SUMMER	FALL	WINTER
Southeastern	—	—	—	—
Southcoastal	—	—	—	U
Southwestern ★	C	C	C	C
Central	—	—	+	—
Western ★	C	C	C	—
Northern	—	R	—	—

Habitat: Breeding — inshore marine waters, island cliffs and beaches. Nests in crevices of talus, cliffs and among beach boulders. In winter — inshore and offshore marine waters.

Notes: Spectacular aerial displays occur at colonies with birds spiraling high above the colony then swooshing down to the sea where they alight together, dive in unison and take to the air again.

CRESTED AUKLET
(R. H. Day)

LEAST AUKLET
(James Mackovjak)

LEAST AUKLET

(Aethia pusilla)
LENGTH: 6 IN.

Identification: Black above and white below with an extremely stubby bill. In summer has a wide dusky band across white of the upper breast; in winter has a white stripe above the folded wing.

Status and Distribution:	SPRING	SUMMER	FALL	WINTER
Southeastern	—	—	—	—
Southcoastal	+	+	+	—
Southwestern ★	C	C	C	C
Central	—	—	—	—
Western ★	C	C	C	—
Northern	—	+	—	—

Habitat: Breeding — inshore marine waters, islands. Nests in cliff crevices, among boulders above high tide line and on talus slopes. In winter — inshore and offshore marine waters.

Notes: Most abundant of the auklets in some breeding colonies. Parents take turns incubating and the change occurs in the evening.

WHISKERED AUKLET

(Aethia pygmaea)
LENGTH: 7 IN.

Identification: Adult has quaillike crest and 3 white plumes on each side of the face. Immature is difficult to distinguish from young Crested Auklets although traces of 3 white head stripes are sometimes visible.

Status and Distribution:	SPRING	SUMMER	FALL	WINTER
Southeastern	—	—	—	—
Southcoastal	—	—	—	—
Southwestern ★	U	U	U	+
Central	—	—	—	—
Western	—	+	—	—
Northern	—	—	—	—

Habitat: Breeding — inshore marine waters, islands. Nests in cliff crevices, on talus slopes, between boulders above high tide. In winter — inshore and offshore marine waters.

RHINOCEROS AUKLET
(D.H.S. Wehle)

WHISKERED AUKLET
(G. V. Byrd)

RHINOCEROS AUKLET

(Cerorhinca monocerata)

LENGTH: 15 IN.

Identification: Appears all dark on the water; white center of the belly is visible in flight. Much larger and longer-billed than Cassin's Auklet with which it occurs. In summer bill becomes brighter, yellowish-orange to pink, and a short upright horn appears at its base. Two white head plumes also appear at this time and if the upper plume is not clear, this bright-billed bird might be mistaken for a Parakeet or Crested auklet, which have even brighter, shorter bills.

Status and Distribution:	SPRING	SUMMER	FALL	WINTER
Southeastern ★	U	U	U	—
Southcoastal ★	R	R	R	—
Southwestern ★	R	R	R	R
Central	—	—	—	—
Western	—	—	—	—
Northern	—	—	—	—

Habitat: Breeding — inshore marine waters, islands. Nests in deep burrows on sea islands. In migration — inshore and offshore marine waters. Breeds mainly in southeastern Alaska, primarily on Saint Lazaria and Forrester islands. Sizeable colonies also exist in the Barren and Chiswell islands and on Middleton Island in the Gulf of Alaska.

HORNED PUFFIN
(Paul Arneson)

HORNED PUFFIN

(Fratercula corniculata)

LENGTH: 14½ IN.

Identification: Large triangular orange-red and yellow bill, clear white underparts and broad black collar are diagnostic. In summer cheeks are white, and a small dark fleshy appendage appears above each eye. In winter face and bill are darker. Juvenile has even darker face and narrow darkish bill. In all plumages the contrasting white belly distinguishes it from Tufted Puffins. Horned Puffin is chunkier than a murre, which it often accompanies in flying flocks.

Status and Distribution:	SPRING	SUMMER	FALL	WINTER
Southeastern ★	R	R	R	R
Southcoastal ★	U	U	U	R
Southwestern ★	C	C	C	U
Central	—	—	—	—
Western ★	C	C	C	—
Northern	—	R	—	—

Habitat: Breeding — inshore marine waters, islands. Nests on sea islands in rock crevices or in burrows among boulders, on sea cliffs, and on grassy slopes. In winter — inshore and offshore marine waters.

TUFTED PUFFIN
(W. E. Townsend)

TUFTED PUFFIN

(Fratercula cirrhata)

LENGTH: 15 IN.

Identification: Breeding adult has long curved yellowish tufts that hang behind the eyes and entirely dark body. In winter distinguished from Horned Puffin by dusky rather than white sides. Smaller Rhinoceros Auklet has a considerably narrower bill.

Status and Distribution:	SPRING	SUMMER	FALL	WINTER
Southeastern ★	R	U	R	R
Southcoastal ★	C	C	C	R
Southwestern ★	C	C	C	U
Central	—	—	—	—
Western ★	C	C	C	—
Northern	—	+	—	—

Habitat: Breeding — inshore marine waters, islands. Nests principally in burrows in the soil but rock crevices are also used. In winter — inshore and offshore marine waters.

FAMILY *COLUMBIDAE*

PIGEONS, DOVES

(3 + 1)

These are short-legged birds with pointed wings and a small, rounded head which they bob when walking.

BAND-TAILED PIGEON
(Ted & Lois Matthews)

BAND-TAILED PIGEON

(Columba fasciata)

LENGTH: 14½ IN.

Identification: More rounded wings and longer tail than a Rock Dove. Flocks at a distance appear all gray-brown, lacking color variation of Rock Dove flocks. At close range the yellow, black-tipped bill; yellow feet and white ring on hind neck are visible. In flight the tail shows a wide, pale gray band at its tip. Call is a deep owllike hooting.

Status and Distribution:	SPRING	SUMMER	FALL	WINTER
Southeastern ★	R	R	R	—
Southcoastal	—	—	+	—
Southwestern	—	—	—	—
Central	—	—	—	—
Western	—	—	+	—
Northern	—	+	—	—

Habitat: Open woodlands, forest edges. Nests in conifers or deciduous trees.

Notes: Always perches in trees although it will feed on the ground.

ROCK DOVE

(Columba livia)

LENGTH: 13 IN.

Identification: Color of individual birds may vary considerably from mostly white to browns and blacks. Most common color is a blue or ash gray with a white rump, dark head and black bars across the wing. Distinguished from less common Band-tailed Pigeon and Mourning Dove by 2 dark wing bars, reddish legs and dark bill. Rock Dove is never plain brown or brownish gray as are Band-tailed Pigeon and Mourning Dove. At a distance flocks of pigeons will be Rock Doves if variably colored, pointed winged and shorter tailed, and especially if they perch on human-made objects or cliffs or glide with the wings up in a "V".

Status and Distribution:	SPRING	SUMMER	FALL	WINTER
Southeastern ★	C	C	C	C
Southcoastal ★	C	C	C	C
Southwestern	—	—	—	—
Central ★	C	C	C	C
Western	—	—	—	—
Northern	—	—	—	—

Habitat: Cities, towns. Nests on building ledges.

Notes: Only "wild" Alaska bird that is feral, having been introduced locally in each community in which it occurs.

ROCK DOVE

MOURNING DOVE
(Ed Burroughs)

MOURNING DOVE

(Zenaida macroura)

LENGTH: 12 IN.

Identification: Smaller and slimmer than pigeons. Entirely brown with a pointed tail bordered extensively with white. Call is a mournful *coo-a-coo, coo, coo.*

Status and Distribution:	SPRING	SUMMER	FALL	WINTER
Southeastern	R	R	R	—
Southcoastal	R	R	R	—
Southwestern	—	—	+	—
Central	R	R	R	—
Western	—	—	+	—
Northern	—	—	—	—

Habitat: Open woodlands, commonly perches in trees. Not known to breed in Alaska.

FAMILY *CUCULIDAE* CUCKOOS

(2)

Slender, long-tailed birds with 2 toes forward and 2 behind. The 2 species that have occurred in Alaska are casual visitors from Asia.

COMMON CUCKOO

(Cuculus canorus)

LENGTH: 13 IN.

Identification: Long and slender with a long tail and pointed wings, almost falcon-like. In the adult the upperparts, head and breast are gray, the underparts barred gray and white. Tail is spotted rather than barred as in most hawks. Bill is slender and not hawklike. Young and some females (brown phase) are rufous, extensively barred with brown, including the tail. Thinner, lighter bars on the underparts than in Oriental Cuckoo. The 2 species of cuckoos are very difficult to identify in the field. Brown phase told from similar Oriental Cuckoo by unbarred rump and uppertail coverts.

Status and Distribution:	SPRING	SUMMER	FALL	WINTER
Southeastern	—	—	—	—
Southcoastal	—	—	—	—
Southwestern	+	+	—	—
Central	—	—	—	—
Western	—	+	—	—
Northern	—	—	—	—

Habitat: Has occurred in the western and central Aleutian Islands, on Saint Paul Island, Pribilofs; and on the Yukon-Kuskokwim River Delta. Not known to breed in Alaska.

COMMON CUCKOO
Gray and Brown Phase
(John C. Pitcher)

ORIENTAL CUCKOO
(John C. Pitcher)

ORIENTAL CUCKOO

(Cuculus saturatus)

LENGTH: 13 IN.

Identification: See Common Cuckoo. Bars on the underparts are broader and darker than in Common Cuckoo. Generally smaller and more buffy below than Common Cuckoo. Has immaculate white alula (wrist at front of wing).

Status and Distribution:	SPRING	SUMMER	FALL	WINTER
Southeastern	—	—	—	—
Southcoastal	—	—	—	—
Southwestern	—	+	—	—
Central	—	—	—	—
Western	—	+	—	—
Northern	—	—	—	—

Habitat: Has occurred on Saint Lawrence Island, Rat Island in the Aleutians group, the Pribilof Islands and near Cape Prince of Wales on the Seward Peninsula.

FAMILY *STRIGIDAE*

TYPICAL OWLS

(11 + 2)

These are large-headed and short-necked birds of prey. Many are nocturnal and more often heard than seen. Large forward-facing eyes are immovable so the entire head must move to look in another direction. Owls excel at hunting and approach prey silently because the modified downy edges of the primaries eliminate sound caused by the straight-edged primaries of other birds.

WESTERN SCREECH-OWL
(Jerrold Olson)

WESTERN SCREECH-OWL

(Otus kennicottii)

LENGTH: 8½ IN.

Identification: Smaller than a Boreal Owl with conspicuous ear tufts. Voice is a series of short notes accelerating toward the end of the series.

Habitat: Coniferous forests. Nests in holes in trees.

Status and Distribution:	SPRING	SUMMER	FALL	WINTER
Southeastern ★	R	R	R	R
Southcoastal	—	+	+	—
Southwestern	—	—	—	—
Central	—	—	—	—
Western	—	—	—	—
Northern	—	—	—	—

ORIENTAL SCOPS-OWL
(Robert Schulmeister)

ORIENTAL SCOPS-OWL

(Otus sunia)

LENGTH: 7-8 IN.

Identification: Very small owl, streaked and barred brownish-gray, with short ear tufts and yellow eyes. Upperparts are a mottled gray and many of the fine streaks on the underparts are edged with rufous.

Habitat: Has been found in Aleutians on Buldir and Amchitka islands.

Status and Distribution:	SPRING	SUMMER	FALL	WINTER
Southeastern	—	—	—	—
Southcoastal	—	—	—	—
Southwestern	+	+	—	—
Central	—	—	—	—
Western	—	—	—	—
Northern	—	—	—	—

GREAT HORNED OWL
Immature

GREAT HORNED OWL

(Bubo virginianus)

LENGTH: 18-25 IN.

Identification: Large with prominent ear tufts. Voice is a series of deeply resonant *hoo* notes, often 5 in males and 8 in females. Also has a scream.

Habitat: Coniferous and deciduous forests. Nests in abandoned hawk nests or cliff crevices.

Status and Distribution:	SPRING	SUMMER	FALL	WINTER
Southeastern ★	C	C	C	C
Southcoastal ★	C	C	C	C
Southwestern ★	U	U	U	U
Central ★	C	C	C	C
Western ★	U	U	U	U
Northern	—	—	+	—

Notes: Primarily night hunters that prey on living mammals and birds such as rabbits, squirrels, minks, weasels, porcupines, mice, domestic cats, ducks, geese, domestic poultry, shorebirds and songbirds. Very aggressive. Will attack humans in defense of nest.

SNOWY OWL
(Doug Murphy)

SNOWY OWL

(Nyctea scandiaca)

LENGTH: 22-25 IN.

Identification: White with a round head and no ear tufts. Adult male is almost immaculate white; adult female usually has at least scattered brown spots and bars. Immature may be heavily marked with brown. Face of the brownish birds is usually white. Silent except on breeding grounds when it utters loud croaking and whistling sounds.

Habitat: Open country. Breeding — tundra. In winter — marshes and beaches. Nests on the ground in dry areas of tundra or on rocky ledges or cliffs.

Status and Distribution:	SPRING	SUMMER	FALL	WINTER
Southeastern	+	—	—	U
Southcoastal	R	+	R	U
Southwestern ★	R	R	R	U
Central	R	—	+	R
Western ★	U	U	U	U
Northern ★	U	U	U	+

Notes: Perches on the ground or fence posts, even on buildings, and does most hunting during the day or at dusk. Chief prey is lemmings.

NORTHERN HAWK-OWL

(Surnia ulula)

LENGTH: 16 IN.

Identification: Slender, long-tailed with barred underparts and without ear tufts. At rest and in flight similar to a hawk because of the long tail. Voice is a hawklike cry sounding like *ki-ki-ki-ki.*

Status and Distribution:	SPRING	SUMMER	FALL	WINTER
Southeastern ★	U	+	U	U
Southcoastal ★	U	U	U	C
Southwestern ★	R	R	R	U
Central ★	C	C	C	C
Western ★	U	U	U	U
Northern	+	—	—	—

Habitat: Open coniferous and deciduous forests. Nests in tree cavities, on the tops of tree stubs and occasionally cliffs or among limbs of a conifer.

Notes: When perching, often flicks its tail.

NORTHERN HAWK-OWL
(Gilbert Staender)

NORTHERN PYGMY-OWL
(Doug Murphy)

NORTHERN PYGMY-OWL

(Glaucidium gnoma)

LENGTH: 7 IN.

Identification: Lacks ear tufts. Coloration similar to the Boreal and Northern Saw-whet owls but has a smaller head, obviously longer tail and a pair of black patches on the hind neck which look like eyes at a distance. Call is a single, short whistle repeated at intervals of about 1 second.

Status and Distribution:	SPRING	SUMMER	FALL	WINTER
Southeastern ★	R	+	R	R
Southcoastal	—	—	+	—
Southwestern	—	—	—	—
Central	—	—	—	—
Western	—	—	—	—
Northern	—	—	—	—

Habitat: Open coniferous forests and forest edges.

Notes: Daytime activity is a diagnostic feature.

BARRED OWL
Immature

BARRED OWL

(Strix varia)

LENGTH: 17-24 IN.

Identification: Large owl. Brown eyes, barring across chest and lengthwise streaks on belly distinguish Barred Owl in Alaska. Call, as recorded in Juneau, had very emphatic hoots that gradually rose in intensity in the pattern *hoo hoo hoo hoo hoo hoo ho hooo.*

Habitat: Has been seen or heard several times in coniferous forests around Juneau.

Status and Distribution:	SPRING	SUMMER	FALL	WINTER
Southeastern	+	+	+	+
Southcoastal	—	—	—	—
Southwestern	—	—	—	—
Central	—	—	—	—
Western	—	—	—	—
Northern	—	—	—	—

GREAT GRAY OWL
(Daniel Gibson)

GREAT GRAY OWL

(Strix nebulosa)

LENGTH: 24-33 IN.

Identification: Appears to be the largest owl in Alaska although both Great Horned and Snowy owls are heavier and stronger. Lacks ear tufts. Dusky gray with streaked underparts. Has a very large facial disk with concentric gray circles, overall gray appearance and relatively long tail. Voice is a deep *hooo* note at irregular intervals.

Status and Distribution:	SPRING	SUMMER	FALL	WINTER
Southeastern ★	R	R	R	R
Southcoastal ★	R	R	R	R
Southwestern	—	—	—	—
Central ★	R	R	R	R
Western	—	—	—	—
Northern	—	—	—	—

Habitat: Coniferous and deciduous forests and forest edges. Nests in trees usually 20 feet or more from the ground.

Notes: Hunts — preferably for mice or ground squirrels — at dusk or at night but sometimes will forage during daylight, a characteristic of all owls that are residents at high latitudes.

SHORT-EARED OWL

(Asio flammeus)

LENGTH: 15 IN.

Identification: Buffy-brownish color and mothlike flapping flight, with very deep wing strokes, are diagnostic. Has light facial disks, yellow eyes, buffy patches on the upper side of the wing and black wrist marks on the lower side of the wing. Marsh hawk inhabits similar open areas but it has a conspicuous white rump patch and different flight. Voice is a sharp bark *kyow!*

Status and Distribution:	SPRING	SUMMER	FALL	WINTER
Southeastern	C	R	C	R
Southcoastal ★	C	C	C	R
Southwestern ★	C	C	C	R
Central ★	C	C	C	—
Western ★	C	C	C	—
Northern ★	C	C	C	—

Habitat: Open country. Lowland tundra, tidal flats, muskegs, freshwater marshes. Nests on ground in grass-lined depression.

BOREAL OWL

(Aegolius funereus)

LENGTH: 10 IN.

Identification: Dark brown and white with a short tail, no ear tufts and a striped belly. Black framing of the facial disks, yellow bill and white forehead spotting are diagnostic. Voice sounds like the ringing of a soft bell. Also emits a high-pitched whistle.

Status and Distribution:	SPRING	SUMMER	FALL	WINTER
Southeastern	—	+	—	U
Southcoastal ★	U	U	U	U
Southwestern ★	U	U	U	U
Central ★	C	C	C	C
Western ★	R	R	R	R
Northern	—	—	—	—

Habitat: Coniferous and mixed coniferous-deciduous forests. Nests in holes in trees.

BOREAL OWL
(Gilbert Staender)

Notes: Seems quite tame and is easily approached. Feeds on mice when available; small birds and insects at other times.

SHORT-EARED OWL
(Robert Gill)

NORTHERN SAW-WHET OWL
(Edgar Jones)

NORTHERN SAW-WHET OWL

(Aegolius acadicus)

LENGTH: 7½ IN.

Identification: Smaller version of the Boreal Owl with dark bill and streaked forehead. Call is similar in quality to Boreal Owl's, but is of separate notes, not run together in a tremolo.

Habitat: Coniferous and deciduous forests. Nests in holes in trees.

Notes: Only active at night. May be discovered roosting in a dense thicket during the day.

Status and Distribution:	SPRING	SUMMER	FALL	WINTER
Southeastern ★	R	R	R	R
Southcoastal ★	R	R	R	R
Southwestern	—	—	+	—
Central	—	—	—	—
Western	—	—	+	—
Northern	—	—	—	—

FAMILY *CAPRIMULGIDAE*

GOATSUCKERS

(1 + 2)

Members of this family are typically nocturnal birds but the 1 species most likely to be seen in Alaska, the Common Nighthawk, often feeds during the day.

COMMON NIGHTHAWK
(Dennis Paulson)

COMMON NIGHTHAWK

(Chordeiles minor)

LENGTH: 9 IN.

Identification: Mottled and barred brown. May be seen perched flat on the ground or lengthwise on a branch where the large head, very tiny bill, long, pointed wings and manner of resting are distinctive. In flight, at times high in the air, appears very long- and narrow-winged with a conspicuous white spot halfway between the bend of the wing and the wing tip. Male has conspicuous white throat and a white band across the tail. Call is loud, buzzy *peent.*

Status and Distribution:	SPRING	SUMMER	FALL	WINTER
Southeastern	—	+	R	—
Southcoastal	—	—	+	—
Southwestern	—	—	—	—
Central	+	+	+	—
Western	—	—	—	—
Northern		+	—	—

Habitat: Open woodlands. Mostly seen near the mouths of mainland rivers in southeastern Alaska from mid-August through mid-September. Not known to breed in Alaska.

FAMILY *APODIDAE*
SWIFTS
(4 + 2)

These birds resemble swallows but the wings are narrow, slightly decurved and held very stiffly. They appear to beat the wings alternately but this is an illusion. They feed exclusively on insects while flying.

BLACK SWIFT
(Cypseloides niger)
LENGTH: 7 IN.

Identification: Appears entirely black. Has a deeply notched tail, and is considerably larger than Vaux's Swift or any swallow in Alaska except casual Purple Martin. In flight has faster wingbeats than swallows and glides less than they do. See Vaux's Swift.

Habitat: Mountains, open woodlands. Nests on cliffs in a niche or cavity.

Status and Distribution:	SPRING	SUMMER	FALL	WINTER
Southeastern ★	R	R	R	—
Southcoastal	—	—	—	—
Southwestern	—	—	—	—
Central	—	—	—	—
Western	—	—	—	—
Northern	—	—	—	—

Notes: Usually flies fairly high but sometimes, especially in rainy weather, will fly low over water or open ground.

BLACK SWIFT
(John C. Pitcher)

VAUX'S SWIFT
(John C. Pitcher)

VAUX'S SWIFT

(Chaetura vauxi)

LENGTH: 4 IN.

Identification: Smaller than any of Alaska's swallows with no apparent tail and pale brown underparts. See Black Swift.

Status and Distribution:	SPRING	SUMMER	FALL	WINTER
Southeastern ★	U	U	U	—
Southcoastal	—	—	+	—
Southwestern	—	—	—	—
Central	—	—	—	—
Western	—	—	—	—
Northern	—	—	—	—

Habitat: Mountains, open woodland. Nests on the inner wall of a hollow tree.

Notes: Usually flies fairly high but sometimes, especially in rainy weather, will fly low over water or open ground.

FORK-TAILED SWIFT
(John C. Pitcher)

FORK-TAILED SWIFT

(Apus pacificus)

LENGTH: 7 IN.

Identification: Large like a Black Swift, but much longer-winged and has a conspicuous white rump and a much more deeply forked tail.

Status and Distribution:	SPRING	SUMMER	FALL	WINTER
Southeastern	—	—	—	—
Southcoastal	—		—	—
Southwestern	+	+	+	—
Central	—	—	—	—
Western	—	—	—	—
Northern	—	—	—	—

Habitat: Found in the Pribilof Islands and western Aleutian Islands. Not known to breed in Alaska.

WHITE-THROATED NEEDLETAIL
(Wild Bird Society of Japan)

WHITE-THROATED NEEDLETAIL

(Hirundapus caudacutus)

LENGTH: 8¼ IN.

Identification: Large swift distinguished from others in Alaska by white throat, pale back, and white V on undersides near square cut tail.

Habitat: Has been seen in western Aleutians on Shemya and Attu islands.

Status and Distribution:	SPRING	SUMMER	FALL	WINTER
Southeastern	—	—	—	—
Southcoastal	—	—	—	—
Southwestern	+	—	—	—
Central	—	—	—	—
Western	—	—	—	—
Northern	—	—	—	—

FAMILY *TROCHILIDAE*
HUMMINGBIRDS
(2 + 1)

These are the smallest birds found in Alaska. They are known for the ability to hover and fly backwards while rapidly beating their wings. The long slender bill and extensile tongue are especially adapted for sipping nectar from flowers.

ANNA'S HUMMINGBIRD
(Calypte anna)
LENGTH: 4 IN.

Identification: Male has green back, whitish underparts and rose-red crown and throat. Female is similar but lacks the red. Neither sex has any rufous on the back, belly or tail.

Habitat: All Alaska records are from feeders. Not known to breed in Alaska.

Status and Distribution:	SPRING	SUMMER	FALL	WINTER
Southeastern	+	+	R	R
Southcoastal	—	—	+	—
Southwestern	—	—	—	—
Central	—	—	—	—
Western	—	—	—	—
Northern	—	—	—	—

ANNA'S HUMMINGBIRD
(Merrick Hersey)

ANNA'S HUMMINGBIRD
Female
(Merrick Hersey)

RUFOUS HUMMINGBIRD

RUFOUS HUMMINGBIRD

(Selasphorus rufus)

LENGTH: 3½ IN.

Identification: Adult male distinguished from all other birds by rufous color and extensive flaming orange-red throat patch. Adult female lacks throat patch and has a green back, dull rufous sides and considerable rufous at base of the tail. Immatures are similar to females.

Status and Distribution:	SPRING	SUMMER	FALL	WINTER
Southeastern ★	C	C	C	R
Southcoastal ★	C	C	C	—
Southwestern	—	—	—	—
Central	—	R	—	—
Western	—	—	—	—
Northern	—	—	—	—

Habitat: Forest edges and openings from sea level to the mountains, wherever flowers are available. Nests in various trees and bushes.

Notes: Feeds on flower and blossom nectar with a preference for red flowers; also feeds on tiny insects.

RUFOUS HUMMINGBIRD
Female
(Tom Ulrich)

FAMILY *ALCEDINIDAE*

KINGFISHERS

(1)

In Alaska this family is represented by only 1 species, the Belted Kingfisher.

BELTED KINGFISHER

(Ceryle alcyon)

LENGTH: 13 IN.

Identification: Large head and bill, which look out of proportion to body size, short tail and tiny feet are distinctive. Blue-gray above and white below with a white collar. In flight has jerky wingbeats and rattling call. Both sexes have a gray breast band; female has an additional rufous band, one of the rare instances in which the female appears more brightly colored than the male.

Habitat: Rivers, streams, lakes, ponds, sloughs, inshore marine waters. Nests in a burrow which it excavates in sandy, clay or gravelly banks.

Status and Distribution:	SPRING	SUMMER	FALL	WINTER
Southeastern ★	C	C	C	C
Southcoastal ★	U	U	U	U
Southwestern ★	U	U	U	U
Central ★	C	C	C	—
Western ★	U	U	U	—
Northern	—	—	+	—

Notes: Catches small fish by diving straight into the water, sometimes completely submerging. When fish are scarce, feeds on insects, mice and berries.

BELTED KINGFISHER
Female

FAMILY *PICIDAE*

WOODPECKERS

(7 + 1)

Woodpeckers are highly specialized for climbing the trunks and branches of trees and for digging out wood-boring insects. The bill is hard, straight and chisellike; the tongue is slender and fitted with a horny spear at the tip for impaling insect larvae. Legs are short. Feet have 4 toes (rarely 3), 2 in front and 2 behind, that have sharp claws for climbing. Stiff pointed tail feathers serve as a brace against tree trunks.

NORTHERN FLICKER
(Tom Ulrich)

NORTHERN FLICKER

(Colaptes auratus)

LENGTH: 12½ IN.

Identification: Has conspicuous white rump patch and yellow or reddish wing and tail linings. Males have a black (yellow-shafted) or red (red-shafted) mustache. Voice is a loud, far-carrying series of rapid *wucks* or a deliberate *wicka-wicka-wicka.*

Habitat: Coniferous and deciduous forests. Nests in a hole in a tree or stump.

Notes: Essentially a forest bird but may feed on insects on the ground, especially in cleared areas along the highway. Also eats wild berries such as dwarf dogwood, mountain ash and blueberries.

Two races found in Alaska: red-shafted is only found in southeastern Alaska; yellow-shafted occurs throughout forested regions of the state.

Status and Distribution:	SPRING	SUMMER	FALL	WINTER
Southeastern ★	U	U	U	+
Southcoastal	+	R	U	—
Southwestern	—	—	—	—
Central ★	C	C	C	+
Western	—	—	+	—
Northern	—	—	+	—

RED-BREASTED SAPSUCKER

RED-BREASTED SAPSUCKER

(Sphyrapicus ruber)

LENGTH: 9 IN.

Identification: Red hood covering the head, neck and breast and a long white stripe down the folded wing are diagnostic. Flight is undulating but the wings appear to be held closed for a slightly longer interval than in other woodpeckers. Sexes are alike. Call is a squealing *chee-ar,* most often heard during breeding season.

Habitat: Coniferous and mixed deciduous-coniferous forests. Nests in a hole in a tree.

Status and Distribution:	SPRING	SUMMER	FALL	WINTER
Southeastern ★	U	U	U	R
Southcoastal	+	—	+	+
Southwestern	—	—	—	—
Central	—	+	—	—
Western	—	—	—	—
Northern	—	—	—	—

Notes: Is responsible for the horizontal rows of squarish holes frequently found on tree trunks. Drinks sap from these holes and also may obtain insects that are attracted by the sap.

YELLOW-BELLIED SAPSUCKER
(O.S. Pettingill, Jr., Cornell Lab of Ornithology)

YELLOW-BELLIED SAPSUCKER

(Sphyrapicus varius)

LENGTH: 9 IN.

Identification: Red forehead, two white horizontal stripes across face, black bib across upper breast and straw-yellow underparts separate Yellow-bellied Sapsucker from Red-breasted Sapsucker. Throat is red in male and white in female.

Habitat: Very rare in eastern central Alaska. Breeds as close to Alaska as northwestern British Columbia.

Status and Distribution:	SPRING	SUMMER	FALL	WINTER
Southeastern	—	—	—	—
Southcoastal	—	—	—	—
Southwestern	—	—	—	—
Central	+	+	—	—
Western	—	—	—	—
Northern	—	—	—	—

HAIRY WOODPECKER

(Picoides villosus)

LENGTH: 9 IN.

Identification: Vivid black and white markings, white back and large bill. Immaculate white outer tail feathers. Bill is nearly as long as the head. Downy Woodpecker's bill is more stubby and obviously shorter than the head. Adult males of both species have a bright red patch, which may be divided into 2 spots, on the nape. Young males of both species just out of the nest usually have a red crown. Call is a far-carrying *pick.*

Habitat: Coniferous and deciduous forests. Nests in a hole in a tree.

Status and Distribution:	SPRING	SUMMER	FALL	WINTER
Southeastern ★	U	U	U	U
Southcoastal ★	U	U	U	U
Southwestern	—	—	—	—
Central ★	U	U	U	U
Western	—	—	—	—
Northern	—	—	—	—

HAIRY WOODPECKER

DOWNY WOODPECKER
(Ed Burroughs)

DOWNY WOODPECKER

(Picoides pubescens)

LENGTH: 6½ IN.

Identification: Smaller version of Hairy Woodpecker with stubby bill that is obviously shorter than the head. Barred outer tail feathers. Call is similar to but much softer than that of Hairy Woodpecker.

Status and Distribution:	SPRING	SUMMER	FALL	WINTER
Southeastern ★	U	U	U	U
Southcoastal ★	U	U	U	U
Southwestern ★	R	R	R	R
Central ★	U	U	U	U
Western ★	R	R	R	R
Northern	—	—	—	—

Habitat: Coniferous and deciduous forests, shrub thickets. Nests in a hole in a tree.

Notes: Often comes to suet in winter.

BLACK-BACKED WOODPECKER
(Merrick Hersey)

BLACK-BACKED WOODPECKER
(Picoides arcticus)
LENGTH: 9½ IN.

Identification: Larger and darker than Three-toed Woodpecker. Has solid, glossy black back. Sides are barred. Adult male has yellow cap.

Habitat: Coniferous and mixed deciduous-coniferous forests. Nests in tree cavities, usually of a conifer.

Status and Distribution:	SPRING	SUMMER	FALL	WINTER
Southeastern	R	—	R	—
Southcoastal ★	+	+	+	—
Southwestern	+	—	—	—
Central ★	R	R	R	R
Western	—	—	—	—
Northern	—	—	—	—

THREE-TOED WOODPECKER

THREE-TOED WOODPECKER
(Picoides tridactylus)
LENGTH: 8½ IN.

Identification: Appears darker than the Hairy Woodpecker with a dull black-and-white-barred back and barred sides. Adult male has a yellow cap. Call is a sharp *pik* or *kik,* uttered much less frequently than that of Hairy Woodpecker.

Habitat: Coniferous and mixed deciduous-coniferous forests. Nests in tree cavities, usually of a conifer.

Status and Distribution:	SPRING	SUMMER	FALL	WINTER
Southeastern ★	U	U	U	U
Southcoastal ★	R	R	R	R
Southwestern ★	U	U	U	U
Central ★	U	U	U	U
Western ★	U	U	U	U
Northern	—	—	—	—

FAMILY *TYRANNIDAE*

TYRANT FLYCATCHERS

(8 + 3)

Flycatchers typically perch in an upright position on bare branches and make frequent short flights after flying insects, usually returning to the same perch. They have broad flat bills especially adapted for catching insects.

The 3 similar-looking small flycatchers that breed in Alaska have conspicuous wing bars and white eye ring and are known collectively by their generic name, *Empidonax*.

EASTERN KINGBIRD
(Michael Hopiak, Cornell Lab of Ornithology)

EASTERN KINGBIRD

(Tyrannus tyrannus)

LENGTH: 8½ IN.

Identification: Dark gray above and white below with a white band at tip of the black tail. Call is a loud, harsh *dzeeb,* at times uttered in rapid progression.

Habitat: Open areas with trees, shrubs or posts for perching. Not known to breed in Alaska.

Status and Distribution:	SPRING	SUMMER	FALL	WINTER
Southeastern	—	R	—	—
Southcoastal	—	+	+	—
Southwestern	—	+	—	—
Central	—	+	+	—
Western	—	+	—	—
Northern	—	+	+	—

Notes: Usually perches on fences or utility wires and flies out substantial distances after insects.

WESTERN KINGBIRD
(John C. Pitcher)

WESTERN KINGBIRD

(Tyrannus verticalis)

LENGTH: 8½ IN.

Identification: Olive-gray above with light gray breast and yellow belly. Tail is black with white edges. Call is a sharp *wit* or *wik.*

Habitat: Open areas with trees, shrubs and posts for perching. Not known to breed in Alaska.

Status and Distribution:	SPRING	SUMMER	FALL	WINTER
Southeastern	+	—	—	—
Southcoastal	—	—	+	—
Southwestern	—	—	—	—
Central	—	+	—	—
Western	—	—	—	—
Northern	—	—	—	—

SAY'S PHOEBE

(Sayornis saya)

LENGTH: 7½ IN.

Identification: Gray-brown on back and breast, light cinnamon on belly with a black tail. Voice is mellow, whistled *pee-ur.*

Status and Distribution:	SPRING	SUMMER	FALL	WINTER
Southeastern ★	R	R	R	—
Southcoastal ★	R	R	R	—
Southwestern	—	+	+	—
Central ★	U	U	U	—
Western ★	U	U	U	—
Northern ★	U	U	U	—

Habitat: Open areas and cliffs in mountains and uplands. Nests on shelves or crevices of cliffs and on buildings.

Notes: Sits in the open on dead limbs, electrical wires or posts and makes short flights after insects.

YELLOW-BELLIED FLYCATCHER

(Empidonax flaviventris)

LENGTH: 5½ IN.

Identification: Much like Western Flycatcher but with slightly more yellowish underparts. Any yellowish empidonax in Alaska's interior is more likely to be a Yellow-bellied Flycatcher than a Western Flycatcher. Song is soft *chu-wee,* rising distinctly on the second syllable.

Habitat: Has occurred at Coal Creek near the Yukon River in east central Alaska. Not known to breed in Alaska.

Status and Distribution:	SPRING	SUMMER	FALL	WINTER
Southeastern	—	—	—	—
Southcoastal	—	—	—	—
Southwestern	—	—	—	—
Central	—	+	—	—
Western	—	—	—	—
Northern	—	—	—	—

YELLOW-BELLIED FLYCATCHER
(John C. Pitcher)

Notes: This species now considered accidental in Alaska.

SAY'S PHOEBE

ALDER FLYCATCHER

ALDER FLYCATCHER

(Empidonax alnorum)

LENGTH: 6 IN.

Identification: Four small flycatchers regularly occur in Alaska. Three of them have a conspicuous white eye ring. Alder Flycatcher is much like Hammond's Flycatcher and might also be mistaken for Western Flycatcher. Song is a *fee-bee-o* and call is a short sharp *whit* or *wee-o.*

Habitat: Alder and willow thickets, usually in moist areas. Nests in the upright crotch of a shrub.

Status and Distribution:	SPRING	SUMMER	FALL	WINTER
Southeastern ★	U	U	U	—
Southcoastal ★	U	U	U	—
Southwestern ★	U	U	U	—
Central ★	C	C	C	—
Western ★	U	U	U	—
Northern	+	+	—	—

HAMMOND'S FLYCATCHER
(Empidonax hammondii)
LENGTH: 5 IN.

Identification: Very similar to Alder Flycatcher and Yellow-bellied Flycatcher. Typical 3-part song begins and ends with a double note and has a short or slightly rolling middle part described as *seedick, prrt, pewit.* Call note is lower-pitched and quite different from that of the Alder Flycatcher.

Status and Distribution:	SPRING	SUMMER	FALL	WINTER
Southeastern ★	U	U	U	—
Southcoastal	—	—	—	—
Southwestern	—	—	—	—
Central ★	C	C	C	—
Western	—	—	—	—
Northern	—	+	—	—

Habitat: Riparian deciduous forests. Also dry upland mixed or deciduous forests with closed canopy.

Notes: Hammond's Flycatcher is an early migrant arriving in central Alaska about the first of May; Alder Flycatcher is a late migrant arriving near the end of May.

HAMMOND'S FLYCATCHER

WESTERN FLYCATCHER
(Peter M. LaTourrette)

WESTERN FLYCATCHER
(Empidonax difficilis)
LENGTH: 5½ IN.

Identification: Has extensive yellowish underparts, including the throat. Song is 3 thin notes, *pseet-ptsick-seet*; call is a sharp lisping *ps-seet.*

Status and Distribution:	SPRING	SUMMER	FALL	WINTER
Southeastern ★	C	C	C	—
Southcoastal	—	+	—	—
Southwestern	—	—	—	—
Central	—	—	—	—
Western	—	[illegible]	—	—
Northern	—	—	—	—

Habitat: Open coniferous forests. Nests on rock ledges near streams, in the roots of upturned trees, and on stumps or buildings.

WESTERN WOOD-PEWEE

WESTERN WOOD-PEWEE

(Contopus sordidulus)

LENGTH: 6¼ IN.

Identification: Slightly larger and even duller than empidonax flycatchers. Lacks their white eye ring. Voice is nasal *pee-wee*.

Status and Distribution:	SPRING	SUMMER	FALL	WINTER
Southeastern ★	U	U	U	—
Southcoastal ★	—	R	R	—
Southwestern	—	—	—	—
Central ★	U	U	U	—
Western	+	+	—	—
Northern	+	+	—	—

Habitat: Open coniferous and deciduous forests, forest edges. Nests on a horizontal limb and occasionally in an upright crotch of a deciduous or coniferous tree.

OLIVE-SIDED FLYCATCHER
(Edgar Jones)

OLIVE-SIDED FLYCATCHER

(Contopus borealis)

LENGTH: 7½ IN.

Identification: Stout, with a large bill and dark chest patches separated by narrow white stripe. Song is emphatic whistled *whip-three-beers,* with the middle note the highest in pitch. Call is incessant *pilt, pilt.*

Habitat: Coniferous forests. Nests in a conifer.

Status and Distribution:	SPRING	SUMMER	FALL	WINTER
Southeastern ★	U	U	U	—
Southcoastal ★	R	R	R	—
Southwestern ★	R	R	R	—
Central ★	U	U	U	—
Western ★	R	R	R	—
Northern	—	+	—	—

FAMILY *ALAUDIDAE*

LARKS

(2)

These are sparrow-sized ground birds that rarely perch in trees or bushes.

EURASIAN SKYLARK
Fall
(John C. Pitcher)

EURASIAN SKYLARK

(Alauda arvensis)

LENGTH: 7 IN.

Identification: Brown, streaked above and on the breast, with a slight crest. Bill is thinner than that of a longspur or sparrow. Larger than a pipit and does not wag its tail. Extremely elongated, straight hind claw. Lacks indistinct head markings of an immature Horned Lark. Call is liquid *chirrup*.

Habitat: Asiatic lark that occurs in the western Aleutian Islands and has occurred in the Pribilof Islands.

Notes: Ground bird which prefers open country.

Status and Distribution:	SPRING	SUMMER	FALL	WINTER
Southeastern	—	—	—	—
Southcoastal	—	—	—	—
Southwestern ★	R	+	+	—
Central	—	—	—	—
Western	+	—	—	—
Northern	—	—	—	—

HORNED LARK
(Anton Szabados)

HORNED LARK
(Eremophila alpestris)
LENGTH: 7½ IN.

Identification: Has a black shield below a light throat and a black face patch curving downward from the bill to below the eye. "Horns" are not always visible. In flight black tail is conspicuous against sandy brown back or white belly. Immature is streaky brown with a typical lark shape and behavior, and often is vaguely marked with the adult head pattern. Song is a series of tinkling notes given from high in the air.

Status and Distribution:	SPRING	SUMMER	FALL	WINTER
Southeastern ★	U	R	U	—
Southcoastal	R	R	R	—
Southwestern ★	R	R	R	—
Central ★	C	C	C	—
Western ★	U	U	U	—
Northern ★	U	U	U	—

Habitat: Breeding — alpine tundra. Nests on the ground in the tundra. In migration — drier grassy areas of tidal flats, alpine meadows.

FAMILY *HIRUNDINIDAE*

SWALLOWS

(7 + 1)

Swallows are excellent flyers that capture insects on the wing. They have long pointed wings, a flattish head, a small flat bill, wide mouth and most have notched or forked tails. They commonly perch on wires.

VIOLET-GREEN SWALLOW
(Doug Herr)

VIOLET-GREEN SWALLOW

(Tachycineta thalassina)

LENGTH: 5½ IN.

Identification: One of 2 swallow species that look dark above and entirely white below from a distance. White patch on either side of the rump shows from above in flight, and green and violet upperparts are visible at close range. White of the face extends around the eye, which distinguishes this species from similar Tree Swallow. Female is considerably duller, especially around the head.

Status and Distribution:	SPRING	SUMMER	FALL	WINTER
Southeastern ★	U	U	U	—
Southcoastal ★	C	C	C	—
Southwestern ★	U	U	U	—
Central ★	C	C	C	—
Western	—	—	—	—
Northern	—	+	—	—

Habitat: Forages for insects in open areas, over water, above tree tops. Nests in holes, cavities and crevices in trees, cliffs, buildings.

TREE SWALLOW
(Doug Murphy)

TREE SWALLOW

(Tachycineta bicolor)

LENGTH: 5½ IN.

Identification: Steely-blue on back and white on belly. May be confused with Violet-green Swallow but lacks white patches that almost meet over the base of the tail of that species. Dark cap extends down over the eyes, presenting a very different appearance from Violet-green Swallow. First year female is much duller; mature female and all males are fully colored.

Status and Distribution:	SPRING	SUMMER	FALL	WINTER
Southeastern ★	C	C	C	—
Southcoastal ★	C	C	C	—
Southwestern ★	C	C	C	—
Central ★	C	C	C	—
Western ★	C	C	C	—
Northern	+	+	+	—

Habitat: Forages for insects over water or moist ground. Lakes, larger streams, marshes and wet muskegs. Nests in tree cavities and sometimes in buildings and bird boxes. Closely tied to human settlements in tundra areas.

BANK SWALLOW

(Riparia riparia)

LENGTH: 5 IN.

Identification: Brown back, white throat and clearly defined dark breast band. Smallest and dullest swallow found in Alaska.

Habitat: Usually near water. Nests in holes in clay and sand banks near rivers, creeks and lakes and along highways.

Status and Distribution:	SPRING	SUMMER	FALL	WINTER
Southeastern ★	R	R	R	—
Southcoastal ★	U	U	U	—
Southwestern ★	U	U	U	—
Central ★	C	C	C	—
Western ★	U	U	U	—
Northern	+	+	+	—

NORTHERN ROUGH-WINGED SWALLOW

(Stelgidopteryx serripennis)

LENGTH: 5½ IN.

Identification: All brown above with an entirely brown throat. Flight is batlike.

Status and Distribution:	SPRING	SUMMER	FALL	WINTER
Southeastern ★	R	R	R	—
Southcoastal	+	+	—	—
Southwestern	—	+	—	—
Central	—	—	—	—
Western	—	—	—	—
Northern	—	+	—	—

Habitat: Forages over water and open land. Nests in burrows in sand, gravel or clay and in other cavities.

Notes: Usually occurs in single pairs; not colonial like the Bank Swallow.

NORTHERN ROUGH-WINGED SWALLOW
(Dennis Paulson)

BANK SWALLOW

BARN SWALLOW

(Hirundo rustica)

LENGTH: 6 IN.

BARN SWALLOW
Immature
(Doug Murphy)

Identification: Has deeply forked tail, steely iridescent blue back and light orange belly. Immature has much shorter tail and paler belly. Easily recognized at great distances by leisurely flight with slow wingbeats for a swallow.

Habitat: Forages over marshes, open land and water. Nests in buildings and under bridges.

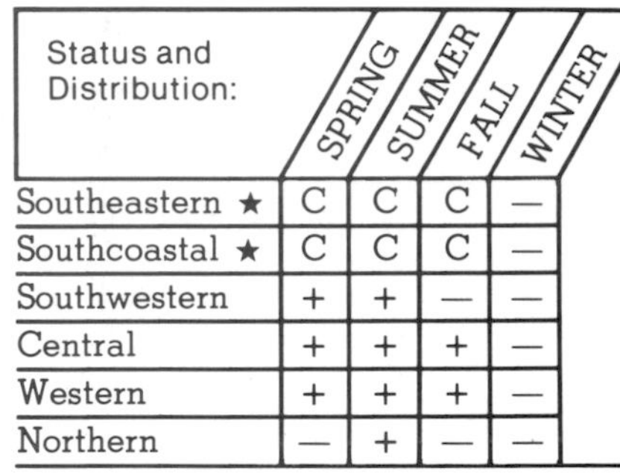

Status and Distribution:	SPRING	SUMMER	FALL	WINTER
Southeastern ★	C	C	C	—
Southcoastal ★	C	C	C	—
Southwestern	+	+	—	—
Central	+	+	+	—
Western	+	+	+	—
Northern	—	+	—	—

CLIFF SWALLOW

(Hirundo pyrrhonota)

LENGTH: 5½ IN.

CLIFF SWALLOW

Identification: Appears plump because of short, almost square tail. Blue-black above and white below, with a dark chestnut throat, whitish forehead and conspicuous buffy rump patch. More likely to soar than other small swallows.

Habitat: Forages over water and open land. Nests on buildings and under bridges.

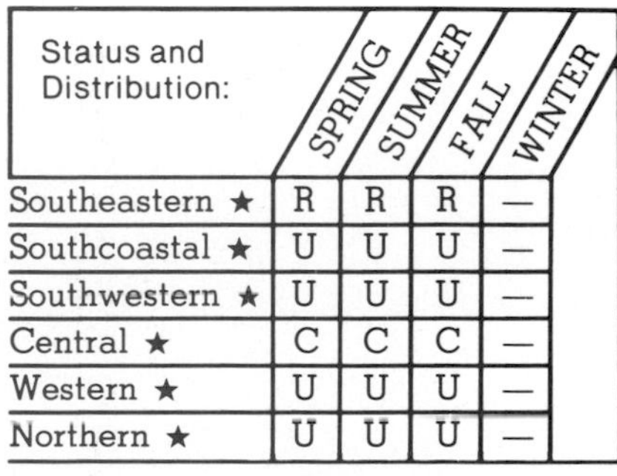

Status and Distribution:	SPRING	SUMMER	FALL	WINTER
Southeastern ★	R	R	R	—
Southcoastal ★	U	U	U	—
Southwestern ★	U	U	U	—
Central ★	C	C	C	—
Western ★	U	U	U	—
Northern ★	U	U	U	—

PURPLE MARTIN

(Progne subis)

LENGTH: 8 IN.

Identification: Male is entirely blue-black; female is brownish-black above and gray below. Soars much more than the smaller species.

Habitat: Open areas of forests, water, marshes. Not known to breed in Alaska.

Status and Distribution:	SPRING	SUMMER	FALL	WINTER
Southeastern	—	—	—	—
Southcoastal	+	—	—	—
Southwestern	—	+	+	—
Central	+	+	—	—
Western	—	+	—	—
Northern	—	+	—	—

PURPLE MARTIN
(John C. Pitcher)

FAMILY *CORVIDAE*

JAYS, MAGPIES, CROWS

(6)

Members of this family are medium to large, gregarious birds with heavy bills. They will feed on meat (including carrion), eggs and young of other birds, insects, fruits and seeds.

GRAY JAY

(Perisoreus canadensis)

LENGTH: 11 IN.

Identification: Adults are long tailed, primarily gray, with darker back and crown and rather short bill. Immature — from fledging to September — is very dark gray, almost black, all over. Utters a variety of shrill, high-pitched notes and whistles including a soft *whee-oh* and a harsh, scolding *cla, cla, cla, cla.*

Status and Distribution:	SPRING	SUMMER	FALL	WINTER
Southeastern	+	—	+	R
Southcoastal ★	R	R	R	R
Southwestern ★	U	U	U	U
Central ★	C	C	C	C
Western ★	U	U	U	U
Northern ★	+	+	+	+

Habitat: Openings in coniferous and deciduous forests. Campgrounds. Nests in conifers.

GRAY JAY
Adult
(Doug Murphy)

STELLER'S JAY
(Cyanocitta stelleri)
LENGTH: 13 IN.

Identification: Dark blue to black with a conspicuous crest. Flight is series of wing-flappings interspersed with long, straight glides. Voice is a harsh *shack-shack-shack-shack* or *chook-chook-chook*. Also mimics the screams of hawks.

Status and Distribution:	SPRING	SUMMER	FALL	WINTER
Southeastern ★	C	C	C	C
Southcoastal ★	C	C	C	C
Southwestern	—	—	—	—
Central	—	—	+	—
Western	—	—	—	—
Northern	—	—	—	—

Habitat: Coniferous and mixed coniferous-deciduous forests. Nests 10 feet or more above the ground in conifers.

STELLER'S JAY
(John Helle)

GRAY JAY
Immature

BLACK-BILLED MAGPIE

BLACK-BILLED MAGPIE

(Pica pica)

LENGTH: 20 IN.

Identification: Very long tail and black-and-white color at rest or in flight are diagnostic. Young share the adult color pattern but have a much shorter tail. Voice is a rapid, nasal *mag? mag? mag?* or *yak yak yak.*

Status and Distribution:	SPRING	SUMMER	FALL	WINTER
Southeastern ★	U	R	U	C
Southcoastal ★	C	C	C	C
Southwestern ★	C	C	C	C
Central ★	C	C	C	C
Western	—	—	—	R
Northern	—	+	—	—

Habitat: Shrub thickets, open woodlands, forest edges along saltwater beaches. Nests in tall bushes.

COMMON RAVEN
(Doug Murphy)

COMMON RAVEN

(Corvus corax)

LENGTH: 22-27 IN.

Identification: Can be confused only with Northwestern Crow but is much larger with a proportionately larger bill and wedge-shaped tail. Soars like a buteo. From the ground Common Raven often takes 2 or 3 hops to become airborne; crow jumps directly into the air. Most common call is hoarse, croaking *kraaak.* Utters a variety of other sounds including a hollow, knocking sound and a melodious *kloo-klok,* usually in flight.

Status and Distribution:	SPRING	SUMMER	FALL	WINTER
Southeastern ★	C	C	C	C
Southcoastal ★	C	C	C	C
Southwestern ★	C	C	C	C
Central ★	C	C	C	C
Western ★	C	C	C	C
Northern ★	C	C	C	U

Habitat: Marine shores to mountain ridges and glaciers. Garbage dumps. Nests in trees or on cliffs.

NORTHWESTERN CROW
(Corvus caurinus)
LENGTH: 17 IN.

Identification: All black. Sometimes, when silent and in dim light, may be confused with Common Raven but the square-cut tail and shorter bill are distinguishing. Voice is a raucous *kaah*, sometimes repeated endlessly. Imitates a variety of sounds.

Habitat: Marine shores; rarely ventures inland. Coniferous forests, beaches and tidal flats, rocky shores and reefs. Nests in a conifer or sometimes under boulders or windfalls close to shore.

Status and Distribution:	SPRING	SUMMER	FALL	WINTER
Southeastern ★	C	C	C	C
Southcoastal ★	C	C	C	C
Southwestern ★	R	R	—	—
Central	—	—	—	—
Western	—	—	—	—
Northern	—	—	—	—

Notes: Diet consists chiefly of dead fish, clams, mussels, small crabs; elderberries, salmonberries and some insects in summer. Opens clams and mussels by carrying them aloft and dropping them on the rocks below.

NORTHWESTERN CROW

CLARK'S NUTCRACKER
(Don Cunningham)

CLARK'S NUTCRACKER

(Nucifraga columbiana)

LENGTH: 12½ IN.

Identification: Gray, wings and tail black with large white patches. Bill is much longer and tail much shorter than Gray Jay. Call is loud, harsh *kraaa.*

Habitat: Open coniferous forests. Not known to breed in Alaska.

Status and Distribution:	SPRING	SUMMER	FALL	WINTER
Southeastern	+	+	+	+
Southcoastal	—	—	—	—
Southwestern	—	—	+	—
Central	—	—	+	+
Western	—	—	+	—
Northern	—	—	—	—

FAMILY *PARIDAE*

CHICKADEES

(5)

These are small, dull-colored, acrobatic birds with black bibs and dark caps. They are quite tame and readily come to feeders. They typically inhabit the forested regions of Alaska.

BLACK-CAPPED CHICKADEE

BLACK-CAPPED CHICKADEE

(Parus atricapillus)

LENGTH: 5 IN.

Identification: Solid black cap, gray back and pale buffy sides are diagnostic. Most common call is clear *tsick-a-dee-dee-dee.* Male in spring sings clear, 2-noted whistles *fee-bee.*

Status and Distribution:	SPRING	SUMMER	FALL	WINTER
Southeastern ★	U	U	U	U
Southcoastal ★	U	U	U	U
Southwestern ★	U	U	U	U
Central ★	C	C	C	C
Western ★	U	U	U	U
Northern	—	—	+	—

Habitat: Prefers deciduous woods; secondarily coniferous forests, particularly the edges. Cottonwoods and alders along the mainland river systems in southeastern Alaska. Nests in a hole in the dead wood of trees or tree stubs.

Notes: Easily attracted to feeders.

MOUNTAIN CHICKADEE

MOUNTAIN CHICKADEE

(Parus gambeli)

LENGTH: 5½ IN.

Identification: Very similar to Black-capped Chickadee but has a conspicuous white line over the eye separated from white of the cheek. Sides are gray, lacking the buffy wash of Black-capped Chickadee. Song is 4-note whistle, and the *chick-a-dee* call is buzzier than that of Black-capped Chickadee, more like *chick-a-zhee-zhee-zhee.* Not known to breed in Alaska.

Status and Distribution:	SPRING	SUMMER	FALL	WINTER
Southeastern	+	+	+	+
Southcoastal	—	—	—	—
Southwestern	—	—	—	—
Central	—	—	—	—
Western	—	—	—	—
Northern	—	—	—	—

Habitat: Open coniferous forests, deciduous woods and thickets. Nests in tree holes. Has been found at sea level near Juneau and in the mountains near Skagway.

SIBERIAN TIT

(Parus cinctus)

LENGTH: 5½ IN.

Identification: Larger, longer-tailed, washed-out version of more frequently encountered Boreal Chickadee. Gray-brown cap, very little brown on the sides, white on the cheek extends onto sides of the neck.

Status and Distribution:	SPRING	SUMMER	FALL	WINTER
Southeastern	—	—	—	—
Southcoastal	—	—	—	—
Southwestern	—	—	—	—
Central ★	R	R	R	R
Western ★	R	R	R	R
Northern	—	—	—	—

Habitat: Breeding — spruce forests at or near timberline. In winter — willow and alder thickets along valley floors. Nests in the holes of dead trees.

Notes: Locally distributed and rarely seen.

BOREAL CHICKADEE

(Parus hudsonicus)

LENGTH: 5 IN.

Identification: Has brown cap, brown back and reddish-brown flanks, generally duller and paler than Chestnut-backed Chickadee. Voice is somewhat similar to Chestnut-backed Chickadee.

Habitat: Coniferous forests, deciduous-coniferous woodlands. Nests in holes in trees.

Status and Distribution:	SPRING	SUMMER	FALL	WINTER
Southeastern	—	+	—	+
Southcoastal ★	R	R	R	R
Southwestern ★	U	U	U	U
Central ★	C	C	C	C
Western ★	U	U	U	U
Northern	—	—	—	—

BOREAL CHICKADEE
(Pete Robinson)

SIBERIAN TIT
(John C. Pitcher)

CHESTNUT-BACKED CHICKADEE

CHESTNUT-BACKED CHICKADEE

(Parus rufescens)

LENGTH: 5 IN.

Identification: Chestnut back and sides and very dark brown cap. Darkest appearing chickadee. Voice is *tsIda-tsida-see.*

Habitat: Coniferous forests, deciduous trees and thickets. Nests in a hole in a tree.

Status and Distribution:	SPRING	SUMMER	FALL	WINTER
Southeastern ★	C	C	C	C
Southcoastal ★	C	C	C	C
Southwestern	—	—	—	—
Central	—	—	—	—
Western	—	—	—	—
Northern	—	—	—	—

Notes: Readily comes to feeders with sunflower seeds and suet.

FAMILY *SITTIDAE*

NUTHATCHES

(1)

These are small, tree-climbing birds with short tails and long, straight bills.

RED-BREASTED NUTHATCH
(Michael Hopiak, Cornell Lab of Ornithology)

RED-BREASTED NUTHATCH

(Sitta canadensis)

LENGTH: 4½ IN.

Identification: Short tail, straight, slender bill, blue-gray back and reddish underparts with a prominent white eye stripe are diagnostic. A worn bird may have much paler underparts. More often heard than seen. Call, audible for considerable distances, is a high nasal *yank-yank-yank.*

Habitat: Coniferous and deciduous trees. Nests in tree cavities.

Status and Distribution:	SPRING	SUMMER	FALL	WINTER
Southeastern ★	U	U	U	R
Southcoastal ★	R	R	U	R
Southwestern	+	—	+	—
Central ★	+	+	+	+
Western	—	—	+	—
Northern	—	—	—	—

Notes: Expert climber. Runs nimbly up and down tree trunks and on underside of limbs searching for insects, their eggs, or seeds of pine and spruce. Makes short flights to catch insects on the wing. Name derived from the habit of inserting nuts in bark crevices and hammering them with the bill until the shell is broken.

FAMILY *CERTHIIDAE*
CREEPERS
(1)

These are small, tree-climbing birds with long stiff tail feathers and a long slender bill.

BROWN CREEPER
(Certhia americana)
LENGTH: 5½ IN.

Identification: Dark brown streaked back, white breast, long slender down-curved bill and long tail are distinguishing. Blends in well with the bark of trees. Best way to detect presence of the creeper is the faint, high-pitched call, *ts-ts*. Golden-crowned Kinglet has similar call but usually with more syllables and not quite so pure.

Habitat: Coniferous forests, mixed deciduous-coniferous woodlands. Nests in trees behind a strip of loosened bark.

Status and Distribution:	SPRING	SUMMER	FALL	WINTER
Southeastern ★	U	U	U	U
Southcoastal ★	U	U	U	U
Southwestern ★	U	U	U	U
Central ★	R	R	R	R
Western	—	—	—	—
Northern	—	—	—	—

Notes: Searches cracks in tree bark for insects by starting at the bottom of a tree and working upwards in a spiral fashion; then flying to the base of the next tree to repeat the pattern. Sometimes forages along the underside of a horizontal branch.

BROWN CREEPER
(Ed Burroughs)

FAMILY *CINCLIDAE*

DIPPERS

(1)

These are stocky, wrenlike birds with short tails. They are perching birds that have adapted to feeding under water, with compact plumage, strong toes for holding onto rocks in a current, and special oil glands.

AMERICAN DIPPER

AMERICAN DIPPER

(Cinclus mexicanus)

LENGTH: 7½ IN.

Identification: Is solid gray with a short tail. Call is a loud, sharp *zeet* given singly or repeatedly.

Habitat: Fast moving streams and occasionally ponds, lakeshores, saltwater beaches, especially in winter when streams are frozen. Nests on a rock wall or perpendicular bank bordering a stream, often behind a waterfall.

Status and Distribution:	SPRING	SUMMER	FALL	WINTER
Southeastern ★	C	C	C	C
Southcoastal ★	C	C	C	C
Southwestern ★	C	C	C	C
Central ★	U	U	U	U
Western ★	U	U	U	U
Northern ★	R	R	R	R

Notes: Can walk, completely submerged, along the bottom of a rushing stream by grasping stones or rough places with long toes while probing under stones for aquatic insects, small fish and fish eggs.

FAMILY *TROGLODYTIDAE*

WRENS

(1)

These are small, restless, brownish birds that hold their tail straight up when not in flight. Represented in Alaska by the Winter Wren.

WINTER WREN

WINTER WREN

(Troglodytes troglodytes)

LENGTH: 4 IN.

Identification: All brown with the tail cocked over the back. Song is a rapid succession of high tinkling warbles and trills. Call is a loud *chimp-chimp,* easily imitated.

Habitat: The ground or low branches of heavily forested areas. Beaches in the Aleutian Islands and Pribilof Islands where it feeds among beach rocks and nests in cliffs and talus slopes. Usually nests among the roots of an upturned tree, in old stumps, brush piles, abandoned buildings.

Status and Distribution:	SPRING	SUMMER	FALL	WINTER
Southeastern ★	C	C	C	U
Southcoastal ★	U	U	U	U
Southwestern ★	C	C	C	C
Central	—	—	—	—
Western	—	—	—	—
Northern	—	+	—	—

FAMILY *MUSCICAPIDAE*

THRUSHES, OLD WORLD FLYCATCHERS AND WARBLERS, KINGLETS

(19 + 4)

The thrush, solitaire and bluebird group consists of songbirds characterized by large eyes and slender bills. Color varies widely among adults of these species but birds in juvenile plumage all have spotted breasts. This group encompasses some of the finest singers in the bird world. Old world flycatchers and warblers, and kinglets are small, drab perching birds with slender bills. They are very active and flit from branch to branch after insects.

AMERICAN ROBIN

(Turdus migratorius)

LENGTH: 10 IN.

Identification: Brick red breast, dark gray back and yellow bill are distinguishing. Male has blackish head and brighter underparts than female. The spotted-breasted young, very common in middle to late summer, are usually associated with adults. Song is a procession of 2- or 3-syllable phrases that suggest *cheer-up* or *cheerily* with variations in pitch. Common calls are the alarm *pip, pip* and the sibilant flight call *swee weep*.

Status and Distribution:	SPRING	SUMMER	FALL	WINTER
Southeastern ★	C	C	C	R
Southcoastal ★	C	C	C	R
Southwestern ★	C	C	C	—
Central ★	C	C	C	+
Western ★	C	C	C	—
Northern ★	R	R	R	—

Habitat: From above timberline to forest edges, muskegs, tundra and saltwater beaches and tidal flats. Nests in a crotch in a tree, less commonly on a horizontal limb or the ledge of a building or bridge.

AMERICAN ROBIN

EYE-BROWED THRUSH

(Turdus obscurus)

LENGTH: 7½ IN.

Identification: Warm olive-brown above, with a distinct white eye line, gray head and throat; orange breast and sides and white belly. Built like, but smaller than, an American Robin.

Habitat: Asiatic thrush that has occurred in the western and cental Aleutian Islands, in the Pribilof Islands, at Wales and at Barrow. Not known to breed in Alaska.

Status and Distribution:	SPRING	SUMMER	FALL	WINTER
Southeastern	—	—	—	—
Southcoastal	—	—	—	—
Southwestern	R	—	+	—
Central	—	—	—	—
Western	+	—	—	—
Northern	+	—	—	—

DUSKY THRUSH

(Turdus naumanni)

LENGTH: 9 IN.

Identification: Mottled blackish-brown above, with a bold white eye line and throat, dark breast band and spotted sides. Wings are washed with bright cinnamon color. Very distinctive bird. Not known to breed in Alaska.

Habitat: Asiatic thrush that has been found in the Aleutian Islands, on Saint Lawrence Island and at Barrow.

Status and Distribution:	SPRING	SUMMER	FALL	WINTER
Southeastern	—	—	—	—
Southcoastal	—	—	—	—
Southwestern	+	—	—	—
Central	—	—	—	—
Western	+	—	—	—
Northern	+	—	—	—

EYE-BROWED THRUSH
(John C. Pitcher)

DUSKY THRUSH
(John C. Pitcher)

VARIED THRUSH

(Ixoreus naevius)

LENGTH: 9½ IN.

Identification: Resembles robin in size, shape and orange-brown breast. Is slightly smaller and shorter-tailed than robin and has a broad black breast band (gray in the female), orange-buff line above and behind the eye, and orange-brown wing bars and wing patches. Light markings on wing are conspicuous in flight. Song, which is penetrating and has a ventriloquial quality, is a long, somewhat burry, whistled note, followed after a pause, by another note on a lower or higher pitch.

Status and Distribution:	SPRING	SUMMER	FALL	WINTER
Southeastern ★	C	C	C	U
Southcoastal ★	C	C	C	U
Southwestern ★	C	C	C	U
Central ★	C	C	C	—
Western ★	C	C	C	—
Northern	+	—	—	—

Habitat: Forests from sea level to alpine; prefers shady damp forests. Usually nests in a conifer from 5 to 15 feet above the ground. Forages on the tundra, muskegs, tidal flats and beaches.

VARIED THRUSH
(Jack VanHoesen)

HERMIT THRUSH

HERMIT THRUSH

(Catharus guttatus)

LENGTH: 7 IN.

Identification: Three brown, spotted-breasted thrushes occur in Alaska. Hermit Thrush is distinguished by reddish tail which is often slowly raised and lowered. Song is loud, slow, repetitive phrases spiraling down the scale. Call is a soft *cheep* or *chup-chup,* or catlike mew.

Habitat: Edges of coniferous forests, mixed deciduous-coniferous woodlands, shrub thickets. Nests usually on the ground; sometimes in a tree.

Status and Distribution:	SPRING	SUMMER	FALL	WINTER
Southeastern ★	C	C	C	—
Southcoastal ★	C	C	C	—
Southwestern ★	C	C	C	—
Central ★	U	U	U	—
Western ★	R	R	R	—
Northern	+	+	—	—

SWAINSON'S THRUSH

(Catharus ustulatus)

LENGTH: 7 IN.

Identification: Distinguished from other spotted Alaskan thrushes by entirely brown back and tail and buffy eye ring and face. Sings almost continuously in the morning and evening and often throughout the night. Song is breezy, flutelike phrases starting with a clear long note on 1 pitch, then spiraling up the scale, becoming fainter until the last notes fade out. Call is a *whit.*

Status and Distribution:	SPRING	SUMMER	FALL	WINTER
Southeastern ★	C	C	C	—
Southcoastal ★	U	U	U	—
Southwestern ★	U	U	U	—
Central ★	C	C	C	—
Western ★	R	R	R	—
Northern	—	+	—	—

Habitat: Mixed deciduous-coniferous woodlands, shrub thickets, coniferous forests. Nests low in trees or bushes close to the trunk.

SWAINSON'S THRUSH

GRAY-CHEEKED THRUSH
(Doug Murphy)

GRAY-CHEEKED THRUSH

(Catharus minimus)

LENGTH: 7½ IN.

Identification: All brown above with grayish cheeks, lacking the conspicuous buffy eye ring of Swainson's Thrush. Song is a thin nasal *wee-oh, chee, chee, wee-oh,* that usually rises abruptly at the end. Call is *wee-a* and, when alarmed, *chuck.*

Status and Distribution:	SPRING	SUMMER	FALL	WINTER
Southeastern ★	U	U	U	—
Southcoastal ★	U	U	U	—
Southwestern ★	C	C	C	—
Central ★	C	C	C	—
Western ★	C	C	C	—
Northern ★	C	C	C	—

Habitat: Mixed deciduous-coniferous woodlands, shrub thickets, coniferous forests. Forages for food in open areas near thickets and on the tundra. Nests in bushes or low trees.

MOUNTAIN BLUEBIRD

(Sialia currucoides)

LENGTH: 7 IN.

Identification: Male is bright sky-blue all over. Female is much duller than the male with an overall brownish appearance but with enough blue wash on the wings and tail to be recognizable.

Status and Distribution:	SPRING	SUMMER	FALL	WINTER
Southeastern	R	—	R	+
Southcoastal	—	—	+	—
Southwestern	—	—	—	—
Central ★	R	R	+	—
Western	—	—	+	—
Northern	+	—	—	—

Habitat: Open woodlands. Perches conspicuously on dead limbs, tree tops, fences, utility wires. Nests in tree holes, rock crevices and in buildings.

MOUNTAIN BLUEBIRD
(Tom Ulrich)

NORTHERN WHEATEAR
Female
(Dick Wood)

NORTHERN WHEATEAR

(Oenanthe oenanthe)

LENGTH: 6 IN.

Identification: In all plumages shows a white rump patch and black-and-white tail pattern like an inverted "T". Breeding male has black wings, black face patch and gray back. Young are buffy-brown, paler below. Song is short, abrupt twitter, sounding like an ungreased door hinge; alarm call is *tuck, tuck.*

Status and Distribution:	SPRING	SUMMER	FALL	WINTER
Southeastern	—	—	+	—
Southcoastal ★	R	R	R	—
Southwestern	R	—	R	—
Central ★	U	U	U	—
Western ★	C	U	C	—
Northern ★	U	U	U	—

Habitat: Above timberline, rock fields in the tundra and rocky mountain ridges. Nests in crevices under rocks or in rubble.

Notes: Has a habit of frequently bobbing, spreading its tail feathers, and moving its tail up and down.

BLUETHROAT
(Kenneth Fink)

NORTHERN WHEATEAR
(Martin Grosnick)

BLUETHROAT

(Luscinia svecica)

LENGTH: 5½ IN.

Identification: Summer male has bright blue throat patch with a chestnut-colored spot in the center. Both sexes are plain brown above, with rusty patches at the base of the tail, conspicuous in flight. Female has a white throat bordered by black and a white eye stripe. No other plain brown thicket-inhabiting bird with these characteristics occurs in Alaska. Musical song is introduced by notes sounding like *dip, dip, dip*; alarm call is *buyt-tock.*

Status and Distribution:	SPRING	SUMMER	FALL	WINTER
Southeastern	—	—	—	—
Southcoastal	—	—	—	—
Southwestern	—	—	—	—
Central	—	—	—	—
Western ★	R	R	R	—
Northern ★	R	R	R	—

Habitat: Shrub thickets in the uplands and foothills of western and northern Alaska. Nests on the ground.

SIBERIAN RUBYTHROAT

(Luscinia calliope)

LENGTH: 6 IN.

Identification: Much like Bluethroat in appearance, habits, and habitat, but larger. Male has bright red throat and black-and-white mustaches. Female has white throat, not bordered on chest by dark as in female Bluethroat, and both sexes have white lines both over and under the eye.

Status and Distribution:	SPRING	SUMMER	FALL	WINTER
Southeastern	—	—	—	—
Southcoastal	—	—	—	—
Southwestern	R	—	+	—
Central	—	—	—	—
Western	+	—	—	—
Northern	—	—	—	—

Habitat: Asiatic species that has been found in the western Aleutian Islands, Pribilof Islands and at Gambell on Saint Lawrence Island. Not known to breed in Alaska.

SIBERIAN RUBYTHROAT
(Robert Schulmeister)

TOWNSEND'S SOLITAIRE

TOWNSEND'S SOLITAIRE

(Myadestes townsendi)

LENGTH: 8½ IN.

Identification: Slim gray bird with short bill, long tail and white eye ring. In flight shows a conspicuous buffy wing patch and white tail edges. Song of fluted rising and falling phrases is loud and melodious; call is a bell-like *heep*.

Status and Distribution:	SPRING	SUMMER	FALL	WINTER
Southeastern ★	R	R	R	+
Southcoastal ★	R	R	R	+
Southwestern	—	—	—	—
Central ★	R	R	R	+
Western	—	—	—	—
Northern	—	—	—	—

Habitat: Open forests usually near the timberline, especially during breeding season. Nests on the ground under overhanging banks, rocks, tree roots.

Notes: Solitary bird not often observed, probably because of its retiring habits and rather sparse distribution.

ARCTIC WARBLER

(Phylloscopus borealis)

LENGTH: 4¾ IN.

Identification: Plain, rather like a Warbling Vireo although the 2 species do not occur together. Has dark line through the eye and light greenish-yellow stripe over the eye. Has pale legs. Of the species with which Arctic Warbler occurs, perhaps it is most similar to Orange-crowned Warbler but Arctic is brown above and white below rather than greenish. Song is a trill introduced by a note sounding like *zick* or *zick-zick-zick*; call is also *zick* or *zirrup*.

Status and Distribution:	SPRING	SUMMER	FALL	WINTER
Southeastern	—	—	—	—
Southcoastal	—	—	—	—
Southwestern ★	U	U	U	—
Central ★	C	C	C	—
Western ★	C	C	C	—
Northern ★	C	C	C	—

Habitat: Willow thickets. Nests on the ground in grass or moss in willow thickets.

ARCTIC WARBLER
(Doug Murphy)

DUSKY WARBLER

(Phylloscopus fuscatus)

LENGTH: 4½ IN.

Identification: Small, drab old world warbler best identified by absence of greenish or yellowish colors; and by fine bill, buffy line above eye, rounded tail tip; and by distinctive harsh call *tsack* which it utters frequently. This species skulks and is difficult to observe.

Habitat: Has been found on Shemya Island in western Aleutians and at Gambell on Saint Lawrence Island. Breeds in northern Asia.

Status and Distribution:	SPRING	SUMMER	FALL	WINTER
Southeastern	—	—	—	—
Southcoastal	—	—	—	—
Southwestern	—	—	+	—
Coastal	—	—	—	—
Western	+	—	—	—
Northern	—	—	—	—

DUSKY WARBLER
(John C. Pitcher)

MIDDENDORFF'S GRASSHOPPER-WARBLER
(Wild Bird Society of Japan)

MIDDENDORFF'S GRASSHOPPER-WARBLER

(Locustella ochotensis)

LENGTH: 6 IN.

Identification: Rather large old world warbler with a whitish line over the eye and a white-tipped, fan-shaped tail. Dark olive-brown above; whitish below with an olivaceous wash on the sides. Fall immatures have a buffy yellow throat, indistinctly streaked breast and white-tipped tail. A skulker, this warbler keeps close to ground cover and is difficult to flush.

Habitat: Has been found in western Aleutians and on Nunivak and Saint Lawrence islands in western Alaska. Breeds in northeast Asia.

Status and Distribution:	SPRING	SUMMER	FALL	WINTER
Southeastern	—	—	—	—
Southcoastal	—	—	—	—
Southwestern	—	—	+	—
Central	—	—	—	—
Western	+	—	+	—
Northern	—	—	—	—

GOLDEN-CROWNED KINGLET
(Dennis Paulson)

GOLDEN-CROWNED KINGLET

(Regulus satrapa)

LENGTH: 3½ IN.

Identification: Olive-green and gray with a white eyebrow stripe which distinguishes this species from Ruby-crowned Kinglet and any other small species. Male has yellow and orange crown with black border; female has a yellow crown with black border. Voice is thin *see-see-see*, so high-pitched that some people cannot hear it.

Status and Distribution:	SPRING	SUMMER	FALL	WINTER
Southeastern ★	C	C	C	U
Southcoastal ★	U	U	U	U
Southwestern ★	U	U	U	U
Central	—	R	R	—
Western	—	—	—	—
Northern	—	—	—	—

Habitat: Coniferous forests. Nests in branches of conifers.

Notes: Flicks its wings almost constantly. Feeds mostly on insects and their eggs and larvae found on conifer branches.

RUBY-CROWNED KINGLET

(Regulus calendula)

LENGTH: 4 IN.

Identification: Olive above and gray below. Conspicuous white eye ring and lack of head stripes separate this species from Golden-crowned Kinglet. Ruby crown of male usually concealed. Song is usually in 3 parts: *tee tee tee, chur chur chur, teedadee teedadee teedadee.* First notes are high, like those of the Golden-crowned Kinglet, but the rest is a loud, finchlike warble. Call is a harsh, usually 2-syllabled chatter.

Status and Distribution:	SPRING	SUMMER	FALL	WINTER
Southeastern ★	C	C	C	+
Southcoastal ★	C	C	C	+
Southwestern ★	R	R	R	—
Central ★	U	U	U	—
Western ★	U	U	U	—
Northern	+	—	+	—

Habitat: Coniferous forests, mixed coniferous-deciduous woodlands, shrub thickets. Widespread in Alaska occurring wherever spruce forests exist. Nests in conifers usually 20-60 feet from the ground.

Notes: Characteristically flicks its wings nervously.

GRAY-SPOTTED FLYCATCHER
(John C. Pitcher)

RUBY-CROWNED KINGLET

GRAY-SPOTTED FLYCATCHER

(Muscicapa griseisticta)

LENGTH: 4½ IN.

Identification: Drab, about the size of an *Empidonax*. Perches upright like a Tyrant Flycatcher but has streaked underparts and white spectacles.

Habitat: Asiatic flycatcher that has occurred in the western Aleutian Islands. Not known to breed in Alaska.

Status and Distribution:	SPRING	SUMMER	FALL	WINTER
Southeastern	—	—	—	—
Southcoastal	—	—	—	—
Southwestern	R	—	—	—
Central	—	—	—	—
Western	—	—	—	—
Northern	—	—	—	—

RED-BREASTED FLYCATCHER
Male, right; Female, left
(Hans Reinhard, Bruce Coleman, Inc.)

RED-BREASTED FLYCATCHER

(Ficedula parva)

LENGTH: 4½ IN.

Identification: Small old world flycatcher best distinguished by black tail and white patches at base of the outer tail feathers. Frequently flicks tail upward. Adult male has orange throat, grayish head, back and upper breast, white belly and under tail coverts. Females are grayish brown above, white below, with a creamy wash on the throat and breast.

Habitat: Has been found in western Aleutians on Shemya and Attu islands and at Gambell on Saint Lawrence Island. Breeds in northern Eurasia.

Status and Distribution:	SPRING	SUMMER	FALL	WINTER
Southeastern	—	—	—	—
Southcoastal	—	—	—	—
Southwestern	+	—	—	—
Central	—	—	—	—
Western	+	—	—	—
Northern	—	—	—	—

FAMILY *PRUNELLIDAE*
ACCENTORS
(1)

This Old World family has only 1 representative in Alaska, the Siberian Accentor.

SIBERIAN ACCENTOR
(Prunella montanella)
LENGTH: 6 IN.

Identification: Ground-dwelling bird with a thin bill. Dark reddish-brown above, grayer at the rump and tail, and warm buffy to whitish below with streaked sides. Has distinct buffy eye stripe and black mask through the eyes.

Habitat: Asiatic species that has occurred on Saint Lawrence Island and at Point Barrow. Not known to breed in Alaska.

Status and Distribution:	SPRING	SUMMER	FALL	WINTER
Southeastern	—	—	—	—
Southcoastal	—	—	+	—
Southwestern	—	—	—	—
Central	—	—	—	—
Western	—	—	+	—
Northern	—	—	+	—

SIBERIAN ACCENTOR
Immature
(John C. Pitcher)

FAMILY *MOTACILLIDAE*

WAGTAILS, PIPITS

(8 + 1)

These are sparrow-sized ground birds with slender bills that walk instead of hop. They wag their tails almost constantly. All have dark tails and white outer tail feathers.

WHITE WAGTAIL

(Motacilla alba)

LENGTH: 7 IN.

Identification: Gray above, white below with a black crown and throat vaguely like a chickadee; the female with less black. When disturbed, flies up in great undulating arcs uttering a loud *tizzick.*

Habitat: Open areas with short vegetation usually along the coast. Nests near or on the ground in crevices or niches in old buildings.

Status and Distribution:	SPRING	SUMMER	FALL	WINTER
Southeastern	—	—	—	—
Southcoastal	—	—	—	—
Southwestern	+	—	—	—
Central	+	—	—	—
Western ★	R	R	R	—
Northern	R	—	R	—

Notes: Slender, hyperactive ground bird that wags its very long tail constantly. Wary. Recent taxonomic splitting of White and Black-backed wagtails has resulted in records of "White" Wagtails in southeastern, southcoastal and southwestern Alaska that cannot now be assigned to species.

WHITE WAGTAIL
(Jim Erckmann)

BLACK-BACKED WAGTAIL
Female
(Wild Bird Society of Japan)

BLACK-BACKED WAGTAIL
Male
(Wild Bird Society of Japan)

BLACK-BACKED WAGTAIL

(Motacilla lugens)

LENGTH: 7 IN.

Identification: Adult male differs from White Wagtail by having an all black or mostly black back, more black on the nape and may have some dark shading on the face. Adult female has a white chin whereas almost all White Wagtails have a black chin. Adult black-backed of both sexes has a much larger white wing patch than White Wagtail. After the fall molt, males and females of both species are gray-backed with a white throat which makes identification very difficult. Juveniles of both species are virtually identical.

Status and Distribution:	SPRING	SUMMER	FALL	WINTER
Southeastern	—	+	—	—
Southcoastal	—	—	—	—
Southwestern	R	—	—	—
Central	—	—	—	—
Western	+	—	—	—
Northern	—	—	—	—

Habitat: Much less common than White Wagtail. Most sightings have been in spring on western Aleutian Islands.

GRAY WAGTAIL
(John C. Pitcher)

GRAY WAGTAIL

(Motacilla cinerea)

LENGTH: 7 IN.

Identification: Has pale rump and white wing bars conspicuous only in flight. Summer male is distinguished from Yellow Wagtail by black throat. Females and winter birds have a white throat but differ from Yellow Wagtail in the gray rather than olive backs. Call is sharper and more metallic than those of Yellow and White wagtails, but is double-noted like White Wagtails'.

Status and Distribution:	SPRING	SUMMER	FALL	WINTER
Southeastern	—	—	—	—
Southcoastal	—	—	—	—
Southwestern	+	—	+	—
Central	—	—	—	—
Western	+	—	—	—
Northern	—	—	—	—

Habitat: Asiatic species that has occurred in the Aleutian Islands, Pribilof Islands, and on Saint Lawrence Island. Not known to breed in Alaska.

YELLOW WAGTAIL
(Motacilla flava)
LENGTH: 6½ IN.

Identification: Olive-gray back, white eye line and yellow underparts are diagnostic. Call, a loud single note, *tzeep*, is often heard as the bird flies overhead.

Status and Distribution:	SPRING	SUMMER	FALL	WINTER
Southeastern	—	—	—	—
Southcoastal	—	+	—	—
Southwestern	R	—	R	—
Central	+	+	+	—
Western ★	C	C	C	—
Northern ★	U	U	U	—

Habitat: Willow thickets on the tundra. Nests on open tundra under grass, overhanging banks.

Notes: Tail is constantly in motion.

YELLOW WAGTAIL
(Henry Kyllingstad)

WATER PIPIT

WATER PIPIT
(Anthus spinoletta)
LENGTH: 6½ IN.

Identification: Resembles a sparrow because of the brown, streaked color, but is slender and longer-tailed than a sparrow, walks instead of hops, and has a very slender bill. In flight the white outer tail feathers are conspicuous. Has a plain back unlike the other, much rarer, Alaskan pipits. Song is a series of simple notes, given in flight; call is a soft *tsi-tsip*, hence "pipit".

Status and Distribution:	SPRING	SUMMER	FALL	WINTER
Southeastern ★	C	C	C	+
Southcoastal ★	C	C	C	+
Southwestern ★	C	C	C	+
Central ★	C	C	C	—
Western ★	C	C	C	—
Northern ★	C	C	C	—

Habitat: Tundra, tidal flats and beaches, fields, alpine meadows, lakeshores, ponds, rivers and streams. Nests on the ground on drier ridges and foothills and above timberline.

Notes: One of the most common and widely distributed birds in Alaska. Tail is wagged frequently but not continuously.

OLIVE TREE-PIPIT

(Anthus hodgsoni)

LENGTH: 6½ IN.

Identification: Only pipit with an obscurely streaked olive back and strongly streaked breast. Prominent eye stripe ends just behind the eye. Call is similar to but thinner than that of the Red-throated Pipit.

Habitat: Asiatic species that has occurred in the western Aleutian Islands and on Saint Lawrence Island. Not known to breed in Alaska.

Status and Distribution:	SPRING	SUMMER	FALL	WINTER
Southeastern	—	—	—	—
Southcoastal	—	—	—	—
Southwestern	+	—	+	—
Central	—	—	—	—
Western	+	—	—	—
Northern	—	—	—	—

OLIVE TREE-PIPIT
(John C. Pitcher)

PECHORA PIPIT
(John C. Pitcher)

PECHORA PIPIT

(Anthus gustavi)

LENGTH: 5¾ IN.

Identification: Heavily striped breast and back, with 2 distinctive whitish streaks on the back, and buff rather than white outer tail feathers are diagnostic. Call is a hard 1- or 2-noted *pwit*, given 2 to 3 times in series.

Status and Distribution:	SPRING	SUMMER	FALL	WINTER
Southeastern	—	—	—	—
Southcoastal	—	—	—	—
Southwestern	+	—	—	—
Central	—	—	—	—
Western	+	—	—	—
Northern	—	—	—	—

Habitat: Asiatic pipit that has occurred at Gambell on Saint Lawrence Island, and on Attu Island in the Aleutians. Not known to brood in Alaska.

RED-THROATED PIPIT

(Anthus cervinus)

LENGTH: 6 IN.

Identification: In summer can be distinguished from the Water Pipit by the reddish or pinkish color on the face, throat and breast, especially in the male, and the heavily striped back. Call is *teez,* similar to a Yellow Wagtail.

Status and Distribution:	SPRING	SUMMER	FALL	WINTER
Southeastern	—	—	—	—
Southcoastal	—	—	R	—
Southwestern	R	—	R	—
Central	—	—	—	—
Western ★	U	U	U	—
Northern	—	—	+	—

Habitat: Shrubby areas on the tundra. Nests on the ground in tussock-sheltered areas.

RED-THROATED PIPIT
(John C. Pitcher)

FAMILY *BOMBYCILLIDAE* WAXWINGS (2)

These are crested birds with black masks and yellow tips to the tails. The red waxlike spots on the wings of the adult give the birds their name.

BOHEMIAN WAXWING

(Bombycilla garrulus)

LENGTH: 8 IN.

Identification: Brownish, with a black eye patch, yellow tail tip, and a crest. Larger than Cedar Waxwing, with chestnut rather than whitish undertail coverts and with small white wing patches. Belly is very gray in Bohemian Waxwing; yellowish buffy in Cedar Waxwing. Call is a high and sibilant rattle, often given in flight.

Habitat: Breeding — wet muskeg. Nests in a conifer. In winter — usually any habitat where there are trees or shrubs with berries.

Status and Distribution:	SPRING	SUMMER	FALL	WINTER
Southeastern ★	U	R	U	U
Southcoastal ★	U	U	U	R
Southwestern ★	R	R	R	—
Central ★	C	C	C	R
Western ★	R	R	R	—
Northern	—	—	—	—

Notes: Feeds on fruits and insects. Is an expert flycatcher and takes most of its prey on the wing like flycatchers or circles high in the air like swallows. In winter often gathers in flocks in the towns of southeastern Alaska wherever there are cultivated shrubs with fruit.

BOHEMIAN WAXWING

CEDAR WAXWING
(Michael Hopiak, Cornell Lab of Ornithology)

CEDAR WAXWING

(Bombycilla cedrorum)

LENGTH: 7 IN.

Identification: Smaller than the Bohemian Waxwing with a dull pale yellowish belly and undertail and no white in the wings. Call is similar to the Bohemian Waxwing but higher pitched and even more sibilant.

Habitat: Openings and edges of coniferous forests. Nests in trees, usually in isolated trees in open areas.

Status and Distribution:	SPRING	SUMMER	FALL	WINTER
Southeastern ★	R	R	R	+
Southcoastal	—	—	+	—
Southwestern	—	—	—	—
Central	—	—	—	—
Western	—	—	—	—
Northern	—	—	—	—

FAMILY *LANIIDAE*

SHRIKES

(2)

Shrikes are songbirds with hook-tipped bills that prey on smaller birds and rodents.

NORTHERN SHRIKE

(Lanius excubitor)

LENGTH: 10 IN.

Identification: Robin-sized gray bird with a black mask and black wings and tail that normally perches at the top of a tree or post. Has a hooked bill and the habits of a bird of prey. Song is variable, and has been described as similar to a canary, parakeet, crow and robin.

Habitat: Openings and edges of coniferous forests and mixed deciduous-coniferous woodlands, shrub thickets on the tundra, trees near fresh and saltwater marshes. Usually nests in a small deciduous tree. May be found singly or in pairs in spruce forests over much of Alaska.

Status and Distribution:	SPRING	SUMMER	FALL	WINTER
Southeastern	U	—	U	U
Southcoastal ★	U	U	U	U
Southwestern ★	U	U	U	U
Central ★	U	U	U	R
Western ★	U	U	U	U
Northern ★	U	U	U	+

Notes: Feeds on small rodents and birds. Impales prey on thorns, broken twigs, barbs of barbed-wire fences, or suspends prey from the crotch of a tree. When hunting is good, kills and hangs up more than can be eaten at once, hence the nickname "butcher bird."

NORTHERN SHRIKE

BROWN SHRIKE
(S.S. Menon, Bruce Coleman, Inc.)

BROWN SHRIKE

(Lanius cristatus)

LENGTH: 8 IN.

Identification: Much smaller than Northern Shrike. Reddish brown with black mask and buffy sides. Females and immatures have narrow, dark wavy bars on the sides and across the breast.

Habitat: Has been found at Gambell on Saint Lawrence Island, and on Shemya Island in western Aleutians. Breeds in eastern Asia.

Status and Distribution:	SPRING	SUMMER	FALL	WINTER
Southeastern	—	—	—	—
Southcoastal	—	—	—	—
Southwestern	—	—	+	—
Central	—	—	—	—
Western	+	—	—	—
Northern	—	—	—	—

FAMILY *STURNIDAE*
STARLINGS
(1)

These birds, related to crows, are Old World equivalents of North American blackbirds. One, the European Starling, is now well established in Alaska.

EUROPEAN STARLING

EUROPEAN STARLING
(Sturnus vulgaris)
LENGTH: 8 IN.

Identification: Resembles a blackbird but has a short, stubby tail. From mid-winter to mid-summer a yellow bill separates it from any blackbird. Plumage is highly iridescent, with flashes of green and violet. In late summer bill turns dusky and the plumage becomes white-spotted, unlike any blackbird. In flight short tail is obvious, and wings are more pointed than those of blackbirds. Flight is also more rapid and direct, reminiscent of a Bohemian Waxwing.

Habitat: Open woodlands, fields, beaches and tidal flats, garbage dumps. Nests in natural cavities such as woodpecker holes, Bank Swallow holes, in buildings.

Status and Distribution:	SPRING	SUMMER	FALL	WINTER
Southeastern ★	U	U	U	U
Southcoastal	R	—	R	R
Southwestern	—	—	—	—
Central ★	R	R	R	+
Western	+	+	+	—
Northern	—	+	—	—

Notes: European Starling was considered hypothetical in Alaska by Gabrielson and Lincoln (1959). They stated that its phenomenal spread was almost certain to eventually include parts of Alaska. Their prediction has come true, and the species is now well established in several parts of the State (Kessel and Gibson, 1978).

FAMILY *VIREONIDAE*

VIREOS

(3)

These birds look like rather plain warblers but have heavier bills.

RED-EYED VIREO
(Gary Jones)

RED-EYED VIREO

(Vireo olivaceus)
LENGTH: 6 IN.

Identification: A typical vireo, plain and slow-moving, when compared with the active warblers. Olive-green above and white below, with a distinctly gray cap and black-and-white eye stripes. Song is a series of 2- or 3-syllable whistles, given monotonously for hours.

Habitat: Deciduous trees mostly along the mainland rivers of southeastern Alaska. Nests in forked branches of a tree.

Status and Distribution:	SPRING	SUMMER	FALL	WINTER
Southeastern ★	R	R	R	—
Southcoastal	—	+	+	—
Southwestern	—	—	—	—
Central	—	—	—	—
Western	—	—	—	—
Northern	—	—	—	—

WARBLING VIREO

(Vireo gilvus)
LENGTH: 5 IN.

Identification: Dull brownish olive above and whitish below, with a white eye line and no other distinctive marks. Drabness alone aids identification. The dullest Yellow Warblers are still obviously yellowish, Orange-crowned Warblers are greenish, and neither has a white line over the eye. Song is a short warble, with a characteristic up-and-down pattern.

Habitat: Deciduous trees mostly along the mainland rivers of southeastern Alaska. Nests in forked branches of trees.

Status and Distribution:	SPRING	SUMMER	FALL	WINTER
Southeastern ★	U	U	U	—
Southcoastal	+	+	+	—
Southwestern	—	—	—	—
Central	—	—	—	—
Western	—	—	—	—
Northern	—	—	—	—

WARBLING VIREO
(Edgar Jones)

PHILADELPHIA VIREO
(Betty Cottrille, Cornell Lab of Ornithology)

PHILADELPHIA VIREO

(Vireo philadelphicus)

LENGTH: 4¾ IN.

Identification: Similar in size and shape to Warbling Vireo. Has yellowish throat and breast; Warbling Vireo is always whitish on throat and on center of breast. Philadelphia has a black eyeline that extends to the bill; Warbling Vireo lacks this line. Song is series of 2- or 3-syllable whistles like the Red-eyed Vireo but higher pitched and slower.

Habitat: Has been found at Eagle in central Alaska and on Middleton Island in the southcoastal region. Breeds in western and southern Canada and northeastern United States.

Status and Distribution:	SPRING	SUMMER	FALL	WINTER
Southeastern	—	—	—	—
Southcoastal	—	—	+	—
Southwestern	—	—	—	—
Central	—	+	—	—
Western	—	—	—	—
Northern	—	—	—	—

FAMILY *EMBERIZIDAE*

WOOD WARBLERS, BLACKBIRDS, TANAGERS, SPARROWS, BUNTINGS

(40 + 11)

This is the largest bird family in the world. More than 150 species occur in North America and of these 51 have been found in Alaska.

TENNESSEE WARBLER

(Vermivora peregrina)

LENGTH: 5 IN.

Identification: Bright olive-green above and white below, with a gray head and white eye line. Red-eyed Vireo is much larger with more distinct head stripes. In fall the breast is suffused with yellowish and the head becomes greenish, rather like an Orange-crowned Warbler, but yellower and with a more distinct eye line. The undertail is always white; it is greenish-yellow in the Orange-crowned Warbler. Song begins with buzzy paired notes in series and ends in a dry trill.

Status and Distribution:	SPRING	SUMMER	FALL	WINTER
Southeastern ★	R	R	R	—
Southcoastal	+	—	+	—
Southwestern	—	—	—	—
Central	—	+	+	—
Western	—	—	—	—
Northern	—	—	—	—

Habitat: Deciduous and mixed deciduous-coniferous woodlands. Nests on or near the ground often in a muskeg.

TENNESSEE WARBLER
(Edgar Jones)

ORANGE-CROWNED WARBLER
(Edgar Jones)

ORANGE-CROWNED WARBLER

(Vermivora celata)

LENGTH: 5 IN.

Identification: Only dingy, greenish-yellow warbler with no distinct markings. Crown patch is rarely visible. Only a dull female Yellow Warbler might be confused with an Orange-crowned Warbler but the Yellow Warbler is always more yellow on the breast and has yellow tail patches. Song is a simple trill going up or down the scale toward the end. Call is a sharp *stick.*

Habitat: Deciduous woodlands, shrub thickets, coniferous forest edges where low deciduous growth is present. Nests on the ground or in low shrubs.

Status and Distribution:	SPRING	SUMMER	FALL	WINTER
Southeastern ★	C	C	C	—
Southcoastal ★	C	C	C	—
Southwestern ★	C	C	C	—
Central ★	C	C	C	—
Western ★	U	U	U	—
Northern	+	+	+	—

YELLOW WARBLER

(Dendroica petechia)

LENGTH: 5 IN.

Identification: Only clear yellow bird with yellow markings in the outer tail feathers found in Alaska. Adult male has reddish streaks on the breast, but in female and young the streaks are faint or absent. Has a lively cheerful song of single and double whistles, *sweet-sweet-sweet-sweet-setta-see-see-whew!* Call is loud down-slurred *cheep.*

Habitat: Deciduous woodlands and shrub thickets. Nests in shrubs or trees, usually near the ground.

Status and Distribution:	SPRING	SUMMER	FALL	WINTER
Southeastern ★	C	C	C	—
Southcoastal ★	U	U	U	—
Southwestern ★	C	C	C	—
Central ★	C	C	C	—
Western ★	C	C	C	—
Northern ★	R	R	R	—

MAGNOLIA WARBLER

(Dendroica magnolia)

LENGTH: 5 IN.

Identification: Male is gray and black above with a gray head and black cheek patch and bright yellow below, heavily striped with black. Rump is yellow and wings have an extensive white patch. Tail crossed by a band of white is diagnostic in any plumage. Female and fall immatures are much duller with reduced striping beneath. Usually has a distinct eye ring.

Status and Distribution:	SPRING	SUMMER	FALL	WINTER
Southeastern	—	+	+	—
Southcoastal	—	—	—	—
Southwestern	—	—	—	—
Central	—	—	—	—
Western	—	—	+	—
Northern	—	—	+	—

MAGNOLIA WARBLER
(John C. Pitcher)

Habitat: Coniferous forests and mixed deciduous-coniferous woodlands. Not known to breed in Alaska.

YELLOW WARBLER
(Edgar Jones)

CAPE MAY WARBLER
(Dennis Paulson)

CAPE MAY WARBLER

(Dendroica tigrina)

LENGTH: 5 IN.

Identification: Summer male is distinguished by chestnut cheek patches, olive back and bright yellow underparts heavily striped with black. Female and fall birds are very dull, olive above with a vague yellowish rump patch, lightly but extensively streaked below and with a distinctive yellow patch around the ear area.

Habitat: Has occurred at Fairbanks, Haines and Point Barrow. Not known to breed in Alaska.

Status and Distribution:	SPRING	SUMMER	FALL	WINTER
Southeastern	—	—	+	—
Southcoastal	—	—	—	—
Southwestern	—	—	—	—
Central	—	—	+	—
Western	—	—	—	—
Northern	+	—	—	—

YELLOW-RUMPED WARBLER

(Dendroica coronata)

LENGTH: 5½ IN.

Identification: Brightly marked with black streaks on an overall gray background above. Throat and belly are white, breast is black. Crown, a patch at either side of the breast and the rump are bright yellow; these 4 yellow patches are unique to this species. Female is duller, and young in the fall are very drab brownish-gray, with scattered streaks and the obvious yellow rump. Song is a tinkling trill that either rises or falls in pitch at the end.

Status and Distribution:	SPRING	SUMMER	FALL	WINTER
Southeastern ★	C	C	C	+
Southcoastal ★	U	U	U	+
Southwestern ★	U	U	U	—
Central ★	C	C	C	—
Western ★	C	C	C	—
Northern	+	+	—	—

Habitat: Coniferous forests, mixed deciduous-coniferous woodlands, shrub thickets. Nests in a conifer, usually 4 to 10 feet above the ground.

YELLOW-RUMPED WARBLER

TOWNSEND'S WARBLER
(John C. Pitcher)

TOWNSEND'S WARBLER

(Dendroica townsendi)

LENGTH: 5 IN.

Identification: Only regularly occurring Alaska warbler that is olive above and yellow below with dark streaks. Male has a black throat, cheek patch and cap. Female has an olive cap and cheek and yellow throat. Song is *weazy weazy weazy twea* or *dee dee dee-de de*; call is soft *chip.*

Habitat: Coniferous forests, mixed deciduous-coniferous woodlands. Nests in a conifer.

Status and Distribution:	SPRING	SUMMER	FALL	WINTER
Southeastern ★	C	C	C	—
Southcoastal ★	U	U	U	—
Southwestern	—	—	+	—
Central ★	C	C	C	—
Western	—	—	—	—
Northern	—	—	+	—

BLACKPOLL WARBLER
(Doug Murphy)

BLACKPOLL WARBLER

(Dendroica striata)

LENGTH: 5½ IN.

Identification: Breeding male is olive above and white below, with black streaks. Has a black cap and white cheeks. Female and fall male are drab olive-green with white wing bars, liberally streaked on back and sides. Lacks the distinctive head pattern of female Townsend's Warbler and the yellow patches of fall Yellow-rumped Warbler. Only streaked warbler with pale legs. Song is a high pitched *zi-zi-zi* repeated 6 to 12 times; call is low *chip* and thin *zeep.*

Habitat: Coniferous forests, mixed deciduous-coniferous woodlands, shrub thickets. Nests in small conifers or on the ground near conifers.

Status and Distribution:	SPRING	SUMMER	FALL	WINTER
Southeastern	R	—	R	—
Southcoastal ★	R	R	R	—
Southwestern ★	C	C	C	—
Central ★	U	U	U	—
Western ★	C	C	C	—
Northern	+	+	+	—

NORTHERN WATERTHRUSH
(Dennis Heikes)

NORTHERN WATERTHRUSH

(Seiurus noveboracensis)

LENGTH: 6 IN.

Identification: Dark brown above and heavily streaked below with a prominent buffy eyebrow stripe. Much more vividly marked than a pipit and teeters more like a Spotted Sandpiper. Song is a sequence of quickly uttered, identical, short, chattering phrases repeated many times and speeded toward the end. Call is a loud, sharp *chink.*

Habitat: Deciduous trees bordering streams, lakes, ponds and swamps. Nests on the ground beneath logs, roots, stumps or in a mossy bank.

Status and Distribution:	SPRING	SUMMER	FALL	WINTER
Southeastern ★	R	R	R	—
Southcoastal ★	R	R	R	—
Southwestern ★	C	C	C	—
Central ★	C	C	C	—
Western ★	C	C	C	—
Northern	+	—	—	—

Notes: A difficult bird to see because it frequents dense underbrush. Best found by listening for the song during breeding season.

MacGILLIVRAY'S WARBLER

(Oporornis tolmiei)

LENGTH: 5 IN.

Identification: Olive above and yellow below, with a slate-gray hood and conspicuous white eye ring. Female is duller than the male. No other plain olive and yellow Alaska warbler has gray throat and breast. Song is chanting *tree tree tree tree sweet sweet*; call is a loud *tik*, sharper than the calls of most other western warblers.

Habitat: Shrub thickets. Nests near the ground in shrubs or weed clumps.

Status and Distribution:	SPRING	SUMMER	FALL	WINTER
Southeastern ★	U	U	U	—
Southcoastal	—	—	+	—
Southwestern	—	—	—	—
Central	—	—	—	—
Western	—	—	—	—
Northern	—	+	+	—

MacGILLIVRAY'S WARBLER
(John C. Pitcher)

COMMON YELLOWTHROAT

(Geothlypis trichas)

LENGTH: 5 IN.

Identification: Olive above and yellow below, like several other Alaska species, but both sexes have an obvious white belly, and the male has a black face mask. Other warblers of this general appearance have the undersides yellow all the way to the tail. Song is a well enunciated *witchity-witchity-witchity-witch*; call is a low *djip.*

Status and Distribution:	SPRING	SUMMER	FALL	WINTER
Southeastern ★	U	U	U	—
Southcoastal	—	—	+	—
Southwestern	—	—	—	—
Central	—	+	—	—
Western	—	—	—	—
Northern	—	—	—	—

Habitat: Freshwater marshes and estuarine meadows along mainland rivers of southeastern Alaska and on islands near the mouths of these rivers. Nests on or near the ground in grasses and weeds.

COMMON YELLOWTHROAT
(Dennis Paulson)

WILSON'S WARBLER
(Merrick Hersey)

WILSON'S WARBLER

(Wilsonia pusilla)

LENGTH: 4½ IN.

Identification: Olive above and entirely bright yellow below. Male has a glossy black cap. Female has an olive cap with the yellow of the face extending above the eye. Yellow Warbler has very plain head and yellow tail patches. Song is an evenly spaced series of notes, *chip chip chip chip chip*; call is soft *timp.*

Status and Distribution:	SPRING	SUMMER	FALL	WINTER
Southeastern ★	C	C	C	—
Southcoastal ★	C	C	C	—
Southwestern ★	C	C	C	—
Central ★	C	C	C	—
Western ★	U	U	U	—
Northern ★	+	+	+	—

Habitat: Shrub thickets, mixed deciduous-coniferous woodlands. Nests on or near the ground in shrub thickets.

Notes: Typically holds the tail cocked up like a wren.

AMERICAN REDSTART

(Setophaga ruticilla)

LENGTH: 5 IN.

Identification: Males are black, with a white belly and bright orange patches on the wings and tail. Female and immatures are olive brown above and white below with yellow patches on the wings and tail. Song is similar to that of the much more common Yellow Warbler but less variable, more on 1 pitch.

Status and Distribution:	SPRING	SUMMER	FALL	WINTER
Southeastern ★	U	U	U	—
Southcoastal	—	+	—	—
Southwestern	—	—	—	—
Central	+	+	—	—
Western	—	—	—	—
Northern	—	—	+	—

Habitat: Has occurred mostly in the deciduous forests along the mainland rivers of southeastern Alaska. Nests in a deciduous tree usually 5 to 20 feet up.

Notes: Flits about, droops the wings and spreads the tail feathers almost constantly.

AMERICAN REDSTART
(Stephen Lang)

AMERICAN REDSTART
Female
(Edgar Jones)

WESTERN MEADOWLARK
(David Hatler)

WESTERN MEADOWLARK

(Sturnella neglecta)

LENGTH: 10 IN.

Identification: Shaped like a Starling, streaked brown and white above, with a short tail bearing conspicuous white edges. Mostly yellow below with a conspicuous black "V" on the breast.

Habitat: Has occurred at Craig, Juneau and Ketchikan in southeastern Alaska and in the Brooks Range at Anaktuvuk Pass. An open country ground bird. Not known to breed in Alaska.

Status and Distribution:	SPRING	SUMMER	FALL	WINTER
Southeastern	—	—	+	+
Southcoastal	—	—	—	—
Southwestern	—	—	—	—
Central	—	—	—	—
Western	—	—	—	—
Northern	—	—	+	—

YELLOW-HEADED BLACKBIRD

(Xanthocephalus xanthocephalus)

LENGTH: 10½ IN.

Identification: Male has entirely yellow head and neck and white wing patch, conspicuous in flight. Female is considerably smaller, brown with a yellow throat and breast.

Habitat: Has been found at Fairbanks, Barrow, Juneau and near Cordova. Not known to breed in Alaska.

Status and Distribution:	SPRING	SUMMER	FALL	WINTER
Southeastern	+	—	+	—
Southcoastal	—	+	+	—
Southwestern	—	—	—	—
Central	—	+	+	—
Western	—	—	+	—
Northern	—	+	—	—

YELLOW-HEADED BLACKBIRD
(O.S. Pettingill, Jr., Cornell Lab of Ornithology)

YELLOW-HEADED BLACKBIRD
Female
(Merrick Hersey)

RED-WINGED BLACKBIRD
(Doug Murphy)

RED-WINGED BLACKBIRD

(Agelaius phoeniceus)

LENGTH: 8 IN.

Identification: Has red shoulder patch. When perched, the red may be concealed, but the buffy rear border of the patch is usually visible. Female is dark above and light below, heavily streaked all over. Pointed bill distinguishes the female from vaguely similar sparrows. Young male is the size of an adult (considerably larger than a female) but mottled with brown and with duller shoulder patches. Song is loud, liquid, ringing *ok-a-lee*; common call is *chuck* and a thin *teeyee.*

Habitat: Freshwater marshes and water edges with thick vegetation. Nests in shoreline vegetation or bushes.

RED-WINGED BLACKBIRD
Female
(Michael Hopiak, Cornell Lab of Ornithology)

Status and Distribution:	SPRING	SUMMER	FALL	WINTER
Southeastern ★	U	U	U	+
Southcoastal ★	R	R	R	—
Southwestern	—	-	—	—
Central ★	U	U	U	—
Western	—	+	+	—
Northern	+	+	—	

Notes: This species is either increasing in Alaska or more observations make it seem to be. Gabrielson and Lincoln (1959) list only 3 specimens for Alaska. However, in recent years many sightings have been made and they have been reported from all but the southwestern region (Kessel and Gibson, 1978).

RUSTY BLACKBIRD
(Edgar Jones)

RUSTY BLACKBIRD

(Euphagus carolinus)

LENGTH: 9 IN.

Identification: Has conspicuous yellow eyes. Adult male is black, without iridescence. Adult female is slate colored. Adult and young in winter have close, rust-colored bars, especially on the undersides. Song is short and ends with a note sounding like a squeaky hinge; call is a harsh *chack.*

Habitat: Willow thickets near rivers in coastal areas. Swampy areas inland. Nests in a conifer, willow or alder near water. After nesting season may frequent garbage dumps.

Status and Distribution:	SPRING	SUMMER	FALL	WINTER
Southeastern ★	U	R	U	R
Southcoastal ★	U	R	U	R
Southwestern ★	U	U	U	—
Central ★	U	U	U	R
Western ★	U	U	U	—
Northern ★	R	R	R	—

RUSTY BLACKBIRD
Female
(Heinrich Springer)

BREWER'S BLACKBIRD
Male
(Bill Dyer, Cornell Lab of Ornithology)

BREWER'S BLACKBIRD

(Euphagus cyanocephalus)

LENGTH: 9 IN.

Identification: Male is black with whitish eye, female is brownish gray with dark eye. Female Brewer's and Rusty blackbirds best distinguished from one another by eye color: dark in Brewer's, yellow in rusty. Male Brewer's may show purplish reflection on the head; male rusty may show dull greenish reflections but these are hard to see. In winter, Brewer's lacks extensive rusty color of Rusty Blackbird.

Status and Distribution:	SPRING	SUMMER	FALL	WINTER
Southeastern	+	+	—	—
Southcoastal	—	—	—	—
Southwestern	—	—	—	—
Central	—	—	—	—
Western	—	—	—	—
Northern	—	+	—	—

Habitat: Has been found at Point Barrow in northern Alaska and in southeastern Alaska.

BREWER'S BLACKBIRD
Female
(Bill Dyer, Cornell Lab of Ornithology)

COMMON GRACKLE
(Doug Murphy)

COMMON GRACKLE

(Quiscalus quiscula)

LENGTH: 12 IN.

Identification: Has a yellow eye. Both sexes are conspicuously iridescent like the male Brewer's Blackbird. Larger size, much longer and heavier bill, and long wedge-shaped tail, which is noticeably lengthened in males, are distinctive.

Habitat: Open places, fields, marshes, shores, wet woodlands. Not known to breed in Alaska.

Status and Distribution:	SPRING	SUMMER	FALL	WINTER
Southeastern	—	—	+	—
Southcoastal	—	—	+	—
Southwestern	—	—	—	—
Central	+	+	—	—
Western	—	+	—	—
Northern	—	+	—	—

BROWN-HEADED COWBIRD
(Molothrus ater)
LENGTH: 7 IN.

Identification: Has finchlike bill. Male is shiny black with a brown head. Female is entirely brownish-gray. Only a young rosy finch is as plain, and it has wing bars. Young are light brown, obscurely streaked.

Habitat: Open woodlands, fields, pastures. Often associated with horses and cows where cowbird feeds upon insects stirred up by the hoofed animals. Lays eggs in the nests of other small birds.

Status and Distribution:	SPRING	SUMMER	FALL	WINTER
Southeastern ★	R	R	R	+
Southcoastal	—	+	+	—
Southwestern	—	—	+	—
Central	+	+	+	—
Western	—	+	+	—
Northern	—	—	+	—

BROWN-HEADED COWBIRD
Female
(Ed Burroughs)

BROWN-HEADED COWBIRD
(Ed Burroughs)

WESTERN TANAGER

(Piranga ludoviciana)

LENGTH: 7 IN.

Identification: Male is bright yellow with a red face and black wings and tail. Female has a dull greenish back, dull yellow underparts and 2 white or yellowish wing bars. Female Evening Grosbeak is browner, with much heavier bill, and female Pine Grosbeak is considerably larger, with a gray body and yellow only on the head and rump. Song is robinlike but harsh and burry; call is *per-dick.*

Status and Distribution:	SPRING	SUMMER	FALL	WINTER
Southeastern ★	U	U	U	—
Southcoastal	—	—	—	—
Southwestern	—	—	—	—
Central	—	+	+	—
Western	—	—	—	—
Northern	+	—	—	—

Habitat: Open coniferous forests. Edge of Western Hemlock/Sitka Spruce forests of mainland rivers of southeastern Alaska. Nests in forked conifer branches.

WESTERN TANAGER
(Tom Ulrich)

SAVANNAH SPARROW

(Passerculus sandwichensis)

LENGTH: 5½ IN.

Identification: Streaked sparrow that resembles but is paler than most Song Sparrows. Usually has a yellowish line over the eye and a much shorter, slightly notched tail. Often has breast spot like that of Song Sparrow. Song is a quiet buzzing *tsit-tsit-tsit-tseee-tseee.*

Status and Distribution:	SPRING	SUMMER	FALL	WINTER
Southeastern ★	C	C	C	—
Southcoastal ★	C	C	C	—
Southwestern ★	C	C	C	+
Central ★	C	C	C	+
Western ★	C	C	C	—
Northern ★	C	C	C	—

Habitat: Open places, especially grassy fields. Widespread in Alaska from seashore to mountain ridges. Nests on the ground, usually in open grassy areas.

SAVANNAH SPARROW

DARK-EYED JUNCO
Oregon Subspecies

DARK-EYED JUNCO

(Junco hyemalis)

LENGTH: 5½ IN.

Identification: Adult has no streaks, wing bars, or head markings. Has flashy white outer tail feathers, especially conspicuous in flight. Juncos breeding north of Yakutat Bay are all slate gray with a white belly; those from Yakutat Bay south have a black (male) or gray (female) hood, reddish-brown back and buffy-pink sides. The 2 subspecies have been called Slate-colored and Oregon respectively. Both subspecies occur together in southeastern Alaska when not breeding. Fledgling is colored like an adult but is heavily streaked. Song is a loud, musical trill all on 1 pitch.

Status and Distribution:	SPRING	SUMMER	FALL	WINTER
Southeastern ★	C	C	C	U
Southcoastal ★	U	U	U	U
Southwestern ★	U	U	U	R
Central ★	C	C	C	R
Western ★	U	U	U	—
Northern ★	—	R	R	—

Habitat: Breeding — coniferous forests and forest edges, clearings, muskegs. Nests on the ground. In winter — easily attracted to feeders.

DARK-EYED JUNCO
Slate-colored Subspecies
(Doug Murphy)

AMERICAN TREE SPARROW

(Spizella arborea)

LENGTH: 6 IN.

Identification: Slender sparrow with red cap, single dusky spot in the middle of an unstreaked breast and 2 white wing bars. After young leave the nest, American Tree Sparrows form large flocks and, when feeding, utter a twittering *teedle-eet.*

Habitat: Shrub thickets. Near timberline to sea level, on the tundra wherever willows occur. Nests on the ground or in low bushes.

Status and Distribution:	SPRING	SUMMER	FALL	WINTER
Southeastern	U	—	U	R
Southcoastal ★	U	R	U	R
Southwestern ★	U	U	U	R
Central ★	C	C	C	+
Western ★	U	U	U	—
Northern ★	U	U	U	—

AMERICAN TREE SPARROW
(Doug Murphy)

CHIPPING SPARROW

(Spizella passerina)

LENGTH: 5½ IN.

Identification: Slightly smaller than an American Tree Sparrow with the same overall appearance. Clean gray, not beige, underparts. Has a broad white stripe over the eye and a black stripe through the eye. Lacks the breast spot of the Tree Sparrow. Fall immatures have a streaked crown, less distinct eye stripe and brown cheek patch. Song is an even trill, drier and less musical than that of the junco.

Status and Distribution:	SPRING	SUMMER	FALL	WINTER
Southeastern ★	R	R	R	+
Southcoastal	+	+	+	—
Southwestern	—	—	—	—
Central ★	U	U	U	—
Western	+	—	—	—
Northern	—	—	+	—

Habitat: Openings and edges of woodlands. Nests in deciduous or coniferous trees.

Notes: Found mostly along the mainland rivers of southeastern Alaska and the upper Tanana River valley of eastern central Alaska.

CHIPPING SPARROW
(Edgar Jones)

HARRIS' SPARROW
(John C. Pitcher)

HARRIS' SPARROW

(Zonotrichia querula)

LENGTH: 7½ IN.

Identification: Large, long tailed, easily recognized by black crown, face and throat, streaked sides, and otherwise white underparts. Immature and winter birds have much less black, often restricted to a dark blotch on the upper breast. Only other large, streaked sparrows are the Song Sparrow and Fox Sparrow, both of which are much more heavily streaked below.

Habitat: Has occurred mostly at feeders in southeastern Alaska. Not known to breed in Alaska.

Status and Distribution:	SPRING	SUMMER	FALL	WINTER
Southeastern	R	—	R	R
Southcoastal	+	—	+	+
Southwestern	—	—	—	—
Central	—	—	—	—
Western	—	—	—	—
Northern	+	—	—	—

WHITE-CROWNED SPARROW
(Doug Murphy)

WHITE-CROWNED SPARROW

(Zonotrichia leucophrys)

LENGTH: 6 IN.

Identification: Streaked above, plain gray below, slender, long tailed and larger than Tree and Chipping sparrows. Adult has conspicuously black-and-white striped head. Throat is the same color as the rest of the underparts. Fledgling has finely streaked crown and streaked breast; it will usually be with an adult. First winter bird has plain breast, head is striped with rusty-brown and gray instead of black and white. Bill of all birds is flesh colored. Song is a series of 6 whistled notes, sounding lazy and wheezy, which rises on the second and third notes and falls on the last 3 notes.

Habitat: Forest edges and brush patches. Nests on the ground in grass clump or low shrub.

Status and Distribution:	SPRING	SUMMER	FALL	WINTER
Southeastern	C	—	U	R
Southcoastal ★	U	R	U	R
Southwestern ★	C	C	C	—
Central ★	C	C	C	+
Western ★	C	C	C	—
Northern ★	U	U	U	—

Notes: Often travels with Golden-crowned Sparrows in migration. Readily comes to feeders.

GOLDEN-CROWNED SPARROW

(Zonotrichia atricapilla)

LENGTH: 6½ IN.

Identification: Slightly larger than White-crowned Sparrow. Has a golden crown bordered by a wide black stripe on either side. First winter bird is very dull, darker than a young White-crowned Sparrow with a dark bill. Top of the head is finely streaked, lacking prominent stripes of the White-crowned and White-throated sparrows. Song is normally 3 high whistled notes of minor tone quality, running down the scale like 3 blind mice.

Status and Distribution:	SPRING	SUMMER	FALL	WINTER
Southeastern ★	C	U	C	+
Southcoastal ★	C	C	C	R
Southwestern ★	C	C	C	—
Central ★	U	U	U	+
Western ★	C	C	C	—
Northern	R	R	R	—

Habitat: Willow and alder thickets usually near timberline. Nests on the ground under shrubs. Favors brushy areas in migration.

Notes: In migration travels in flocks often with White-crowned Sparrows. Readily comes to feeders.

GOLDEN-CROWNED SPARROW

WHITE-THROATED SPARROW
(Ed Burroughs)

WHITE-THROATED SPARROW

(Zonotrichia albicollis)

LENGTH: 6½ IN.

Identification: Superficially like the White-crowned Sparrow, but in all plumages the throat is white, sharply distinct from the gray breast. Bill is darker, head is rounder, never looking angular as it often does in the White-crowned Sparrow.

Habitat: Has occurred in a variety of places including Colville River Delta, Fairbanks, Cordova, Kodiak, Juneau, Sitka and Ketchikan. Not known to breed in Alaska.

Status and Distribution:	SPRING	SUMMER	FALL	WINTER
Southeastern	—	—	+	+
Southcoastal	—	—	+	+
Southwestern	—	—	—	—
Central	—	+	+	—
Western	—	—	—	—
Northern	+	—	+	—

FOX SPARROW

FOX SPARROW

(Passerella iliaca)

LENGTH: 7 IN.

Identification: Has brown or grayish brown back and very heavily spotted to streaked underparts. Northern and interior subspecies have bright, reddish-brown tail that contrasts sharply with the back; striped back, and partially striped head. Coastal forms are much darker and browner, without the strong contrast between the back color and the tail and with no stripes on the head or back. Darkest and smallest Fox Sparrows are found in lower southeastern Alaska. Races to the north are grayer and larger. Southern birds are distinguished from Song Sparrows by the plain head and back, and all Fox Sparrows are recognizable by the light lower mandible. Song opens with 1 or more clear whistles and follows with several short *trills* or *churrs;* call is a sharp *chink.*

Status and Distribution:	SPRING	SUMMER	FALL	WINTER
Southeastern ★	C	C	C	R
Southcoastal ★	C	C	C	R
Southwestern ★	C	C	C	—
Central ★	C	C	C	+
Western ★	C	C	C	—
Northern ★	U	U	U	—

Habitat: Shrub thickets. Nests on the ground under shrubs or low in a tree or shrub.

LINCOLN'S SPARROW
(Melospiza lincolnii)
LENGTH: 5½ IN.

Identification: Small, trim, finely streaked. Paler than a Song Sparrow with fine streaks, seldom massed into a central spot, across a buffy band on the breast and sides. Side of the head looks gray. Song is a low, gurgling stanza that ends after some rising phrases; calls are *tik* and buzzy *tzeee.*

Habitat: Shrubs, salt and freshwater marshes. Nests on the ground in marshy places.

Status and Distribution:	SPRING	SUMMER	FALL	WINTER
Southeastern ★	C	C	C	+
Southcoastal ★	C	C	C	+
Southwestern ★	U	U	U	—
Central ★	C	C	C	—
Western ★	U	U	U	—
Northern	—	+	—	—

LINCOLN'S SPARROW

SONG SPARROW

SONG SPARROW
(Melospiza melodia)
LENGTH: 6-7½ IN.

Identification: Brownish back, heavy streaks on the breast, usually a prominent spot in the center of the breast streaks. Head and back are streaked, bill is dark. Song Sparrow in the Aleutian Islands is huge, as big as the biggest Fox Sparrow, and very long billed; that from southern Alaska is obviously smaller than a Fox Sparrow. Song is staccato but musical, usually beginning with 2 or 3 loud notes which sound like *sweet, sweet, sweet,* followed by a trill, then several short notes; call is harsh single note.

Status and Distribution:	SPRING	SUMMER	FALL	WINTER
Southeastern ★	C	C	C	C
Southcoastal ★	C	C	C	C
Southwestern ★	C	C	C	C
Central	—	—	—	—
Western	—	—	—	—
Northern	—	—	—	—

Habitat: Marine beaches, only occasionally ventures inland. Beach rocks, shrub thickets. Nests on the ground in grass clumps.

LAPLAND LONGSPUR

(Calcarius lapponicus)

LENGTH: 6½ IN.

Identification: Breeding male has black crown, face and breast and chestnut hind neck. Female is more nondescript, like many sparrows, but usually is accompanied by a male. Savannah Sparrow might be mistaken for a longspur, but the sparrow is smaller with heavily streaked breast and no white in the tail. Autumn male is colored like a female. In flight appears bulkier and shorter-tailed than a lark or pipit and flies in tighter, faster flocks. Song is beautiful series of tinkling notes given in flight. Call on the breeding grounds is a liquid *teew;* migrants utter a dry rattle.

Status and Distribution:	SPRING	SUMMER	FALL	WINTER
Southeastern	C	—	C	+
Southcoastal ★	U	R	U	+
Southwestern ★	C	C	C	+
Central ★	C	C	C	—
Western ★	C	C	C	—
Northern ★	C	C	C	—

LAPLAND LONGSPUR
(Skip Gray)

Habitat: Breeding — tundra. Nests on small clumps of grass or dry knolls. In migration — grassy fields, wetlands, alpine meadows and ridges.

Notes: One of the most common and widespread breeding land birds on the tundra. In migration often associated with Horned Larks and Snow Buntings. All longspurs spend much time on the ground and usually run or walk instead of hopping.

SMITH'S LONGSPUR

(Calcarius pictus)

LENGTH: 6 IN.

Identification: Distinguished from the Lapland Longspur and other open country birds by buffy underparts, brighter in summer. Breeding male has conspicuous black-and-white head pattern. Song is warblerlike with sweet notes. Call on breeding ground is distinct 2-note rattle.

Habitat: Brooks Range — damp tussock meadows, usually on wide alpine valley floors, often on flat meadows surrounding lakes. Central Alaska — dry ridgetop tundra. Nests on the ground.

Status and Distribution:	SPRING	SUMMER	FALL	WINTER
Southeastern	+	—	+	—
Southcoastal	—	—	—	—
Southwestern	—	—	—	—
Central ★	R	R	R	—
Western	—	—	—	—
Northern ★	U	U	U	—

Notes: Far less abundant in Alaska than Lapland Longspur. Sings from the ground rather than from the air like Lapland Longspur.

SNOW BUNTING
(Jim Erckmann)

SNOW BUNTING
(Plectrophenax nivalis)
LENGTH: 6½ IN.

Identification: Whitest small bird found in Alaska except for McKay's Bunting. Striking black-and-white plumage of breeding male is unmistakable. Breeding female and all winter birds have more brown but in flight show extensive white in the wings and tail. Song is short musical warble, often with some phrases repeated, which is given on the ground or in flight.

Status and Distribution:	SPRING	SUMMER	FALL	WINTER
Southeastern ★	U	R	U	U
Southcoastal ★	U	R	U	R
Southwestern ★	C	C	C	C
Central ★	C	U	U	R
Western ★	C	C	C	U
Northern ★	C	C	C	—

Habitat: Breeding — tundra. Coastlines of northern, western and southwestern Alaska where nests in various locations including buildings, empty gas drums and bird houses. In mountains — nests beneath rocks or in rock crevices. In migration and winter — prefer open fields, shoreline, roadsides.

SMITH'S LONGSPUR
(John C. Pitcher)

MCKAY'S BUNTING
(Cal Lensink)

McKAY'S BUNTING

(Plectrophenax hyperboreus)

LENGTH: 7 IN.

Identification: Breeding male is mostly white except for black wing tips and black on the tip of the central tail feathers. Female and winter birds show some brown on the back and more black in the wings but much less than the Snow Bunting.

Habitat: Breeding — islands of the Bering Sea where nests in small depressions on the ground or in rock crevices. In migration and winter — mainland bordering the Bering Sea.

Status and Distribution:	SPRING	SUMMER	FALL	WINTER
Southeastern	—	—	—	—
Southcoastal	—	—	—	+
Southwestern ★	U	R	U	U
Central	—	—	—	—
Western ★	R	R	R	R
Northern	—	—	—	—

RUSTIC BUNTING

(Emberiza rustica)

LENGTH: 5¾ IN.

Identification: An Old World bunting, more brightly marked about the head than New World sparrows. Summer male has black top and sides of the head, a white eye stripe behind the eye, white throat and underparts and narrow rusty breast band. Female and winter male are similarly rusty with a band of rusty streaks on the breast and sides. Female and winter male Lapland Longspur have darker streaks and never show the slight crest of Rustic Bunting. Call is sharp *tsip, tsip, tsip.*

Status and Distribution:	SPRING	SUMMER	FALL	WINTER
Southeastern	—	—	—	—
Southcoastal	—	—	—	—
Southwestern	R	—	R	—
Central	—	—	—	—
Western	+	—	—	
Northern	—	—	—	—

Habitat: Asiatic bunting that has occurred in the western and central Aleutian Islands and at Gambell on Saint Lawrence Island. Not known to breed in Alaska.

Notes: Buntings, like sparrows, hop; longspurs walk or run.

PALLAS' REED-BUNTING

(Emberiza pallasi)

LENGTH: 5½ IN.

Identification: Very similar to Common Reed-Bunting but smaller. Male has a more extensive black throat and a pale yellow rather than white nape. Female has less rusty edges to the wing and back feathers. Bill is more slender and pointed than in the Reed Bunting.

Habitat: Asiatic bunting that has been found at Barrow and at Gambell on Saint Lawrence Island. Not known to breed in Alaska.

Status and Distribution:	SPRING	SUMMER	FALL	WINTER
Southeastern	—	—	—	—
Southcoastal	—	—	—	—
Southwestern	—	—	—	—
Central	—	—	—	—
Western	+	—	—	—
Northern	+	—	—	—

PALLAS' REED-BUNTING
(John C. Pitcher)

RUSTIC BUNTING
(John C. Pitcher)

GRAY BUNTING
(Emberiza variabilis)
LENGTH: 6 IN.

Identification: Breeding plumaged males distinctive dark slate gray. Winter males have dark brown back with black streaks. Females are dark brown above, paler below, very similar to other female buntings but lack the white in the tail of other species. In flight, females and immature males best distinguished by chestnut-colored rump.

Habitat: Has been found in western Aleutians on Attu and Shemya islands. Breeds in northeast Asia.

Status and Distribution:	SPRING	SUMMER	FALL	WINTER
Southeastern	—	—	—	—
Southcoastal	—	—	—	—
Southwestern	+	—	—	—
Central	—	—	—	—
Western	—	—	—	—
Northern	—	—	—	—

GRAY BUNTING
(Wild Bird Society of Japan)

COMMON REED-BUNTING
(John C. Pitcher)

COMMON REED-BUNTING
(Emberiza schoeniclus)
LENGTH: 6 IN.

Identification: Entire head and throat are black except for a white line extending back and down from the bill and a white hind neck. Female and winter male are heavily streaked, longer tailed than longspurs and lack the reddish nape patch and pale crown stripe of the Lapland Longspur. Call is loud *tseek,* somewhat like that of the Yellow Wagtail.

Status and Distribution:	SPRING	SUMMER	FALL	WINTER
Southeastern	—	—	—	—
Southcoastal	—	—	—	—
Southwestern	+	—	—	—
Central	—	—	—	—
Western	—	—	—	—
Northern	—	—	—	—

Habitat: Asiatic bunting that has occurred in the western Aleutian Islands. Not known to breed in Alaska.

FAMILY *FRINGILLIDAE*

FINCHES

(14)

Members of this family have a short, heavy, conical beak, which is used for cracking seeds, their main food.

BRAMBLING
Winter
(John C. Pitcher)

BRAMBLING

(Fringilla montifringilla)

LENGTH: 5¾ IN.

Identification: Small finch with a conspicuous white rump, rusty or orange breast and white wing bars in any plumage. Summer male is contrastingly marked with black head, back, wings and tail. Winter male and all females are duller, with gray to brown, streaked head and back. Flight call is *tchuck, tchuck*; another common call is harsh *tsweep.*

Status and Distribution:	SPRING	SUMMER	FALL	WINTER
Southeastern	—	—	—	+
Southcoastal	—	—	+	+
Southwestern	R	—	R	—
Central	—	—	—	—
Western	+	—	—	—
Northern	+	—	+	—

Habitat: Asiatic finch that has been found mostly in the western and central Aleutian Islands. Other sightings have occurred in the Pribilof Islands, at Hooper Bay, Gambell, Barrow, Cordova, Girdwood and Juneau. Not known to breed in Alaska.

HAWFINCH

(Coccothraustes coccothraustes)

LENGTH: 7 IN.

Identification: Stocky and short-tailed with a huge gray bill. Built like Evening Grosbeak to which it is closely related. Brown with black wings and conspicuous white patches on the shoulder and in the primaries. Tail is brown with a white tip. Call is a loud, metallic *tik*.

Habitat: Asiatic finch found in the western and central Aleutian Islands and in the Pribilof Islands. Not known to breed in Alaska.

Status and Distribution:	SPRING	SUMMER	FALL	WINTER
Southeastern	—	—	—	—
Southcoastal	—	—	—	—
Southwestern	+	+	+	—
Central	—	—	—	—
Western	+	—	—	—
Northern	—	—	—	—

HAWFINCH
(John C. Pitcher)

EVENING GROSBEAK
Male
(Michael Hopiak, Cornell Lab of Ornithology)

EVENING GROSBEAK

(Coccothraustes vespertinus)

LENGTH: 7½ IN.

Identification: Size and shape of the Hawfinch. Bill is large and pale greenish to ivory. Male is brown and yellow with a conspicuous yellow eye line and black wings with large white bases. Female is duller, gray-brown with less white in the wing. Loud, ringing call is often a clue to the presence of these nomadic birds.

Habitat: Has been found at Sitka, Ketchikan and Juneau in southeastern Alaska. Not known to breed in Alaska.

Status and Distribution:	SPRING	SUMMER	FALL	WINTER
Southeastern	—	—	+	+
Southcoastal	—	—	—	—
Southwestern	—	—	—	—
Central	—	—	—	—
Western	—	—	—	—
Northern	—	—	—	—

EVENING GROSBEAK
Female

EURASIAN BULLFINCH
(John C. Pitcher)

EURASIAN BULLFINCH

(Pyrrhula pyrrhula)

LENGTH: 5¾ IN.

Identification: Slightly stouter with distinctly shorter, stouter bill than Brambling. Has a black cap and white rump and wing bars in all plumages. Male is gray above, rosy below. Female is dull brownish above, more buffy below. Movements are slow and deliberate. Call is soft, piping whistle.

Habitat: Asiatic finch that has been found mostly on Bering Sea islands and western Aleutian Islands. Has occurred at Nulato, Anchorage and Petersburg. Not known to breed in Alaska.

Status and Distribution:	SPRING	SUMMER	FALL	WINTER
Southeastern	—	—	—	+
Southcoastal	—	—	+	+
Southwestern	+	—	+	—
Central	—	—	—	+
Western	+	—	+	—
Northern	—	—	—	—

COMMON ROSEFINCH
(John C. Pitcher)

COMMON ROSEFINCH

(Carpodacus erythrinus)

LENGTH: 5¾ IN.

Identification: Males are rosy below and brown above. Female is brown above, obscurely streaked with brown below. Both sexes have 2 obscure wing bars. Call is soft and 2-syllabled, rising at the end to a squeak.

Habitat: Asiatic finch that has been found mostly on Saint Lawrence Island and in Aleutian Islands. Not known to breed in Alaska.

Status and Distribution:	SPRING	SUMMER	FALL	WINTER
Southeastern	—	—	—	—
Southcoastal	—	—	—	—
Southwestern	R	+	+	—
Central	—	—	—	—
Western	R	—	—	—
Northern	—	—	—	—

PURPLE FINCH
(Merrick Hersey)

PURPLE FINCH

(Carpodacus purpureus)

LENGTH: 6 IN.

Identification: Similar to Common Rosefinch but male is more distinctly streaked above and female is more distinctly streaked all over, with a conspicuous white eye line. The 2 finches are unlikely to occur in the same regions. Flight call is sharp *tip*.

Habitat: Has occurred in the Juneau area. Not known to breed in Alaska.

Status and Distribution:	SPRING	SUMMER	FALL	WINTER
Southeastern	+	—	+	+
Southcoastal	—	—	+	—
Southwestern	—	—	—	—
Central	—	—	—	—
Western	—	—	—	—
Northern	—	—	—	—

PURPLE FINCH
Female
(Merrick Hersey)

PINE GROSBEAK

(Pinicola enucleator)

LENGTH: 9 IN.

Identification: Plump, stocky, about the size of a robin, appearing slim and long-tailed in flight overhead. Male is rosy red with gray belly and 2 conspicuous white wing bars. Female is gray with white wing bars but head and rump are tinged with yellow instead of the red found in adult male. Song is a 3-noted whistle similar to that of the Greater Yellowlegs.

Habitat: Coniferous forests. Nests in a conifer, usually not more than 10 to 15 feet above ground. In winter travels in flocks and feeds on buds and fruits of trees. Fond of Mountain Ash berries.

Status and Distribution:	SPRING	SUMMER	FALL	WINTER
Southeastern ★	U	U	C	C
Southcoastal ★	U	U	U	U
Southwestern ★	U	U	U	U
Central ★	U	U	U	U
Western ★	U	U	U	U
Northern	R	R	R	—

PINE GROSBEAK
Male

PINE GROSBEAK
Female

ROSY FINCH

(Leucosticte arctoa)

LENGTH: 6 IN.

Identification: Dark brown with a rosy wash on the wings, belly and rump. Head is mostly gray in male from southern Alaska; an interior bird has gray only bordering the crown from behind. Female is duller, with much less gray on head than male. In late summer immatures, entirely dull brown with buffy wing bars, can be confusing. Song is canarylike warble. Flying flocks give harsh *cheep, cheep* notes.

Status and Distribution:	SPRING	SUMMER	FALL	WINTER
Southeastern ★	U	U	U	R
Southcoastal ★	U	U	U	R
Southwestern ★	C	C	C	C
Central ★	U	U	U	—
Western ★	U	U	U	—
Northern ★	R	R	R	—

ROSY FINCH
(Doug Murphy)

Habitat: Alpine tundra, mountain ridges above timberline, near snowfields. Beaches in the Aleutian Islands and Bering Sea islands. Nests in cliff crevices or rock slides. In winter — lower elevations, often seen in flocks near towns.

ORIENTAL GREENFINCH
(John C. Pitcher)

ORIENTAL GREENFINCH

(Carduelis sinica)

LENGTH: 6 IN.

Identification: Has bright yellow patches in wings and tail. Male has a gray crown and nape with yellowish-green cheeks and throat and a brown body with greenish yellow rump. Female is light brown with yellow wing and tail patches. Call is thin, metallic tinkle.

Habitat: Asiatic finch that has occurred in the western Aleutian Islands. Not known to nest in Alaska.

Status and Distribution:	SPRING	SUMMER	FALL	WINTER
Southeastern	—	—	—	—
Southcoastal	—	—	—	—
Southwestern	+	—	+	—
Central	—	—	—	—
Western	—	—	—	—
Northern	—	—	—	—

HOARY REDPOLL

(Carduelis hornemanni)

LENGTH: 5½ IN.

Identification: Stubby-billed finch with bright red cap, blackish chin and dark streaks on the sides. Adult male often shows a pinkish suffusion on the breast. Paler than Common Redpoll on the average but there is much overlap. Has a pure white rump with no streaking, unstreaked undertail coverts. Configuration of head and very short bill makes the face look pushed in. Bill is smaller than that of Common Redpoll. Song is a trill, followed by rattling *chit-chit-chit-chit*; call is loud *chit-chit-chit-chit* and a *swee-e-et,* often given in flight.

Status and Distribution:	SPRING	SUMMER	FALL	WINTER
Southeastern	—	—	—	R
Southcoastal	R	—	—	R
Southwestern	U	—	U	C
Central ★	C	R	U	C
Western ★	C	C	C	C
Northern ★	C	C	C	—

Habitat: Tundra shrub thickets, mixed deciduous-coniferous woodlands, open fields and grasslands, near cities and villages especially in winter. Nests on the ground or in the lower branches of bushes. May be found with Common Redpoll at any time of the year.

COMMON REDPOLL
(Carduelis flammea)
LENGTH: 5 IN.

Identification: Stubby-billed finch with bright red cap, blackish chin and dark streaks on the sides. Adult male often has pinkish wash on the breast. Larger bill than the Hoary Redpoll. Song is a trill, followed by a rattling *chit-chit-chit-chit*; call is loud *chit-chit-chit-chit* and a *swee-e-et,* often given in flight.

Status and Distribution:	SPRING	SUMMER	FALL	WINTER
Southeastern ★	C	U	C	C
Southcoastal ★	C	U	U	C
Southwestern ★	C	C	C	C
Central ★	C	C	C	C
Western ★	C	C	C	C
Northern ★	U	U	U	—

Habitat: Tundra shrub thickets, mixed deciduous-coniferous woodlands, open fields and grasslands, near cities and towns especially in winter. Nests on the ground or in lower branches of bushes. May be found with Hoary Redpoll at any time of the year.

Notes: In most of Alaska outnumbers the Hoary Redpoll but in some Arctic localities the reverse may be true.

COMMON REDPOLL

Redpolls have an enlarged esophagus that acts similar to a crop, something which birds of this family do not normally have. This allows them to take in more food in winter and digest its contents through the night.

HOARY REDPOLL

PINE SISKIN

(Carduelis pinus)

LENGTH: 5 IN.

Identification: Streaked finch with a touch of yellow in the wings and tail base. Even if the yellow is not visible, siskin is smaller than any sparrow and more heavily streaked than any redpoll. Presence usually detected by long, buzzy *schhrreeee*; in flight utters a scratchy *shick-shick* and a thin *tseee*.

Habitat: Coniferous forests. Nests in conifer, usually well out on a branch. During non-nesting season may be found in deciduous trees and on the ground.

Status and Distribution:	SPRING	SUMMER	FALL	WINTER
Southeastern ★	C	C	C	C
Southcoastal ★	C	C	C	U
Southwestern	+	+	+	—
Central ★	R	R	R	+
Western	—	+	—	—
Northern	—	+	—	—

Notes: Unlike sparrows, roams in tight flocks searching for plant seeds. Nesting is erratic and may occur during many months.

PINE SISKIN

RED CROSSBILL
(Dennis Paulson)

RED CROSSBILL

(Loxia curvirostra)

LENGTH: 6 IN.

Identification: Large-headed and heavy-billed with crossed mandibles and stubby tail. Male is brick red and female dull olive-gray with a yellowish rump. Immature is striped above and below. Call is repeated *kip-kip* or *jeep-jeep* and whistled notes sometimes interspersed with warbled passages.

Status and Distribution:	SPRING	SUMMER	FALL	WINTER
Southeastern ★	C	C	C	C
Southcoastal ★	R	R	R	R
Southwestern	—	R	+	—
Central	—	—	—	—
Western	—	—	+	—
Northern	—	—	—	—

Habitat: Coniferous forests. Nests in a conifer, usually well out on a branch. May nest almost any time of the year.

Notes: Often hangs upside down on conifer cones. Flies in flocks and feeds on seeds of conifers that are extracted by the specialized bill and tongue. Number of birds varies with abundance of the cone crop. Often feeds quietly in tree tops or flies high in the air between trees and presence can only be detected by call.

RED CROSSBILL
Female
(Gary Jones)

WHITE-WINGED CROSSBILL
Female

WHITE-WINGED CROSSBILL

(Loxia leucoptera)

LENGTH: 6 IN.

Identification: Similar to Red Crossbill but both sexes have conspicuous white wing bars. Male is much pinker red than male Red Crossbill, more like color of a Pine Grosbeak. Song is variable, melodious, with warbling trilling; flight call is soft *twee* or a loud, harsh *cheet, cheet.*

Status and Distribution:	SPRING	SUMMER	FALL	WINTER
Southeastern ★	C	C	C	C
Southcoastal ★	U	U	U	U
Southwestern ★	U	U	U	U
Central ★	U	U	U	U
Western ★	U	U	U	U
Northern	—	—	+	—

Habitat: Coniferous forests. Nests in a conifer from 5 to 80 feet up. May nest almost any time of the year.

Notes: Usually seen in small flocks feeding near the tops of spruce trees. Numbers may fluctuate considerably from one year to the next depending on the cone crop.

ACCIDENTALS

ACCIDENTALS

These species have been sighted once or a very few times in Alaska. They are far from their normal range and further observations are unlikely. Most of these species have come from Asia.

Cook's Petrel *(Pterodroma cookii).* Central Aleutian Islands.

American White Pelican *(Pelecanus erythrorhynchos).* Petersburg.

Great Egret *(Casmerodius albus).* Juneau.

Chinese Egret *(Egretta eulophotes).* Agattu Island, Aleutian Islands.

Snowy Egret *(Egretta thula).* Juneau.

Cattle Egret *(Bubulcus ibis).* Ketchikan.

Turkey Vulture *(Cathartes aura).* Delta Junction.

Eurasian Coot *(Fulica atra).* Pribilof Islands.

Common Crane *(Grus grus).* Fairbanks.

Little Ringed Plover *(Charadrius dubius).* Buldir Island, Aleutian Islands.

American Avocet *(Recurvirostra americana).* Valdez.

Marsh Sandpiper *(Tringa stagnatilis).* Buldir Island, Aleutian Islands.

Willet *(Catoptrophorus semipalmatus).* Minto Lakes west of Fairbanks.

Eskimo Curlew *(Numenius borealis).* Pribilof Islands.

Spoonbill Sandpiper *(Eurynorhynchus pygmeus).* Wainwright. Buldir Island, Aleutian Islands.

Jack Snipe *(Lymnocryptes minimus).* Pribilof Islands.

Western Gull *(Larus occidentalis).* Bristol Bay.

White-winged Tern *(Chlidonias leucopterus).* Nizki Island, Aleutian Islands.

White-winged Dove *(Zenaida asiatica).* Skagway.

Common Barn-Owl *(Tyto alba).* Delta Junction.

Long-eared Owl *(Asio otus).* Southeastern Alaska.

Whip-poor-will *(Caprimulgus vociferus).* Southeastern Alaska.

Jungle Nightjar *(Caprimulgus indicus).* Buldir Island, Aleutian Islands.

Chimney Swift *(Chaetura pelagica).* Saint George Island.

Common Swift *(Apus apus).* Pribilof Islands.

Ruby-throated Hummingbird *(Archilochus colubris).* Saint Michael.

Hoopoe *(Upupa epops).* Old Chevak.

Eurasian Wryneck *(Jynx torquilla).* Wales.

Yellow-bellied Flycatcher *(Empidonax flaviventris).* Coal Creek, eastcentral Alaska

Least Flycatcher *(Empidonax minimus).* Anchorage.

Dusky Flycatcher *(Empidonax oberholseri).* Icy Cape, northwestern Alaska.

Common House-Martin *(Delichon urbica).* Nome. Saint Paul Island, Pribilof Islands.

Wood Warbler *(Phylloscopus sibilatrix).* Shemya Island, Aleutian Islands.

Siberian Flycatcher *(Muscicapa sibirica).* Shemya Island, Aleutian Islands.

Red-flanked Bluetail *(Tarsiger cyanurus).* Attu Island, Aleutian Islands.

Fieldfare *(Turdus pilaris).* Point Barrow.

Northern Mockingbird *(Mimus polyglottos).* Middleton Island.

Brown Thrasher *(Toxostoma rufum).* Point Barrow.

Brown Tree-Pipit *(Anthus trivialis).* Wales.

Black-throated Green Warbler *(Dendroica virens).* Chichagof Island.

Bay-breasted Warbler *(Dendroica castanea).* Fairbanks.

Black-and-white Warbler *(Mniotilta varia).* Colville River.

Ovenbird *(Seiurus aurocapillus).* Prudhoe Bay.

Kentucky Warbler *(Oporornis formosus).* Beaufort Lagoon.

Canada Warbler *(Wilsonia canadensis).* Point Barrow. Prudhoe Bay.

Scarlet Tanager *(Piranga olivacea).* Point Barrow.

Swamp Sparrow *(Melospiza georgiana).* Anchorage.

Little Bunting *(Emberiza pusilla).* Chukchi Sea. Shemya Island, Aleutian Islands.

Bobolink *(Dolichonyx oryzivorus).* Point Barrow.

Northern Oriole *(Icterus galbula).* Petersburg.

BIBLIOGRAPHY

The following references have been used in the preparation of this book.

American Birding Association, *A.B.A. Checklist: Birds of Continental United States and Canada,* Second Edition, 1982.

Anchorage Audubon Society, *Birds of Anchorage Alaska — A checklist,* 1978.

Bellrose, F.C., *Ducks, Geese and Swans of North America,* Wildlife Management Institute, Washington, D.C., 1976.

Bent, A.C., *Life Histories of North American Birds,* U.S. National Museum Bulletins 107, 113, 121, 126, 130, 135, 142, 146, 162, 167, 170, 174, 176, 179, 191, 195, 196, 197, 203, 211 and 237, 1919-1958.

Dement'ev, G.P. and N.A. Gladkov, eds., *Birds of the Soviet Union,* vol. 6. Translated by Israel Prog. Sci. Trans. U.S. Department of the Interior and National Science Foundation, Washington, D.C., 1968.

Gabrielson, I.N. and F.C. Lincoln, *The Birds of Alaska,* The Stackpole Company, Harrisburg, Pennsylvania, and Wildlife Management Institute, Washington, D.C., 1959.

Gibson, D.D., *Checklist — Birds of Alaska,* University of Alaska Museum, Fairbanks, 1977.

---, The Spring Migration: March 1-May 31, 1978 — Alaska Region, *American Birds,* 32(5), 1978, pp. 1043-1045.

---, The Winter Season: December 1, 1978-February 28, 1979 — Alaska Region, *American Birds,* 33(3), 1979, pp. 304-305.

---, The Spring Migration: March 1-May 31, 1979 — Alaska Region, *American Birds,* 33(5), 1979, pp. 798-799.

---, The Nesting Season: June 1-July 31, 1979 — Alaska Region, *American Birds,* 33(6), 1979, pp. 889-890.

---, The Autumn Migration: August 1-November 30, 1979 — Alaska Region, *American Birds,* 34(2), 1980, pp. 190-191.

---, The Winter Season: December 1, 1979-February 29, 1980 — Alaska Region, *American Birds,* 34(3), 1980, pp. 298-299.

---, The Spring Migration: March 1-May 31, 1980 — Alaska Region, *American Birds,* 34(5), 1980, pp. 806-807.

---, The Nesting Season: June 1-July 31, 1980 — Alaska Region, *American Birds,* 34(6), 1980, pp. 921-922.

---, The Autumn Migration: August 1-November 30, 1980 — Alaska Region, *American Birds,* 35(2), 1981, pp. 214-215.

---, The Winter Season: December 1, 1980-February 28, 1981 — Alaska Region, *American Birds,* 35(3), 1981, pp. 326-328.

---, The Spring Migration: March 1-May 31, 1981 — Alaska Region, *American Birds,* 35(5), 1981, pp. 852-853.

---, The Winter Season: December 1, 1981-February 28, 1982 — Alaska Region, *American Birds,* 36(3), 1982, pp. 321-323.

---, The Spring Migration: March 1-May 31, 1982 — Alaska Region, *American Birds,* 36(5), 1982, pp. 884-885.

---. Migrant Birds at Shemya Island, Aleutian Islands, Alaska, *The Condor,* 83(1), 1981, pp. 65-77.

---, *Master List of Alaska Birds,* University of Alaska Museum, November 4, 1982.

Godfrey, W.E., *The Birds of Canada,* National Museum of Canada Bulletin No. 203, Biological Series No. 73, 1966.

Isleib, M.E., *Birds of the Chugach National Forest Alaska - A Checklist,* U.S. Forest Service, U.S. Department of Agriculture, n.d.

Isleib, M.E. and B. Kessel, *Birds of the North Gulf Coast - Prince William Sound Region, Alaska,* Biological Papers No. 14, University of Alaska, Fairbanks, 1973.

Johnsgard, P.A., *Waterfowl of North America,* Indiana University Press, Bloomington, Indiana, 1975.

Johnson, D.H., D.E. Timm and P.F. Springer, *Morphological Characteristics of Canada Geese in the Pacific Flyway,* Typewritten Manuscript, 1978.

Juneau Audubon Society; U.S. Forest Service, U.S. Department of Agriculture; Alaska Department of Fish and Game; *Birds of Southeast Alaska: A checklist,* 1978.

Kessel, B., *Birds of Interior Alaska.* University of Alaska Museum, 1980.

Kessel, B. and D.D. Gibson, *Status and Distribution of Alaska Birds,* Studies in Avian Biology No. 1, Cooper Ornithological Society, Los Angeles, 1978.

King, B.F. and E.C. Dickinson, *A Field Guide to the Birds of South-East Asia,* Houghton Mifflin Company, Boston, 1975.

MacIntosh, R., *Birds of the Kodiak Island Archipelago - A Checklist,* 1978.

Morlan, J., Status and Identification of Forms of White Wagtail in Western North America, *Continental Birdlife* 2(2), April 1981, pp. 37-50.

Murphy, D. and K. Kertell, *Bird Checklist for Denali National Park,* Alaska Natural History Association in cooperation with the National Park Service, 1980.

Murphy, D. and K. Kertell, *Birds of Mount McKinley National Park, Alaska - A Checklist,* 1977.

National Park Service, U.S. Department of the Interior, *Birds of Glacier Bay National Monument* - A Checklist, 1978.

Naveen, R., Storm-Petrels of the World an Introductory Guide to their Field Identification, *Birding* XIV (2), 1982, pp. 56-62.

Ogilvie, M.A., *The Winter Birds - Birds of the Arctic,* Praeger Publishers, New York, 1976.

Peterson, R.T., *A Field Guide to Western Birds,* Houghton Mifflin Company, Boston, 1961.

Peterson, R.T., *A Field Guide to the Birds East of the Rockies,* Houghton Mifflin Company, Boston, 1980.

Peterson, R.T., G. Mountfort and P.A.D. Hollom, *A Field Guide to the Birds of Britain and Europe,* Houghton Mifflin Company, Boston, 1974.

Pitelka, F.A., *An Avifaunal Review for the Barrow Region and North Slope of Arctic Alaska,* Arctic and Alpine Research vol. 6, Barrow, 1974, pp. 161-184.

Pough, R.H., *Audubon Western Bird Guide,* Doubleday & Co., Garden City, New York, 1957.

Prater, A.J., J.H. Marchant and J. Vuorinen, *Guide to the Identification and Ageing of Holarctic Waders,* British Trust for Ornithology Field Guide Seventeen, 1977.

Robbins, C.S., B. Bruun and H.S. Zim, *A Guide to Field Identification, Birds of North America,* Golden Press, New York, 1966.

Roberson, D., Rare Birds of the West Coast of North America, Woodcock Publications, Pacific Grove, California, 1980.

Stromsem, N.E., *A Guide to Alaskan Seabirds,* Alaska Natural History Association in cooperation with the U.S. Fish and Wildlife Service, 1982.

Terres, J.K., *The Audubon Society Encyclopedia of North American Birds,* Alfred A. Knopf, New York, 1980.

Udvardy, Mlklos D.F., *The Audubon Society Field Guide to North American Birds — Western Region,* Alfred A. Knopf, Inc., New York, 1977.

Weeden, R.B. and L.N. Ellison, *Upland Game Birds of Forest and Tundra,* Wildlife Booklet Series No. 3, Alaska Department of Fish and Game, Juneau, 1968.

Wild Bird Society of Japan, *A Field Guide to the Birds of Japan,* Wild Bird Society of Japan, Tokyo, 1982.

Yamashina, Y., *Birds in Japan - A Field Guide,* Tokyo News Service, Ltd., Tokyo, Japan, 1961.

INDEX BY SCIENTIFIC NAME

INDEX BY COMMON NAME